PENGUIN CLASSICS

STRUGGLES AND TRIUMPHS

Carl Bode is the author of two books on nineteenth-century social history, *The American Lyceum: Town Meeting of the Mind* and *Antebellum Culture,* and the editor of two more, *American Life in the 1840s* and *Midcentury America: Life in the 1850s.* A founder and first president of the American Studies Association, he is also a past president of the Popular Culture Association. He teaches American literature and American Studies at the University of Maryland.

STRUGGLES
AND TRIUMPHS

Or,
Forty Years' Recollections
of

P. T. BARNUM

Edited and abridged
with an Introduction by
CARL BODE

PENGUIN BOOKS

PENGUIN BOOKS
Published by the Penguin Group
Viking Penguin Inc., 40 West 23rd Street, New York, New York 10010, U.S.A.
Penguin Books Ltd, 27 Wrights Lane, London W8 5TZ, England
Penguin Books Australia Ltd, Ringwood, Victoria, Australia
Penguin Books Canada Ltd, 2801 John Street,
Markham, Ontario, Canada L3R 1B4
Penguin Books (N.Z.) Ltd, 182–190 Wairau Road,
Auckland 10, New Zealand

Penguin Books Ltd, Registered Offices:
Harmondsworth, Middlesex, England

First edition published under the title
The Life of P.T. Barnum Written by Himself 1855
Second edition published under the title
Struggles and Triumphs: Or,
Forty Years' Recollections of P.T. Barnum 1869
Abridged edition published in The Penguin American Library 1981
Reprinted in Penguin Classics 1987

3   5   7   9   10   8   6   4   2

Introduction copyright © Viking Penguin Inc., 1981
All rights reserved

LIBRARY OF CONGRESS CATALOGING IN PUBLICATION DATA
Barnum, P.T. (Phineas Taylor), 1810–1891.
Struggles and triumphs, or,
Forty Years' recollections of P.T. Barnum.
(Penguin Classics)
Bibliography: p.
1. Barnum, P.T. (Phineas Taylor), 1810–1891.
2. Circus owners—United States—Biography.
I. Bode, Carl, 1911–   .   II.   Title.
GV1811.B3A3   1981   791.3′092′4 [B]   81-12065
ISBN 0 14 039.004 9   AACR2

Printed in the United States of America
Set in CRT Caslon

Contents

Acknowledgments

For help while I worked on this book I am especially grateful to these colleagues of mine at the University of Maryland: Betsy Swart and Heather Kurent, my research assistants; Betty Baehr, Loan Librarian at McKeldin Library; Gene Wise, Director of the American Studies Program; John Howard, Acting Chairman of the English Department; and Shirley Kenny, Provost for Arts and Humanities.

C. B.

INTRODUCTION:

Barnum Uncloaked

I t is Phineas Taylor Barnum's distinction, for better or worse, that he became our first great purveyor of mass entertainment. In doing so, and with unstinting help from himself, he became an international celebrity.

The Barnum the world perceived was a beefy, bustling figure, his smile wide and his receding hair curly. He radiated energy; he was constantly trying to do bigger and more novel things in the field of entertainment. He showed a zest for fresh sensations, personally as well as professionally. He toured the south of France once while the grapes were ripening. As he wrote later, "Desiring a new experience, I myself trod out a half barrel or so with my own naked feet, dancing vigorously the while to the sound of a fiddle." The picture of him, shirttails flying, stomping on the grapes, symbolizes what he brought to the American people: a quickened sensibility. Not heightened but quickened. He decided early that they were too practical, too stodgy, too severe, and he worked for decades to make them less so. He schemed to entrance them with oddities, whether genuine or manufactured; he tried to stimulate their sense of wonder when they viewed one of his giants or cameleopards or dioramas of creation. He attempted to amuse them when he could, though this was harder. However, his wittiest entertainer, Tom Thumb, was a universal delight. Barnum yearned to widen the world's eyes and bring a grin to the world's face. He did it, but at a cost.

For the world also saw in him its premier humbug. From the beginning he deceived his customers with innate ease. After he established himself he lied less, but he never gave up exaggeration. At the least he made his oddities odder, his wonders more wonderful; his midgets shrank while his giants expanded. Sometimes his deceptions were so transparent that he seemed to deceive for the fun of it. For instance, he advertised that his popular American Museum in New York contained a miniature Niagara Falls "with Real Water"—as if it might have been artificial water otherwise. He always carried with him the conviction that the public relished a touch of chicanery.

Perhaps he was right, but a good many people regarded him with contempt. There would have been more of them except for his ostentatious Christianity and good deeds. He periodically announced that he took his Bible with him wherever he went and that he opened it often. In a moral age he presented the picture of a very moral man, a dutiful husband and father who attended church each Sunday and kept the more stylish of the Ten Commandments. In an age of sexual repression he saw to it that no stain of sexual scandal attached itself to him. His exhibits and his shows were moral. When he added stage plays, such as *The Drunkard* and *Joseph and his Brethren,* to the American Museum's attractions, he carefully labeled them "Moral Dramas." Not long before he retired he said, "I feel it my mission, as long as I live, to provide clean, moral, and healthful recreation for the public."

By luck or design, once his name was known he found another highroad to public esteem. He became a very effective temperance lecturer. Lecturing on abolition, for example, would have made him as many enemies as friends; but few people, North or South, could quarrel with a crusader against drink. He also lectured, when invited, on the comforts of Christianity, especially as manifest in the Universalist Church to which he belonged. He published a brochure, "The Liquor Business," as well as a pamphlet, "Why I am a Universalist."

He similarly made a point of conspicuous public service. After he and his family settled down in Bridgeport, Connecticut, forty miles from where he had been born, he played the part of ideal citizen. He did everything from serving in the state legislature to creating a model suburb, East Bridgeport. In the legislature he fought against the railroad oligarchs and for the dirt farmers. He even ran for Congress. And back in New York, where he spent most of his working days, people read about him in the newspapers from time to time as the head of this or that civic or professional society.

He needed to do all these things to be effective. Even today a tinge of Puritanism survives in our culture. However, in the mid-nineteenth century, when Barnum first made his mark, the Puritanism was still pronounced, particularly as it affected our diversions. Puritanism is easy to caricature and we must allow for that. But the truth is that it frowned on the spectacle of Americans amusing themselves, let alone paying cash to have others amuse them. The exceptions it allowed were bland ones, such as singing a Stephen Foster ballad while a piano tinkled the accompaniment. Even reading fiction had an improper air, though more and more people were doing it. *Harper's Magazine* illustrated the fact when it printed a comic drawing of a housewife letting dinner burn while she stood at the stove absorbed in the latest novel. Some of the popular "domestic novels" of the time blunted criticism by insisting that they taught a lesson. The lyceum system of public lectures flourished because people supposedly went to the lectures to learn; though the demand for entertainment grew steadily, they told themselves it was incidental. Not until the coarser days after the Civil War could an entertainer prosper in his own right on the lyceum platform. Until then the stand-up comic would have starved, and it took the genius of Mark Twain to make him acceptable.

This was the cultural climate young Barnum encountered. Puritanism helped to make a sharper distinction between what we call high culture and popular culture than exists today, and Barnum recognized that popular culture was his business. He aimed squarely at the crowd. The plainest evidence is that the foundation of his fortune lay in exhibiting freaks. Toward the close of his half century as a showman he specialized in the spectacular—he perfected the three-ring circus and the torchlight pageant—but for decades he depended on human anomalies. Plus an occasional fake.

Joice Heth was his first anomaly, an ancient slave alleged to have been George Washington's nurse. When Barnum bought her in 1835, he announced her age was 161. His first and foremost fake was his "Fejee Mermaid," which he pretended was at least half human. Actually it was the top part of a mummified monkey attached to the bottom part of a dried fish. However, Barnum advertised it with drawings and transparencies of the beautiful mermaids of folklore, and people kept coming to gape at it for years. The freaks he followed with in his prime ranged from midgets like Tom Thumb to giants like Anna Swan, "the tallest woman in the world." In later years his most publicized freaks were the Siamese twins Eng/Chang. Nearly all of them made money for him; he satisfied the taste of the crowd.

That they made much money was a tribute to his masterly skill in attracting attention. His main instrument was the press, which he played on like a calliope. While still young he learned the lesson that any publicity was good publicity. If his enemies abused him in the newspapers as a trickster, he chuckled because they drew attention to his exhibits and that meant more paying customers. If his enemies failed to abuse him, he did the job himself. When the audiences for Joice Heth dwindled he sent an anonymous letter to the papers. In it he stigmatized her as a fraud, though a clever one. "The fact is," he wrote tantalizingly, "Joice Heth is not a human being [but] an automaton, made up of whalebone, india-rubber, and numberless springs." Hundreds who had not seen her became eager to do so, while hundreds who had already seen her paid again to decide whether she shook with springs or senility.

Tom Thumb proved to be his most profitable, and most winning, anomaly. In 1842, when Barnum found him in Bridgeport, he was five years old and stood twenty-five inches tall. He had a well-proportioned body topped by the head of a mischievous cherub. He turned out to be precociously bright as well as talkative and appealing. Moreover, he possessed a wit beyond his years. After Barnum gave him a cram course on how to act and what to say, he took him touring through the East. Then he took him across the ocean to England, where, in a dazzling showman's coup, he got Tom invited to entertain Queen Victoria and her court in Buckingham Palace. She held Tom by the hand, Barnum later reported with pride, and "asked him many questions, the answers to which kept the party in an uninterrupted strain of merriment." Then he delighted the palace with the "songs, dances, and imitations" which Barnum had taught him.

The contrast between the public's taste in entertainment, as seen in Barnum's shows, during his era and ours is striking. Today we would be uncomfortable staring at a collection of human oddities. Who would pay to watch a bearded lady or a shambling giant or a pair of twins grown together? Such viewing has become taboo. Further, our culture focuses on sex for much of its entertainment, while Barnum's exhibits were marked by their sexlessness. Toward the end of his life he produced circuses with acrobats in tights and dancing girls in flimsy costumes, but by then the nineteenth century was almost over.

Naturally we find exceptions during both eras. In Barnum's time actors and actresses were allowed a covert sexuality, and in our time the interest in human oddities and humanoids is being revived by science-fantasy films and fiction such as J. R. R. Tolkien's. The popularity of midgets lasted in both America and England till the 1920s. Long after freaks had been exiled to the sideshows of minor circuses, troupes of midgets and dwarfs entertained sizable audiences. A company called Singer's Midgets became something of an American institution. Then, too, midgets and dwarfs had traditionally enlivened European courts. When Queen Victoria smiled at Tom's clever antics she was following the fashion of her royal predecessors.

Barnum was given to boasting that his prime aim was to make money. He rigged his early exhibits, and such repute as he had came from his profitable humbugging. The public surveyed him with an envious grin. However, exhibiting Tom Thumb widened Barnum's horizons and stirred within him an appetite for the public's respect. Because he recognized that even Tom could not bring him what he wanted, he searched for someone who could. With a stroke of public relations genius he settled on Jenny Lind.

Affectionately nicknamed the Swedish Nightingale, Jenny ranked as Europe's foremost soprano. Along with a delicious voice and superb musicianship, she had precisely the qualities Barnum required: personal and professional integrity. There was not the slightest shadow on her private life and she had the reputation of being not only honest but generous in her financial dealings. His problem was to lure her to the United States under his management. Through an intermediary he sounded her out, but because of his ambiguous reputation she hesitated to trust him. Perhaps he would show her off in a cage. However, during the Tom Thumb tour in England, Barnum had made some English friends as well as English financial connections. Jenny decided to write to several of those friends, including one in the famous banking house of Baring Brothers. They all endorsed him. Risking financial ruin he proffered her $1,000 a night for up to 150 nights, plus all her expenses. He would pay for, among other things, "servants, carriages, secretary, etc., besides also engaging such musical assistants, not exceeding three in number, as she should select, let the terms be what they might." "Let the terms be what they might"—that was a new Barnum, far distant from the bargainer he had been. She signed the contract.

Because Jenny was little known in America, Barnum mounted a stunning advertising campaign, remarkable for its variety and ingenuity. As usual, the newspapers were his main vehicle. Before she disembarked in New York he flooded them with stories. He furnished flattering portraits of her to any paper or magazine willing to print them. He commissioned a leaflet about her life. He even arranged a nationwide contest for the best poem on the theme of "Greeting to America," which, when set to music, she would sing as the finale to her concerts. An aspiring author named Bayard Taylor won with lyrics of unblemished banality. When she walked down the gangplank at the beginning of September 1850, thirty thousand people had gathered to greet her. Barnum escorted her through a pair of arches of greenery festooned with flowers; one arch was inscribed "Welcome to America," the other "Welcome, Jenny Lind." By the time Barnum's carriage took her to her hotel, five thousand more people stood there waiting in the street.

Her initial concert in New York created a sensation; so did the tour that followed. On opening night she began by singing the "Casta Diva" from Bellini's *Norma* and did it so brilliantly that the audience drowned the last part in acclamation. She went through the program with triumph after triumph and concluded with "Greeting to America." When the audience finally tired of applauding her they shouted for Barnum. He stepped onto the stage to announce benignly that she was donating her share of the proceeds, $10,000, to New York charities. His announcement brought down the house.

From Jenny's tour Barnum reaped rich psychic rewards. For example, when he escorted her to Washington, President Millard Fillmore promptly paid her a call. She gave two concerts there; Fillmore, his family, and his entire cabinet attended both. After one of her hauntingly beautiful songs, Daniel Webster, more imposing than any president, rose from the audience to make her a profound bow. Who could blame Barnum for beaming? Later he summed up the effect of his managing Jenny by saying simply, "It placed me before the world in a new light."

The packed houses and presidential applause during the tour had an impact not only on the world's view of Barnum but on Barnum's view of himself. He took himself and his role more seriously than before. He decided to make his exaggerations less gross, as befitted a public figure of increased stature. His experience with Jenny taught him the gratifying lesson that money invested in abundance could bring abundant returns. To hire Jenny he had risked every dollar he owned or could borrow, and even before she sang for him he voluntarily raised her fees. The result was not bankruptcy but opulence. The financial rewards were as rich as the psychic ones.

Then there was the persuasive case of the American Museum. He bought it in 1841, a shabby showhouse on New York's Broadway. The more money he put into it, he discovered, the more money he got back. Gradually he upgraded his exhibits. Not that his taste was transformed, nor his view of the public's taste. He still scoured the country, as he once said, for "educated dogs, industrious fleas, automatons, jugglers, ventriloquists, living statuary," and such. But he abandoned the "Fejee Mermaid" and her kind. He inaugurated and then expanded his evening entertainments, which were essentially early vaudeville, to include the "Moral Dramas" mentioned before. He remodeled the museum's lecture room into a handsome theater. From time to time he hired some of Broadway's best actors and actresses to star in his plays. A decade after he bought it the American Museum had developed into such an attraction, for tourists and native New Yorkers alike, that Barnum's problem was to keep them moving through. So he ordered a sign painted saying, "To the Egress," which led them to the street instead of to the cage of some rare creature.

Barnum could survey the museum with ever-growing satisfaction. Five stories high, with the flags of the world fluttering atop its facade, it possessed a gaudy grandeur which, in Barnum's eye, typified his success. The Jenny Lind episode was heartwarming and elevating, and it marked a turning point for him; but it was an episode. As he himself noted, the American Museum was for years his ladder to fortune. People on both sides of the Atlantic came to refer to him as the "museum man," and that was how he frequently identified himself.

With his image noticeably improved after the advent of Jenny, he determined that the time had come to tell his story to the world. Seldom gnawed by guilt, he felt little need to apologize for any of his actions. On the other hand, he wanted to explain some of them. He hoped, perhaps by frankness, to minimize the effect of such early hoaxes as Joice Heth and the mermaid and such later ones as the "Woolly Horse" and the "Grand Hoboken Buffalo Hunt." And he intended to expatiate on his growing number of good deeds and superior exhibits.

Always an anecdotalist, he foresaw no trouble in composing his memoirs. He had been writing sporadically since boyhood. Over the years he had prepared many a press release to advertise his exhibits. In the mid-1840s, while managing Tom Thumb's debut abroad, he had penned a hundred letters about his travels for the *New York Atlas*. Now he let publishers know that an autobiography was on the way. J. S. Redfield of New York emerged as the top bidder for the privilege of publishing it when finished.

Barnum wrote as vigorously as he did other things, and by January 1855 America could read *The Life of P. T. Barnum Written by Himself.* So could Britain, for a British edition came out at the same time. British intellectuals had not forgiven him for beguiling Queen Victoria. It was bad enough that he had appealed to the lowest levels of British taste, but the picture of Tom Thumb and Barnum in Buckingham Palace still made them squirm. The reviewer in *Blackwood's Magazine* was merely more eloquent than the rest when he wrote that the book aroused "disgust for the frauds which it narrates, amazement for its audacity, loathing for its hypocrisy, abhorrence for the moral obliquity which it betrays, and sincere pity for the wretched man who compiled it."

Even Barnum could hardly chuckle at such a stricture but he shrugged it off. The critical reception in his own country proved to be mixed. *The New York Times* sniffed that the book attested to a success attained "by the systematic, adroit, and persevering plan of obtaining money under false pretences from the public." However, most newspapers treated it with amiable condescension. After all, Barnum was one of America's own; he represented the wily Yankee side of the national character; and he had always been careful as a showman to woo the papers, if mainly for the sake of his shows. The magazines took a loftier tone than the press, as a rule dismissing the book rather than berating it in the British manner. They refused to speculate—perhaps out of reluctance to inquire into American taste, perhaps out of inability to offer an answer—on why people were buying the book in droves.

The most illuminating exception was Baltimore's *Metropolitan Magazine.* It ran a review by a high-nosed local intellectual, Severn Teakle Wallis, which appraised Barnum's book along with a new book of travels by Harriet Beecher Stowe. He found both books dreadful but Mrs.

Stowe's worse. At the least Barnum was clear-sighted
about his deceits but Mrs. Stowe—the Southern-leaning
Wallis could not forgive her for *Uncle Tom's Cabin*—was
always "rapt in the wisdom of her own twaddle." Why
was Barnum's book selling? Because the public enjoyed
reading the confessions of a celebrated rogue. Its qualms
about his sleazy actions were quieted by his fulsome
Christianity. Wallis quoted him: "In all my journeys as a
showman, the Bible has been my companion." The lesson Barnum's book taught, Wallis added with a grimace,
was "Fear God and cheat your neighbor."

Regardless of what the critics said, the public continued to buy the book. Barnum made it easier by providing
artful assistance in the form of indirect advertising. He
itched to have multitudes read it. And he went on to dem-
onstrate how significant the book was to him by rewriting
and revising it at intervals during the rest of his life. He
found that he liked to write almost as much as he liked to
talk, and he was a garrulous man. The *Life* sold a gratifying 160,000 copies in the United States. Two printings
appeared in England despite reviewers' glares, and
translations were issued in Germany and France.

After the sales finally stopped, Barnum bought the
plates of the book from the publisher and destroyed
them. As usual, he thought he could go on to produce
something bigger and better. Moreover, he had come
to regret some of the candor of the first version. In 1869
he had a revised and expanded version published by Burr
& Company of Hartford, Connecticut. Barnum said in
the preface that the first version had been hasty and im-
perfect but that the second version was the "matured
and leisurely review of almost half a century of work
and struggle, and final success, in spite of fraud." It
should be added at once that the fraud he meant was
the fraud by others. The reference to it reflected
the fact that during the intervening years he had rashly
invested in a clock company run by a set of swindlers. Its
crash had left him with liabilities of $500,000. He had

converted the debacle into a qualified triumph by repaying every cent in the next few years. Appropriately he titled the 1869 version *Struggles and Triumphs*. And he altered the dedication. In 1855 it had been "To the Universal Yankee Nation." By 1869 he had learned that some Yankees did not deserve to have anything dedicated to them, so the new dedication was "To my Wife and Family."

He made other changes. He condensed the story of his boyhood in Connecticut, where he had learned sharpness by being surrounded by sharpers. The Connecticut Yankee of that time stood for cunning, and Barnum recognized that cunning had played too much of a part in both his career and his book. He allotted Tom Thumb and Jenny Lind more space, giving his deceptions less. He philosophized more about life; he dwelt on the importance of Christianity. He expounded further on success and how to win it. He had grown a bit pontifical and the revised book reflected the fact. Yet he could not avoid acting the showman; he still advertised his monkeys as mermaids. In the preface to the 1869 version he assured his readers that they would find not only his life story but "amusing anecdotes, funny passages, felicitous jokes, captivating narratives, novel experiences, and remarkable interviews."

Several times after 1869 he brought the story up to date by writing additions, which he ordered to be bound in at the end of the book. In 1889 he published the last of the three versions of his autobiography. This time he did a good deal of condensing and editing, so that although the title remained *Struggles and Triumphs* the struggles were briefer and fewer. Also, a shorter book could be sold for less. Because he realized that he stood at the summit of his renown, the dedication for this final version could not have been grander: "To the Whole Civilized World in General and to the Universal Yankee Nation in Particular." He had even forgiven those Yankees in the clock company who had swindled him.

The most interesting addition in the 1889 book was the detailed account of his most durable contribution to American entertainment, the circus. He had gotten into the circus business in 1870, as usual on a large scale. During the first half of the nineteenth century the typical circus had been a feeble affair, with perhaps a few clowns, acrobats, and horseback riders, plus a few freaks. After the Civil War several showmen considerably improved it, among them J. A. Bailey, whom Barnum later drew into a partnership. They encountered strenuous competition from Barnum. He mounted, in his own words, "a great show enterprise, comprising a Museum, Menagerie, Caravan, Hippodrome, and Circus, of such proportion as to require five hundred men and horses to transport it through the country."

It was a success wherever it traveled, and Barnum spent freely to improve it. He expanded the ordinary one-ring circus under a modest tent into a three-ring, two-stage extravaganza under a vast cloud of canvas. He brought together the numerous attractions that still draw "children of all ages," as some of his posters phrased it. They included an impressive number of smoothly mus-cled acrobats, bespangled showgirls, clowns, daring bareback riders, elephants, camels, lions, and tigers—in short, just about everything we have today.

Even all this was not enough for Barnum. He un-leashed his showman's imagination and created a series of spectaculars that only Cecil B. De Mille equaled in the movies later on. Barnum billed one of his most glittering extravaganzas as the "Congress of Monarchs." He put a thousand people into it. Under his enormous roof he set the main monarchs of the age as he saw them. They ranged from Queen Victoria to the Emperor of China, from the Emperor Napoleon with his marshals to the Pope with his cardinals. Before them passed a splendid procession, mounted and afoot, of heralds, flag bearers, knights in armor, cavalrymen, and exotically uniformed warriors, along with charioteers driving their chariots.

To bring the pageant to a climax soldiers in Revolutionary War uniforms, flourishing the Stars and Stripes and accompanied by a band of very red Indians, surged into the tent. Inevitably the crowds cheered until hoarse.

Barnum also produced circus parades beyond any seen before or since. When the "Greatest Show on Earth" opened in New York in March 1881, public interest rose so high that window space was actually sold on Broadway to people who had to have the best possible view of the parade. Barnum did not disappoint them. One grandiose wagon after another rolled past, painted in bright colors and gilt. The display looked magnificent. The music was an index to the lavishness of the rest. As one New York paper reported, there were "four brass bands (one composed of genuine Indians), a calliope, a fine chime of bells, a steam organ, a squad of Scotch bag-pipers, and a company of genuine plantation Negro jubilee singers."

As he neared the conclusion of his career Barnum developed, literally, into a spectacle himself; in fact he became something of a folk hero. Before performances he liked to be driven around the main tent while the audience hailed him. His posters testified to his endearing lack of modesty. One set of them advertised: "See the Old Hero . . . Whose Brilliant Deeds are Themes of Poetry and Prose." People stopped him on the street to shake his hand; waiters pointed him out in hotel dining rooms.

Understandably, a note of self-congratulation sounded often in the 1889 version of his book; for the older he grew, the more tokens of esteem he acquired. Even the *Times* of London warmed to him. In 1889 it wished him twice the number of birthdays he had already had, and in his obituary two years later it would announce that his death had removed an "almost classical figure" from the world scene.

Ailing though he was, he shakily penned a short adjunct to the 1889 version, which covered a few months after its publication. Following his death his widow published a sketch of his final period, including a description of the funeral in his home town of Bridgeport. The funeral, according to one local wit, was the grandest show Bridgeport had ever seen.

For the American people during the second half of the nineteenth century Barnum's autobiography became, after the Bible, the most widely read book. The reason lay largely but not totally in its merits. So, before we inquire into its intrinsic appeals, we ought to glance at its promotion, which for persistence and variety exceeded that of any volume but the Bible. Barnum aided in advertising the 1855 version of the book and the publisher did his part—with handsome results but not handsome enough. To put out the 1869 version Barnum chose a new publisher with experience in the newly popular subscription method of merchandising books, as opposed to the older method of using bookstores. Hartford happened to be a center for subscription selling and the smooth-tongued agents of Burr & Company journeyed through the towns and villages to sign up buyers for the book. Armed with an ornate brochure that Barnum had commissioned, they peddled copies at a great rate. After they had marketed all the copies they could, Barnum purchased the plates, and from then on promoted the book beyond anything previously attempted by American publishers.

Gradually he both lowered the price and widened the means of distribution. The 1869 version cost at least $3.50 a copy; he kept whittling away until the 1889 version could be had for as little as fifty cents. Although he reduced the type size as well as cut down the contents, buyers rarely complained. The British statesman W. E. Gladstone was an exception. He grumbled to Barnum that the type was tiny, but Barnum, secure in what his ledgers told him, reported that his reply was merely, "I acknowledged the fact."

Barnum's channels of distribution, above all his circus,

must have been the envy of many another author. He inaugurated the circus only a year after the 1869 version of the book came out and increasingly exploited it as a place to sell *Struggles and Triumphs.* After a while, customers at the circus simply could not avoid the book. It was hawked inside and outside the tent; copies lay piled at the entrances. Each season Barnum grew more openhanded. To the people who streamed in to see the circus he offered the book almost as a giveaway. To those who had not seen the circus he offered a free ticket with each purchase of the book. The older he became the more he craved to have everyone read his story. Finally he even gave away the copyright to any publisher willing to reprint the book.

The consequence was sales of an astronomical order. In 1882 he looked back and reckoned that he had sold half a million copies of the 1869 version, with its various additions; by 1888 it was more than a million. We lack figures on the total sales of the 1889 version and of sales by publishers other than Barnum's. But we can be certain that they were huge.

The appeal the book made throughout Barnum's career, and for decades afterward, was manifold. First of all, it was the autobiography of the most colorful figure in nineteenth-century American life. And the most publicized. He once complimented Ulysses Grant, after his momentous victories in the Civil War and two terms as President, on being the best-known man in the world. Grant replied, "No, sir, your name is familiar to multitudes who never heard of me." Moreover, Barnum was not only a celebrity among celebrities, he was a controversial one during much of his life. Notoriety shifted into renown but both made good copy.

The book was an inside story, especially in its first version, although we find him less candid with his readers later on. Even if they were privy to his deceptions, much of what Barnum admitted about them was new. And seen from within—like much else—the deceptions assumed a fresh perspective. Readers found that some of the most notorious Barnum simply regarded as practical jokes on the public, and he had been weaned on practical jokes. They were widespread in the rustic Connecticut where he grew up. He played them and was the butt of them. His training came early. His grandfather Phineas Taylor solemnly assured the little boy that he had deeded him a tract of the most valuable land in Connecticut. Barnum recalled that the matter became a local joke. "My grandfather always spoke of me (in my presence) to the neighbors and to strangers as the richest child in town." When Barnum finally found the land to be a worthless swamp, everyone hooted. Yet he told the story without showing resentment.

With the passing of the years Barnum grew uncomfortable about the crudest of his hoaxes, above all the mermaid, but he remained complacent about many others. He chuckled about the "Great Hoboken Buffalo Hunt" and invited his readers to chuckle with him. He also tried to indoctrinate them with his hard-bought view that everything had to cost something. There was no such thing as a free lunch. Or a free concert, for that matter. He periodically hired a band to play on the balcony of the American Museum. This was outside, so the crowd did not have to pay to listen, as it would have inside. But Barnum explained to his readers with a grin that he had hired the poorest band possible so that its raucous notes would drive the crowd into the museum to escape. The playing was free but it hurt the ear. Though the stratagem seemed a bit involved it worked. "When people expect to get 'something for nothing' they are sure to be cheated, and generally deserve to be," he observed.

The book also appealed because it was itself a performance. Barnum was his own show, endlessly doing things or making them happen. We might pick a handful of instances, all briskly described in the book. Earlier they had been described in the newspapers as well and that was what he wanted. He introduced the first hippopotamus to

America. . . . He built his showiest private residence, which he called Iranistan, in imitation of the Prince Regent's Oriental pavilion in Brighton. . . . He tried to buy Shakespeare's birthplace in Stratford, hoping to move the whole house into the American Museum. . . . He had not one but two whales caught off the St. Lawrence River, had them shipped to New York, and put them in a large tank in the museum. . . . He tamed the noisy undergraduates at Oxford by his wit on the lecture platform. . . . He promoted the marriage of Tom Thumb to a comely young female midget, Lavinia Warren, and persuaded two Anglican clergymen to officiate. The wedding was solemnized in Grace Church, New York, admission by card only. Several governors attended, as did members of Congress, generals of the army, and other magnificoes. . . . He chartered a ship for a year in a worldwide search for a herd of elephants to exhibit. His agents caught them in Ceylon and shipped them to New York, where he paraded them and then put them into his current traveling menagerie. Thereafter he sold all but one, which—with a typical Barnum touch—he used for some widely publicized plowing on a Connecticut farm he owned.

He built a Roman hippodrome in New York on Madison Avenue, 200 feet wide, 426 feet long. It became his stationary circus tent, at which princes and plebians marveled. . . . He fraternized with celebrities of many sorts, some of them surprising. Among them, the noted British novelist William Makepeace Thackeray, who not only asked his advice about lecturing in the United States but offered to lend him money after the clock company swindle. The starchy British literary critic Matthew Arnold journeyed to Bridgeport to lecture and stayed overnight at Barnum's home. . . . When Barnum was in London the Prince of Wales greeted him with a smile. . . . Barnum organized baby shows at the museum, awarding prizes for the finest baby, the fattest baby, and various other sorts of baby that his ingenuity let him think up. . . . He fought fiercely and victoriously with the irascible press lord of the *New York Herald,* James Gordon Bennett, over a land lease; he made $200,000 in the process. . . . The instances could be extended indefinitely. It almost seemed that the only time he went unnoticed was when he sat writing at his desk—and he wrote in the interest of public notice.

A further appeal of the book lay in the fact that it was a remarkably effective example of a traditional literary type, the picaresque tale, the history of a roguish fellow who passes through one adventure after another. This kind of tale has its artistic unity in the figure of the hero, or rather, the antihero. The author arranges his incidents like gaudy beads on a string. Barnum's was such a tale, with so many incidents that he stopped his narrative at times to bundle them into chapters. In point, he titled one of his chapters "Incidents and Anecdotes," another "A Story Chapter." He described nearly all incidents with gusto.

Barnum's book had a characteristic of the picaresque tale that may have held less attraction for his readers: lack of emotional depth. However, we can certainly argue that readers did not wish to be deeply involved in the actions or feelings of an antihero. The "domestic novels" of the mid-nineteenth century were awash with emotion, but readers identified with their put-upon heroines to a degree that they never identified with Barnum. At any rate, his account of his chief joys and sorrows was cursory enough not to move his readers much. In the book his joys reduced to complacence, his sorrows shrank into summaries. For instance: "On the 11th of April, 1877, my family were stricken with a heavy sorrow in the sudden death of my daughter, Pauline T. Seely, at the age of thirty-one years, leaving a husband and three children. This blow would have been insupportable to me did I not receive it as coming from our good Father in Heaven, who does all things right." That was that; then Barnum turned to describing a trip to England.

He was better at inspirational anecdotes, particularly personal ones, which he retailed with relish. For example, he described the time in North Carolina on a Sunday morning when he spontaneously addressed a Baptist congregation that had just left church. He led the bemused Baptists to a nearby grove, one of God's temples, where he preached a hearty sermon on man's privileges and responsibilities. Similarly, his readers knew he advocated temperance but now they could have the picturesque details. Such as that he decided on total abstinence himself after a sleepless night of debate; that he rose in the morning to knock off the heads of his champagne bottles; and that he emptied their foaming contents onto the ground. Such as that after a temperance lecture of his, one man, surely among many, came forward to say, "Mr. Barnum, you have this night saved me from ruin."

The book was also, to use today's heavy phrase, a manual for career development. Christianity and good works played their part, but there was more, much more. Barnum aimed his manual at men, of course. They could find a good deal to motivate them in his deeds, starting with his struggles for survival in Connecticut and ending with his benefactions, when he was old and wealthy, to his home city of Bridgeport. He helped his readers by his observations about those deeds. But he went beyond that: he provided specific rules for success. They were Yankee rules, for the stress lay on making money. He included them, in a succinct form, in the 1855 version of his book, where they probably inspired a fair number of people. He quoted one person as having exclaimed, "Why can't I go ahead and make money as Barnum did?" He followed the rules and, like Barnum, grew rich.

In the late 1850s Barnum, while on business in England, expanded the rules into a full-scale lecture. He called it "The Art of Money Getting." It became so successful that he delivered it by invitation more than a hundred times. He brought it back to the United States, burnished it, and delivered it here with equal success. A token of the fact was that he advertised that the 1869 version of his book contained "his celebrated lecture on the Art of Money-Getting, along with Rules for Success in Business." And in the 1889 version he promoted his principles to the title page: *Struggles and Triumphs . . . Including . . . the Golden Rules for Money-Making.*

In the lecture he mingled aphorisms with anecdotes. Although the aphorisms were far from novel, the anecdotes kept the readers' attention. He wrote in the same spirited way that he spoke, and when he spoke on money even the *Times* of London listened. It admitted his expertise on the subject, his dry humor, and his clear delivery. In spite of itself, the *Times* acknowledged that Barnum was "one of the most entertaining lecturers that ever addressed an audience on a theme universally intelligible." Naturally he reprinted the acknowledgment in his book.

His theme was that any man, especially in America, could become rich if he really wanted to. He began his lecture by outlining various tested ways of not becoming rich. Cheese-paring economy stood at one extreme, while following fashion at any cost stood at the other. Though he had been guilty of neither one, he sprinkled in enough stories of his own mistakes and shortcomings to give the lecture an air of authenticity and humanity. Mindful of how he had been gulled in the clock company affair he remarked that he ought to speak on "The Art of Money Losing." He had paid his dues and his audiences evidently liked him better for having done so. The rules he propounded to them began with "Don't mistake your vocation." The main ones that followed were: "Avoid debt"; "Persevere"; "Use the best tools"; "Do not scatter your powers"; "Don't endorse without security"; "Advertise your business"; and "Be charitable." Past master of deception though he was, he concluded with the exhortation: "Preserve your integrity." He affirmed that it was more precious than diamonds or rubies.

Sensible living was an important adjunct to the rules. Consider the case of tobacco. In nature its sole user was a "vile worm." But many men either chewed it or smoked it. Legions of chewers walked around spitting their tobacco juice on floors or carpets. They pulled out the noxious quid only to eat—and they could give up roast beef more readily than tobacco. Smokers damaged themselves and injured others. About smoking, Barnum, with his usual shrewdness, made an admission. He himself had smoked in the past until he "trembled like an aspen leaf." On his doctor's earnest advice he had made himself stop. So should his readers, especially the impressionable young. He added sardonically, "No young man ever looked so beautiful, as he thought he did, behind a fifteen cent cigar or a meerschaum!"

Finally, and obviously, the book gave readers a ringside view of the rise of mass entertainment in the nineteenth century. Barnum could guide them because he stood in the center of it. He took them from the scruffy freak shows with which he began through to the glittering extravaganzas, like the "Congress of Monarchs," with which he ended fifty years later. He titillated his readers at the same time that he informed them. He revealed to them what had happened behind the scenes. He trumpeted the tales of his triumphs but also, in a hoarse whisper, confided the facts of his occasional failures. Entertainingly, he told the story of entertainment as he conceived it.

So the book was many things: an autobiography, an apologia, a picaresque novel, a string of anecdotes, a manual on getting rich, an occasional sermon on the merits of Christianity, and a survey of popular entertainment. No wonder it emerged as a best-seller among best-sellers.

On the whole, the book can still appeal to us. We can enjoy the lively picaresque tale that is its platform. But the patent piety of the book can make us yawn. And the rules for business success, which Barnum addressed especially to young men, look paleolithic. His urgings to persevere and, above all, to avoid debt, surely fall on deaf young ears. And on some deaf old ears as well. Another shortcoming, in terms of today's taste, is the absence of colorful private life. The closest thing to a sexual episode in the book is Barnum's coy account of the courtship and marriage of Tom Thumb and Lavinia Warren. Though it doubtless made a fair number of its nineteenth-century readers smirk, it's far from the raw meat that contemporary taste feeds on. And Barnum said not a word, naturally, about his own experience in bed.

Yet it is possible that a new interest in avoiding debt is appearing; and that the taste for detailed sexual description is waning. Even if they are not, the book can make a signal contribution.

For it offers us a view of nineteenth-century popular culture that historians have seldom provided. Today the study of popular culture is growing. We realize that we must take it into account if we want a balanced presentation of the past. Generalizations about the American experience are always shaky but they become shakier still if they ignore popular culture. One of its salient aspects is entertainment. In Barnum's book we see a panorama of it. Equally significant, we see a people's view of life, which can help us to correct the customary omissions of the historians.

Take the outstanding example. Barnum lived and wrote at a time when our nation suffered its gravest trauma, the Civil War. We still feel its effects. The history books are heavy with slavery, abolition, and sectional strife. In Barnum's book they received scant attention. Not that he was insulated or callous; he spoke out for abolition and equal rights for Negroes. However, he gave these matters only one chapter out of forty-seven in the 1869 volume, and proportionately less in the 1889 one. We can see that this neglect did not arise from his artistry as an author who wished to focus on his subject—Barnum was no artist—but from the fact was that the conflict meant little to him. If he had been a Southerner it certainly would have meant more. The fact was that, for multitudes of Northerners, everyday life, including the lighter side to which Barnum catered, went on equably enough in spite of the clash of arms.

During the summer of 1861, after the outbreak of hostilities and the crushing Northern defeat at Bull Run, throngs still pushed into the American Museum to stare at "the first and only genuine hippopotamus that had ever been seen in America." Throughout the war years Barnum diversified and augmented his exhibits. There were more midgets, more exotic fish large and small, more dioramas. There were wax figures of celebrities and an educated seal. There were geological specimens and a family of albinos. There was something for everyone in the crowd. Attendance at the museum set new records. True, New York was not the United States, but travelers from all over the North came in every season to view the exhibits. In the summer of 1865 the museum burned down. Barnum opened another. By autumn, with peace returning, people were flocking into the new museum with enthusiasm. Business as usual, or better than usual. To paraphrase Karl Marx, entertainment was becoming the opium of the people, though not nearly to the extent it is today.

Opium, we know, was not what Barnum wanted. He wanted to provide a quickener rather than a deadener for the American people. And he wanted his book to furnish a good example for them to use. He ended his preface to the 1869 and 1889 versions with: "If this record of trials and triumphs, struggles and successes, shall stimulate any to the exercise of that energy, industry, and courage in their callings, which will surely lead to happiness and

prosperity, one main object I have in yielding to the solicitations of my friends and my publishers will have been
accomplished." There was one added word in the 1889
version. With a lovely and typical touch, he inserted *integrity* before *energy*. Integrity.

—Carl Bode

Suggestions for Further Reading

TEXTS

The Life of P. T. Barnum Written by Himself (New York: Redfield, 1855). The first stage of Barnum's autobiography.

Struggles and Triumphs; or Forty Years' Recollections of P. T. Barnum Written by Himself (Hartford: J. B. Burr, 1869). The second and fullest form of his autobiography.

Struggles and Triumphs or, Sixty Years' Recollections of P. T. Barnum, Including His Golden Rules for Money-Making, Illustrated and Brought up to 1889, Written by Himself (Buffalo: Courier, 1889). The final condensed and sanitized version.

Struggles and Triumphs: or, The Life of P. T. Barnum, Written by Himself. Edited, with an introduction by George S. Bryan (New York: Knopf, 1927). A two-volume composite of major parts of the 1855, 1869, and 1889 autobiographies, with a long preliminary essay and six appendices.

CORRESPONDENCE

Selected letters of P. T. Barnum. Edited, and with an introduction by A. H. Saxon. (New York: Columbia University Press, 1983). More than 300 letters that display Barnum's shrewdness, self-interest, and occasional inclination toward public service.

BIOGRAPHIES

M. R. Werner, *Barnum* (Garden City: Harcourt, Brace, 1923). The first biography of Barnum to offer a researched and generally objective view of the man.

Irving Wallace, *The Fabulous Showman: The Life and Times of P. T. Barnum* (New York: Knopf, 1959). Cogent and well researched, reminding us that the author is a historian as well as a popular novelist.

Neil Harris, *Humbug: The Art of P. T. Barnum* (Boston: Little Brown, 1973). The best biography. Sound scholarship is used to set Barnum in his cultural milieu.

A Note on
the Text

The 1869 version, with Barnum's brief additions to cover two more years, is our basic text. It's entitled *Struggles and Triumphs; or, Forty Years' Recollections of P. T. Barnum Written by Himself.* (Author's edition [biography complete to April 1871]; New York: American News Company, 1871.) It runs to 856 pages, counting illustrations and their blank backs, as Barnum did, and has been shortened because the present publisher believes that more people will read a shorter book.

No version of the three autobiographies Barnum produced—in 1855, 1869, and 1889—is quite satisfactory. The first provides a fuller, franker picture of his early efforts to establish himself than do the others, but it stops in mid-career. The third version takes us to the end of Barnum's activities, but it suffers from the fact that he condensed and edited the text to make himself look as pretty as possible. The middle version is the longest, most comprehensive, and most illuminating, though it necessarily eliminates the conclusion of his career. It is also the best balanced. There have been one or two attempts to carpenter together parts of the three versions, but the results have looked artificial enough to make a straightforward cutting of the 1869 version seem a better idea. The main omissions deal with his travels on the Continent.

Struggles and
Triumphs

TO
MY WIFE AND FAMILY
I DEDICATE
THIS STORY OF A LIFE WHICH HAS BEEN LARGELY
DEVOTED TO THEIR
INTERESTS AND SERVICE.

Contents

43

Preface.

This book is my Recollections of Forty Busy Years. Few men in civil life have had a career more crowded with incident, enterprise, and various intercourse with the world than mine. With the alternations of success and defeat, extensive travel in this and foreign lands; a large acquaintance with the humble and honored; having held the preëminent place among all who have sought to furnish healthful entertainment to the American people, and, therefore, having had opportunities for garnering an ample storehouse of incident and anecdote, while, at the same time, needing a sagacity, energy, foresight and fortitude rarely required or exhibited in financial affairs, my struggles and experiences (it is not altogether vanity in me to think) cannot be without interest to my fellow countrymen.

Various leading publishers have solicited me to place at their disposal my Recollections of what I have been, and seen, and done. These proposals, together with the partiality of friends and kindred, have constrained me, now that I have retired from all active participation in business, to put in a permanent form what, it seems to me, may be instructive, entertaining and profitable.

Fifteen years since, for the purpose, principally, of advancing my interests as proprietor of the American Museum, I gave to the press some personal reminiscences and sketches. Having an extensive sale, they were, however, very hastily, and, therefore, imperfectly, prepared. These are not only out of print, but the plates have been destroyed. Though including, necessarily, in common with them, some of the facts of my early life, in order to make this autobiography a complete and continuous narrative, yet, as the latter part of my life has been the more eventful, and my recollections so various and abundant, this book is new and independent of the former. It is the matured and leisurely review of almost half a century of work and struggle, and final success, in spite of fraud and fire—the story of which is blended with amusing anecdotes, funny passages, felicitous jokes, captivating narratives, novel experiences, and remarkable interviews—the sunny and sombre so intermingled as not only to entertain, but convey useful lessons to all classes of readers.

These Recollections are dedicated to those who are nearest and dearest to me, with the feeling that they are a record which I am willing to leave in their hands, as a legacy which they will value.

And above and beyond this personal satisfaction, I have thought that the review of a life, with the wide contrasts of humble origin and high and honorable success; of most formidable obstacles overcome by courage and constancy; of affluence that had been patiently won, suddenly wrenched away, and triumphantly regained—would be a help and incentive to the young man, struggling, it may be, with adverse fortune, or, at the start, looking into the future with doubt or despair.

All autobiographies are necessarily egotistical. If my pages are as plentifully sprinkled with "I's" as was the chief ornament of Hood's peacock, "who thought he had the eyes of Europe on his tail," I can only say, that the "I's" are essential to the story I have told. It has been my purpose to narrate, not the life of another, but that career in which I was the principal actor.

There is an almost universal, and not unworthy

curiosity to learn the methods and measures, the ups and downs, the strifes and victories, the mental and moral *personnel* of those who have taken an active and prominent part in human affairs. But an autobiography has attractions and merits superior to those of a "Life" written by another, who, however intimate with its subject, cannot know all that helps to give interest and accuracy to the narrative, or completeness to the character. The story from the actor's own lips has always a charm it can never have when told by another.

That my narrative is interspersed with amusing incidents, and even the recital of some very practical jokes, is simply because my natural disposition impels me to look upon the brighter side of life, and I hope my humorous experiences will entertain my readers as much as they were enjoyed by myself. And if this record of trials and triumphs, struggles and successes, shall stimulate any to the exercise of that energy, industry, and courage in their callings, which will surely lead to happiness and prosperity, one main object I have in yielding to the solicitations of my friends and my publishers will have been accomplished.

P. T. BARNUM.

WALDEMERE, BRIDGEPORT,
Connecticut, July 5, 1869.

CHAPTER I.

Early Life.

I was born in the town of Bethel, in the State of Connecticut, July 5, 1810. My name, Phineas Taylor, is derived from my maternal grandfather, who was a great wag in his way, and who, as I was his first grandchild, gravely handed over to my mother at my christening a gift-deed, in my behalf, of five acres of land situated in that part of the parish of Bethel known as the "Plum Trees." I was thus a real estate owner almost at my very birth; and of my property, "Ivy Island," something shall be said anon.

My father, Philo Barnum, was the son of Ephraim Barnum, of Bethel, who was a captain in the revolutionary war. My father was a tailor, a farmer, and sometimes a tavern-keeper, and my advantages and disadvantages were such as fall to the general run of farmers' boys. I drove cows to and from the pasture, shelled corn, weeded the garden; as I grew larger, I rode horse for ploughing, turned and raked hay; in due time I handled the shovel and the hoe, and when I could do so I went to school.

I was six years old when I began to go to school, and the first date I remember inscribing upon my writing-book was 1818. The ferule, in those days, was the assistant school-master; but in spite of it, I was a willing, and, I think, a pretty apt scholar; at least, I was so considered by my teachers and schoolmates, and as the years went on there were never more than two or three in the school who were deemed my superiors. In arithmetic I was unusually ready and accurate, and I remember, at the age of twelve years, being called out of bed one night by my teacher who had wagered with a neighbor that I could calculate the correct number of feet in a load of wood in five minutes. The dimensions given, I figured out the result in less than two minutes, to the great delight of my teacher and to the equal astonishment of his neighbor.

My organ of "acquisitiveness" was manifest at an early age. Before I was five years of age, I began to accumulate pennies and "four-pences," and when I was six years old my capital amounted to a sum sufficient to exchange for a silver dollar, the possession of which made me feel far richer and more independent than I have ever since felt in the world.

Nor did my dollar long remain alone. As I grew older I earned ten cents a day for riding the horse which led the ox team in ploughing, and on holidays and "training days," instead of spending money, I earned it. I was a small peddler of molasses candy (of home make), ginger-bread, cookies and cherry rum, and I generally found myself a dollar or two richer at the end of a holiday than I was at the beginning. I was always ready for a trade, and by the time I was twelve years old, besides other property, I was the owner of a sheep and a calf, and should soon, no doubt, have become a small Croesus, had not my father kindly permitted me to purchase my own clothing, which somewhat reduced my little store.

When I was nearly twelve years old I made my first visit to the metropolis. It happened in this wise: Late one afternoon in January, 1822, Mr. Daniel Brown, of Southbury, Connecticut, arrived at my father's tavern, in Bethel, with some fat cattle he was driving to New York to sell. The cattle were put into our large barnyard, the horses were stabled, and Mr. Brown and his assistant were provided with a warm supper and lodging for the night. After supper I heard Mr. Brown say to my father

that he intended to buy more cattle, and that he would be
glad to hire a boy to assist in driving the cattle. I immediately besought my father to secure the situation for me,
and he did so. My mother's consent was also gained, and
at daylight next morning, after a slight breakfast, I
started on foot in the midst of a heavy snow storm to help
drive the cattle. Before reaching Ridgefield, I was sent on
horseback after a stray ox, and, in galloping, the horse fell
and my ankle was sprained. I suffered severely, but did
not complain lest my employer should send me back. But
he considerately permitted me to ride behind him on his
horse; and, indeed, did so most of the way to New York,
where we arrived in three or four days.

We put up at the Bull's Head Tavern, where we were
to stay a week while the drover was disposing of his cattle, and we were then to return home in a sleigh. It was an
eventful week for me. Before I left home my mother had
given me a dollar which I supposed would supply every
want that heart could wish. My first outlay was for oranges which I was told were four pence apiece, and as
"four-pence" in Connecticut was six cents, I offered ten
cents for two oranges which was of course readily taken;
and thus, instead of saving two cents, as I thought, I actually paid two cents more than the price demanded. I
then bought two more oranges, reducing my capital to
eighty cents. Thirty-one cents was the "charge" for a
small gun which would "go off" and send a stick some
little distance, and this gun I bought. Amusing myself
with this toy in the barroom of the Bull's Head, the arrow
happened to hit the barkeeper, who forthwith came from
behind the counter and shook me and soundly boxed my
ears, telling me to put that gun out of the way or he
would put it into the fire. I sneaked to my room, put my
treasure under the pillow, and went out for another visit
to the toy shop.

There I invested six cents in "torpedoes," with which
I intended to astonish my schoolmates in Bethel. I could
not refrain, however, from experimenting upon the

guests of the hotel, which I did when they were going in to dinner. I threw two of the torpedoes against the wall of the hall through which the guests were passing, and the immediate results were as follows: two loud reports,—astonished guests,—irate landlord,—discovery of the culprit, and summary punishment—for the landlord immediately floored me with a single blow with his open hand, and said:

"There, you little greenhorn, see if that will teach you better than to explode your infernal fire crackers in my house again."

The lesson was sufficient if not entirely satisfactory. I deposited the balance of the torpedoes with my gun, and as a solace for my wounded feelings I again visited the toy shop, where I bought a watch, breastpin and top, leaving but eleven cents of my original dollar.

The following morning found me again at the fascinating toy shop, where I saw a beautiful knife with two blades, a gimlet, and a corkscrew,—a whole carpenter shop in miniature, and all for thirty-one cents. But, alas! I had only eleven cents. Have that knife I must, however, and so I proposed to the shop woman to take back the top and breastpin at a slight deduction, and with my eleven cents to let me have the knife. The kind creature consented, and this makes memorable my first "swap." Some fine and nearly white molasses candy then caught my eye, and I proposed to trade the watch for its equivalent in candy. The transaction was made and the candy was so delicious that before night my gun was absorbed in the same way. The next morning the torpedoes "went off" in the same direction, and before night even my beloved knife was similarly exchanged. My money and my goods all gone I traded two pocket handkerchiefs and an extra pair of stockings I was sure I should not want for nine more rolls of molasses candy, and then wandered about the city disconsolate, sighing because there was no more molasses candy to conquer.

I doubt not that in these first wanderings about the

city I often passed the corner of Broadway and Ann Street—never dreaming of the stir I was destined at a future day to make in that locality as proprietor and manager of the American Museum.

After wandering, gazing and wondering, for a week, Mr. Brown took me in his sleigh and on the evening of the following day we arrived in Bethel. I had a thousand questions to answer, and then and for a long time afterwards I was quite a lion among my mates because I had seen the great metropolis. My brothers and sisters, however, were much disappointed at my not bringing them something from my dollar, and when my mother examined my wardrobe and found two pocket handkerchiefs and one pair of stockings missing she whipped me and sent me to bed. Thus ingloriously terminated my first visit to New York.

Previous to my visit to New York, I think it was in 1820, when I was ten years of age, I made my first expedition to my landed property, "Ivy Island." This, it will be remembered, was the gift of my grandfather, from whom I derived my name. From the time when I was four years old I was continually hearing of this "property." My grandfather always spoke of me (in my presence) to the neighbors and to strangers as the richest child in town, since I owned the whole of "Ivy Island," one of the most valuable farms in the State. My father and mother frequently reminded me of my wealth and hoped I would do something for the family when I attained my majority. The neighbors professed fear that I might refuse to play with their children because I had inherited so large a property.

These constant allusions, for several years, to "Ivy Island" excited at once my pride and my curiosity and stimulated me to implore my father's permission to visit my property. At last, he promised I should do so in a few days, as we should be getting some hay near "Ivy Island." The wished for day at length arrived and my father told me that as we were to mow an adjoining meadow, I might visit my property in company with the hired man during the "nooning." My grandfather reminded me that it was to his bounty I was indebted for this wealth, and that had not my name been Phineas I might never have been proprietor of "Ivy Island." To this my mother added:

"Now, Taylor, don't become so excited when you see your property as to let your joy make you sick, for remember, rich as you are, that it will be eleven years before you can come into possession of your fortune."

She added much more good advice, to all of which I promised to be calm and reasonable and not to allow my pride to prevent me from speaking to my brothers and sisters when I returned home.

When we arrived at the meadow, which was in that part of the "Plum Trees" know as the "East Swamp," I asked my father where "Ivy Island" was.

"Yonder, at the north end of this meadow, where you see those beautiful trees rising in the distance."

All the forenoon I turned grass as fast as two men could cut it, and after a hasty repast at noon, one of our hired men, a good natured Irishman, named Edmund, took an axe on his shoulder and announced that he was ready to accompany me to "Ivy Island." We started, and as we approached the north end of the meadow we found the ground swampy and wet and were soon obliged to leap from bog to bog on our route. A misstep brought me up to my middle in water. To add to the dilemma a swarm of hornets attacked me. Attaining the altitude of another bog I was cheered by the assurance that there was only a quarter of a mile of this kind of travel to the edge of my property. I waded on. In about fifteen minutes more, after floundering through the morass, I found myself half-drowned, hornet-stung, mud-covered, and out of breath, on comparatively dry land.

"Never mind, my boy," said Edmund, "we have only to cross this little creek, and ye'll be upon your own valuable property."

We were on the margin of a stream, the banks of which were thickly covered with alders. I now discovered the use of Edmund's axe, for he felled a small oak to form a temporary bridge to my "Island" property. Crossing over, I proceeded to the centre of my domain; I saw nothing but a few stunted ivies and straggling trees. The truth flashed upon me. I had been the laughing-stock of the family and neighborhood for years. My valuable "Ivy Island" was an almost inaccessible, worthless bit of barren land, and while I stood deploring my sudden downfall, a huge black snake (one of my tenants) approached me with upraised head. I gave one shriek and rushed for the bridge.

This was my first, and, I need not say, my last visit to "Ivy Island." My father asked me "how I liked my property?" and I responded that I would sell it pretty cheap. My grandfather congratulated me upon my visit to my property as seriously as if it had been indeed a valuable domain. My mother hoped its richness had fully equalled my anticipations. The neighbors desired to know if I was not now glad I was named Phineas, and for five years forward I was frequently reminded of my wealth in "Ivy Island."

As I grew older, my settled aversion to manual labor, farm or other kind, was manifest in various ways, which were set down to the general score of laziness. In despair of doing better with me, my father concluded to make a merchant of me. He erected a building in Bethel, and with Mr. Hiram Weed as a partner, purchased a stock of dry goods, hardware, groceries, and general notions and installed me as clerk in this country store.

Of course I "felt my oats." It was condescension on my part to talk with boys who did out-door work. I stood behind the counter with a pen over my ear, was polite to the ladies, and was wonderfully active in waiting upon customers. We kept a cash, credit and barter store, and I drove some sharp bargains with women who brought butter, eggs, beeswax and feathers to exchange for dry goods, and with men who wanted to trade oats, corn, buckwheat, axe-helves, hats, and other commodities for tenpenny nails, molasses, or New England rum. But it was a drawback upon my dignity that I was obliged to take down the shutters, sweep the store, and make the fire. I received a small salary for my services and the perquisite of what profit I could derive from purchasing candies on my own account to sell to our younger customers, and, as usual, my father stipulated that I should clothe myself.

There is a great deal to be learned in a country store, and principally this—that sharp trades, tricks, dishonesty, and deception are by no means confined to the city. More than once, in cutting open bundles of rags, brought to be exchanged for goods, and warranted to be all linen and cotton, I have discovered in the interior worthless woolen trash and sometimes stones, gravel or ashes. Sometimes, too, when measuring loads of oats, corn or rye, declared to contain a specified number of bushels, say sixty, I have found them four or five bushels short. In such cases, some one else was always to blame, but these happenings were frequent enough to make us watchful of our customers. In the evenings and on wet days trade was always dull, and at such times the story-telling and joke-playing wits and wags of the village used to assemble in our store, and from them I derived considerable amusement, if not profit. After the store was closed at night, I frequently joined some of the village boys at the houses of their parents, where, with story-telling and play, a couple of hours would soon pass by, and then as late, perhaps, as eleven o'clock, I went home and slyly crept up stairs so as not to awaken my brother with whom I slept, and who would be sure to report my late hours. He made every attempt, and laid all sorts of plans to catch me on my return, but as sleep always overtook him, I managed easily to elude his efforts.

Like most people in Connecticut in those days, I was brought up to attend church regularly on Sunday, and long before I could read I was a prominent scholar in the Sunday school. My good mother taught me my lessons in the New Testament and the Catechism, and my every effort was directed to win one of those "Rewards of Merit," which promised to pay the bearer one mill, so that ten of these prizes amounted to one cent, and one hundred of them, which might be won by faithful assiduity every Sunday for two years, would buy a Sunday school book worth ten cents. Such were the magnificent rewards held out to the religious ambition of youth.

There was but one church or "meeting-house" in Bethel, which all attended, sinking all differences of creed in the Presbyterian faith. The old meeting-house had neither steeple nor bell and was a plain edifice, comfortable enough in the summer, but my teeth chatter even now when I think of the dreary, cold, freezing hours we passed in that place in winter. A stove in a meeting-house in those days would have been a sacrilegious innovation. The sermons were from an hour and one half to two hours long, and through these the congregation would sit and shiver till they really merited the title the profane gave them of "blue skins." Some of the women carried a "foot-stove" consisting of a small square tin box in a wooden frame, the sides perforated, and in the interior there was a small square iron dish, which contained a few live coals covered with ashes. These stoves were usually replenished just before meeting time at some neighbor's near the meeting-house.

After many years of shivering and suffering, one of the brethren had the temerity to propose that the church should be warmed with a stove. His impious proposition was voted down by an overwhelming majority. Another year came around, and in November the stove question was again brought up. The excitement was immense. The subject was discussed in the village stores and in the juvenile debating club; it was prayed over in conference; and finally in general "society's meeting," in December, the stove was carried by a majority of one and was introduced into the meeting-house. On the first Sunday thereafter, two ancient maiden ladies were so oppressed by the dry and heated atmosphere occasioned by the wicked innovation, that they fainted away and were carried out into the cool air where they speedily returned to consciousness, especially when they were informed that owing to the lack of two lengths of pipe, no fire had yet been made in the stove. The next Sunday was a bitter cold day, and the stove, filled with well-seasoned hickory, was a great gratification to the many, and displeased only a few. After the benediction, an old deacon rose and requested the congregation to remain, and called upon them to witness that he had from the first raised his voice against the introduction of a stove into the house of the Lord; but the majority had been against him and he had submitted; now, if they *must* have a stove, he insisted upon having a large one, since the present one did not heat the whole house, but drove the cold to the back outside pews, making them three times as cold as they were before! In the course of the week, this deacon was made to comprehend that, unless on unusually severe days, the stove was sufficient to warm the house, and, at any rate, it did not drive all the cold in the house into one corner.

During the Rev. Mr. Lowe's ministrations at Bethel, he formed a Bible class, of which I was a member. We used to draw promiscuously from a hat a text of scripture and write a composition on the text, which compositions were read after service in the afternoon, to such of the congregation as remained to hear the exercises of the class. Once, I remember, I drew the text, Luke x. 42: "But one thing is needful; and Mary hath chosen that good part which shall not be taken away from her." *Question*, "What is the one thing needful?" My answer was nearly as follows:

"This question 'what is the one thing needful?' is capable of receiving various answers, depending much upon the persons to whom it is addressed. The merchant might answer that 'the one thing needful' is plenty of customers, who buy liberally, without beating down and pay cash for all their purchases.' The farmer might reply, that 'the one thing needful is large harvests and high prices.' The physician might answer that 'it is plenty of patients.' The lawyer might be of opinion that 'it is an unruly community, always engaged in bickerings and litigations.' The clergyman might reply, 'It is a fat salary with multitudes of sinners seeking salvation and paying large pew rents.' The bachelor might exclaim, 'It is a pretty wife who loves her husband, and who knows how to sew on buttons.' The maiden might answer, 'It is a good husband, who will love, cherish and protect me while life shall last.' But the most proper answer, and doubtless that which applied to the case of Mary, would be, "The one thing needful is to believe in the Lord Jesus Christ, follow in his footsteps, love God and obey His commandments, love our fellow-man, and embrace every opportunity of administering to his necessities.' In short, 'the one thing needful' is to live a life that we can always look back upon with satisfaction, and be enabled ever to contemplate its termination with trust in Him who has so kindly vouchsafed it to us, surrounding us with innumerable blessings, if we have but the heart and wisdom to receive them in proper manner."

The reading of a portion of this answer occasioned some amusement in the congregation, in which the clergyman himself joined, and the name of "Taylor Barnum" was whispered in connection with composition; but at the close of the reading I had the satisfaction of hearing Mr. Lowe say that it was a well written and truthful answer to the question, "What is the one thing needful?"

CHAPTER II.

Incidents and Anecdotes.

In the month of August, 1825, my maternal grandmother met with an accident in stepping on the point of a rusty nail, and, though the matter was at first considered trivial, it resulted in her death. Alarming symptoms soon made her sensible that she was on her death-bed; and while she was in full possession of her faculties, the day before she died she sent for her grandchildren to take final leave of them. I shall never forget the sensations I experienced when she took me by the hand and besought me to lead a religious life, and especially to remember that I could in no way so effectually prove my love to God as by loving all my fellow-beings. The impressions of that death-bed scene have ever been among my most vivid recollections, and I trust they have proved in some degree salutary. A more exemplary woman, or a more sincere Christian than my grandmother, I have never known.

My father, for his time and locality, was a man of much enterprise. He could, and actually did, "keep a hotel"; he had a livery stable and ran, in a small way, what in our day would be called a Norwalk Express; and he also kept a country store. With greater opportunities and a larger field for his efforts and energies, he might have been a man of mark and means. Not that he was successful, for he never did a profitable business; but I, who saw him in his various pursuits, and acted as his clerk, caught something of his enterprising spirit, and, perhaps without egotism, I may say I inherited that characteristic. My business education was as good as the limited field afforded, and I soon put it to account and service.

On the 7th of September, 1825, my father, who had been sick since the month of March, died at the age of forty-eight years. My mother was left with five children, of whom I, at fifteen years of age, was the eldest, while the youngest was but seven. It was soon apparent that my father had provided nothing for the support of his family; his estate was insolvent, and it did not pay fifty cents on the dollar. My mother, by economy, industry, and perseverance, succeeded in a few years afterwards in redeeming the homestead and becoming its sole possessor; but, at the date of the death of my father, the world looked gloomy indeed; the few dollars I had accumulated and loaned to my father, holding his note therefor, were decided to be the property of a minor, belonging to the father and so to the estate, and my small claim was ruled out. I was obliged to get trusted for the pair of shoes I wore to my father's funeral. I literally began the world with nothing, and was barefooted at that.

Leaving Mr. Weed, I went to Grassy Plain, a mile northwest of Bethel, and secured a situation as clerk in the store of James S. Keeler & Lewis Whitlock at six dollars a month and my board. I lived with Mrs. Jerusha Wheeler and her daughters, Jerusha and Mary, and found an excellent home. I chose my uncle, Alanson Taylor, as my guardian. I did my best to please my employers and soon gained their confidence and esteem and was regarded by them as an active clerk and a 'cute trader. They afforded me many facilities for making money on my own account and I soon entered upon sundry speculations and succeeded in getting a small sum of money ahead.

I made a very remarkable trade at one time for my employers by purchasing, in their absence, a whole wagon load of green glass bottles of various sizes, for which I paid in unsalable goods at very profitable prices. How to dispose of the bottles was then the problem, and as it was also desirable to get rid of a large quantity of tin ware which had been in the shop for years and was considerably "shop-worn," I conceived the idea of a lottery in which the highest prize should be twenty-five dollars, payable in any goods the winner desired, while there were to be fifty prizes of five dollars each, payable in goods, to be designated in the scheme. Then there were one hundred prizes of one dollar each, one hundred prizes of fifty cents each, and three hundred prizes of twenty-five cents each. It is unnecessary to state that the minor prizes consisted mainly of glass and tin ware; the tickets sold like wildfire and the worn tin and glass bottles were speedily turned into cash.

As my mother continued to keep the village tavern at Bethel, I usually went home on Saturday night and stayed till Monday morning, going to church with my mother on Sunday. This habit was the occasion of an experience of momentous consequence to me. One Saturday evening, during a violent thunder shower, Miss Mary Wheeler, a milliner, sent me word that there was a girl from Bethel at her house, who had come up on horseback to get a new bonnet; that she was afraid to go back alone; and if I was going to Bethel that evening she wished me to escort her customer. I assented, and went over to "Aunt Rushia's" where I was introduced to "Chairy" (Charity) Hallett, a fair, rosy-cheeked, buxom girl, with beautiful white teeth. I assisted her to her saddle, and mounting my own horse, we trotted towards Bethel.

My first impressions of this girl as I saw her at the house were exceedingly favorable. As soon as we started I began a conversation with her and finding her very affable I regretted that the distance to Bethel was not five miles instead of one. A flash of lightning gave me a distinct view of the face of my fair companion and then I wished the distance was twenty miles. During our ride I

learned that she was a tailoress, working with Mr. Zerah
Benedict, of Bethel. We soon arrived at our destination
and I bid her good night and went home. The next day I
saw her at church, and, indeed, many Sundays afterwards, but I had no opportunity to renew the acquaintance that season. . . .

CHAPTER III.

In Business
for Myself.

Mr. Oliver Taylor removed from Danbury to Brooklyn, Long Island, where he kept a grocery store and also had a large comb factory and a comb store in New York. In the fall of 1826 he offered me a situation as clerk in his Brooklyn store, and I accepted it. I soon became conversant with the routine of my employer's business and before long he entrusted to me the purchasing of all goods for his store. I bought for cash entirely, going into the lower part of New York City in search of the cheapest market for groceries, often attending auctions of teas, sugars, molasses, etc., watching the sales, noting prices and buyers, and frequently combining with other grocers to bid off large lots, which we subsequently divided, giving each of us the quantity wanted at a lower rate than if the goods had passed into other hands, compelling us to pay another profit.

Situated as I was, and well treated as I was by my employer, who manifested great interest in me, still I was dissatisfied. A salary was not sufficient for me. My disposition was of that speculative character which refused to be satisfied unless I was engaged in some business where my profits might be enhanced, or, at least, made to depend upon my energy, perseverance, attention to business, tact, and "calculation." Accordingly, as I had no opportunity to speculate on my own account, I became uneasy, and, young as I was, I began to talk of setting up for myself; for, although I had no capital, several men of means had offered to furnish the money and join me in business. I was in that uneasy, transitory state between boyhood and manhood when I had unbounded confidence in my own abilities, and yet needed a discreet counsellor, adviser and friend.

In the following summer, 1827, I was taken down with the small-pox and was confined to the house for several months. This sickness made a sad inroad upon my means. When I was sufficiently recovered, I started for home to recruit, taking passage on board a sloop for Norwalk, but the remaining passengers were so frightened at the appearance of my face, which still bore the marks of the disease, that I was obliged to go ashore again, which I did, stopping at Holt's, in Fulton Street, going to Norwalk by steamboat next morning, and arriving at Bethel in the afternoon.

During my convalescence at my mother's house, I visited my old friends and neighbors and had the opportunity to slightly renew my acquaintance with the attractive tailoress, "Chairy" Hallett. A month afterwards, I returned to Brooklyn, where I gave Mr. Taylor notice of my desire to leave his employment; and I then opened a porter-house on my own account. In a few months I sold out to good advantage and accepted a favorable offer to engage as clerk in a similar establishment, kept by Mr. David Thorp, 29 Peck Slip, New York. It was a great resort for Danbury and Bethel comb makers and hatters and I thus had frequent opportunities of seeing and hearing from my fellow-townsmen. I lived in Mr. Thorp's family and was kindly treated. I was often permitted to visit the theatre with friends who came to New York, and, as I had considerable taste for the drama, I soon became, in my own opinion, a discriminating critic—nor did I fail to exhibit my powers to my Connecticut friends who accompanied me to the play. Let me gratefully add that my habits were not bad. Though I sold liquors to others, I do not think I ever drank a pint of liquor, wine, or cordials before I was twenty-two years of age. I always had a Bible, which I frequently read, and I attended church regularly. These habits, so far as they go, are in the right direction, and I am thankful to-day that they characterized my early youth. However worthy or unworthy may have been my later years, I *know* that I owe much of the better part of my nature to my youthful regard for Sunday and its institutions—a regard, I trust, still strong in my character.

In February, 1828, I returned to Bethel and opened a retail fruit and confectionery store in a part of my grandfather's carriage-house, which was situated on the main street, and which was offered to me rent free if I would return to my native village and establish some sort of business. This beginning of business on my own account was an eventful era in my life. My total capital was one hundred and twenty dollars, fifty of which I had expended in fitting up the store, and the remaining seventy dollars purchased my stock in trade. I had arranged with fruit dealers whom I knew in New York to receive my orders, and I decided to open my establishment on the first Monday in May—our "general training" day.

It was a "red letter" day for me. The village was crowded with people from the surrounding region and the novelty of my little shop attracted attention. Long before noon I was obliged to call in one of my old schoolmates to assist in waiting upon my numerous customers and when I closed at night I had the satisfaction of reckoning up sixty-three dollars as my day's receipts. Nor, although I had received the entire cost of my goods, less seven dollars, did the stock seem seriously diminished; showing that my profits had been large. I need not say how much gratified I was with the result of this first day's experiment. The store was a fixed fact. I went to New York and expended all my money in a stock of fancy goods, such as pocket-books, combs, beads, rings, pocket-knives, and a few toys. These, with fruit, nuts, etc., made the business good through the summer, and in the fall I added stewed oysters to the inducements.

My grandfather, who was much interested in my success, advised me to take an agency for the sale of lottery tickets, on commission. In those days, the lottery was not deemed objectionable on the score of morality. Very worthy people invested in such schemes without a thought of evil, and then, as now, churches even got up lotteries, with this difference—that then they were called lotteries, and now they go under some other name. While I am very glad that an improved public sentiment denounces the lottery in general as an illegitimate means of getting money, and while I do not see how any one, especially in or near a New England State, can engage in a lottery without feeling a reproach which no pecuniary return can compensate; yet I cannot now accuse myself for having been lured into a business which was then sanctioned by good Christian people, who now join with me in reprobating enterprises they once encouraged. But as public sentiment was forty years ago, I obtained an agency to sell lottery tickets on a commission of ten per cent, and this business, in connection with my little store, made my profits quite satisfactory.

I used to have some curious customers. On one occasion a young man called on me and selected a pocketbook which pleased him, asking me to give him credit for a few weeks. I told him that if he wanted any article of necessity in my line, I should not object to trust him for a short time, but it struck me that a pocket-book was a decided superfluity for a man who had no money; I therefore declined to trust him as I did not see the necessity for his possessing such an article till he had something to put into it. Later in life I have been credited with the utterance of some sagacious remarks, but this with regard to the pocket-book, trivial as the matter is in itself, seems to me quite as deserving of note as any of my ideas which have created more sensation.

My store had much to do in giving shape to my future character as well as career, in that it became a favorite resort; the theatre of village talk, and the scene of many practical jokes. For any excess of the jocose element in my character, part of the blame must attach to my early surroundings as a village clerk and merchant. In that true resort of village wits and wags, the country store, fun, pure and simple, will be sure to find the surface. My Bethel store was the scene of many most amusing incidents, in some of which I was an immediate participant, though in many, of course, I was only a listener or spectator. . . .

CHAPTER IV.

Struggles for a Livelihood.

During this season I made arrangements with Mr. Samuel Sherwood, of Bridgeport, to go on an exploring expedition to Pittsburg, Pennsylvania, where we understood there was a fine opening for a lottery office and where we meant to try our fortunes, provided the prospects should equal our expectations. We went to New York where I had an interview with Mr. Dudley S. Gregory, the principal business man of Messrs. Yates and McIntyre, who dissuaded me from going to Pittsburg, and offered me the entire lottery agency for the State of Tennessee, if I would go to Nashville and open an office. The offer was tempting, but the distance was too far from a certain tailoress in Bethel.

As the Pittsburg trip was given up, Sherwood and I went to Philadelphia for a pleasure excursion and put up at Congress Hall in Chestnut Street where we lived in much grander style than we had been accustomed to. The array of waiters and display of dishes were far ahead of our former experiences and for a week we lived in clover. At the end of that time, however, when we concluded to start for home, the amount of our hotel bill astounded us. After paying it and securing tickets for New York, our combined purses showed a balance of but twenty-seven cents.

Twenty-five cents of this sum went to the boot-black, and as our breakfast was included in our bill we secured from the table a few biscuits for our dinner on the way to New York.

Arriving in New York we carried our own baggage to Holt's Hotel. The next morning Sherwood obtained a couple of dollars from a friend, and went to Newark and borrowed fifty dollars from his cousin, Dr. Sherwood, loaning me one-half the sum. After a few days' sojourn in the city we returned home.

During our stay in New York, I derived considerable information from the city managers with regard to the lottery business, and thereafter I bought my tickets directly from the Connecticut lottery managers at what was termed "the scheme price," and also established agencies throughout the country, selling considerable quantities of tickets at handsome profits. My uncle, Alanson Taylor, joined me in the business, and, as we sold several prizes, my office came to be considered "lucky," and I received orders from all parts of the country.

During this time I kept a close eye upon the attractive tailoress, Charity Hallett, and in the summer of 1829 I asked her hand in marriage. My suit was accepted, and the wedding day was appointed; I, meanwhile, applying myself closely to business, and no one but the parties immediately interested suspecting that the event was so near at hand. Miss Hallett went to New York in October, ostensibly to visit her uncle, Nathan Beers, who resided at No. 3 Allen Street. I followed in November, pressed by the necessity of purchasing goods for my store; and the evening after my arrival, November 8, 1829, the Rev. Dr. McAuley married us in the presence of sundry friends and relatives of my wife, and I became the husband of one of the best women in the world. In the course of the week we went back to Bethel and took board in the family where Charity Barnum as "Chairy" Hallett had previously resided.

I do not approve or recommend early marriages. The minds of men and women taking so important a step in life should be somewhat matured, and hasty marriages, especially marriages of boys and girls, have been the cause of untold misery in many instances. But although I was only little more than nineteen years old when I was married, I have always felt assured that if I had waited twenty years longer I could not have found another woman so well suited to my disposition and so admirable and valuable in every character as a wife, a mother, and a friend.

My business occupations amply employed nearly all my time, yet so strong was my love of fun that when the opportunity for a practical joke presented itself, I could not resist the temptation. On one occasion I engaged in the character of counsel to conduct a case for an Irish peddler whose complaint was that one of our neighbors had turned him out of his house and had otherwise abused him.

The court was just as "real" as the attorney,—no more,—and consisted of three judges, one a mason, the second a butcher, and the third an old gentleman of leisure who was an ex-justice of the peace. The constable was of my own appointment, and my "writ" arrested the culprit who had turned my client out of house and home. The court was convened, but as the culprit did not appear, and as it seemed necessary that my client should get testimonials as to his personal character, the court adjourned nominally for one week, the client consenting to "stand treat" to cover immediate expenses.

I supposed that this was the end of it. But at the time named for the re-assembling of the "court," a *real* lawyer from Newtown put in an appearance. He had been engaged by the Irishman to assist me in conducting the case! I saw at once that the joke was likely to prove a sorry one, and immediately notified the members of the "court," who were quite as much alarmed as I was at the serious turn the thing had taken. I need not say that while the danger threatened we all took precious good care to keep out of the way. However, the affair was explained to Mr. Belden, the lawyer, who in turn set forth the matter to the client, but not in such a manner as to soothe the anger so natural under the circumstances—in fact, he advised the Irishman to get out of the place as soon as possible. The Irishman threatened me and my "court" with prosecution—a threat I really feared he would carry into execution, but which, to the great peace of mind of myself and my companions, he concluded not to follow up. Considering the vexation and annoyance of this Irishman, it was a mitigation to know that he was the party in the wrong and that he really deserved a severer punishment than my practical joke had put upon him.

In the winter of 1829–30, my lottery business had so extended that I had branch offices in Danbury, Norwalk, Stamford and Middletown, as well as agencies in the small villages for thirty miles around Bethel. I had also purchased from my grandfather three acres of land on which I built a house and went to housekeeping. My lottery business, which was with a few large customers, was so arranged that I could safely entrust it to an agent, making it necessary for me to find some other field for my individual enterprise.

So I tried my hand as an auctioneer in the book trade. I bought books at the auctions and from dealers and publishers in New York, and took them into the country, selling them at auction and doing tolerably well; only at Litchfield, Connecticut, where there was then a law school. At Newburgh, New York, several of my best books were stolen, and I quit the business in disgust.

In July, 1831, my uncle, Alanson Taylor, and myself opened a country store in a building, which I had put up in Bethel in the previous spring, and we stocked the "yellow store," as it was called, with a full assortment of groceries, hardware, crockery, and "notions"; but we were not successful in the enterprise, and in October following, I bought out my uncle's interest and we dissolved partnership.

About this time, circumstances partly religious and partly political in their character led me into still another field of enterprise which honorably opened to me that notoriety of which in later life I surely have had a surfeit. Considering my youth, this new enterprise reflected credit upon my ability, as well as energy, and so I may be excused if I now recur to it with something like pride.

In a period of strong political excitement, I wrote several communications for the Danbury weekly paper, setting forth what I conceived to be the dangers of a sectarian interference which was then apparent in political affairs. The publication of these communications was refused and I accordingly purchased a press and types, and October 19, 1831, I issued the first number of my own paper, *The Herald of Freedom*.

I entered upon the editorship of this journal with all the vigor and vehemence of youth. The boldness with which the paper was conducted soon excited widespread attention and commanded a circulation which extended beyond the immediate locality into nearly every State in the Union. But lacking that experience which induces caution, and without the dread of consequences, I frequently laid myself open to the charge of libel and three times in three years I was prosecuted. A Danbury butcher, a zealous politician, brought a civil suit against me for accusing him of being a spy in a Democratic caucus. On the first trial the jury did not agree, but after a second trial I was fined several hundred dollars. Another libel suit against me was withdrawn and need not be mentioned further. The third was sufficiently important to warrant the following detail:

A criminal prosecution was brought against me for stating in my paper that a man in Bethel, prominent in the church, had "been guilty of taking *usury* of an orphan boy," and for severely commenting on the fact in my editorial columns. When the case came to trial the truth of my statement was substantially proved by several witnesses and even by the prosecuting party. But "the greater the truth, the greater the libel," and then I had used the term "usury," instead of extortion, or note-shaving, or some other expression which might have softened the verdict. The result was that I was sentenced to pay a fine of one hundred dollars and to be imprisoned in the common jail for sixty days.

The most comfortable provision was made for me in Danbury jail. My room was papered and carpeted; I lived well; I was overwhelmed with the constant visits of my friends; I edited my paper as usual and received large accessions to my subscription list; and at the end of my sixty days' term the event was celebrated by a large concourse of people from the surrounding country. The court room in which I was convicted was the scene of the celebration. An ode, written for the occasion, was sung; an eloquent oration on the freedom of the press was delivered; and several hundred gentlemen afterwards partook of a sumptuous dinner followed by appropriate toasts and speeches. Then came the triumphant part of the ceremonial, which was reported in my paper of December 12, 1832, as follows:

"P. T. BARNUM and the band of music took their seats in a coach drawn by six horses, which had been prepared for the occasion. The coach was preceded by forty horsemen, and a marshal, bearing the national standard. Immediately in the rear of the coach was the carriage of the Orator and the President of the day, followed by the Committee of Arrangements and sixty carriages of citizens, which joined in escorting the editor to his home in Bethel.

"When the procession commenced its march amidst the roar of cannon, three cheers were given by several hundred citizens who did not join in the procession. The band of music continued to play a variety of national airs until their arrival in Bethel, (a distance of three miles,) when they struck up the beautiful and appropriate tune of 'Home, Sweet Home!' After giving three hearty cheers, the procession returned to Danbury. The utmost harmony and unanimity of feeling prevailed throughout the day, and we are happy to add that no accident occurred to mar the festivities of the occasion."

My editorial career was one of continual contest. I however published the 160th number of *The Herald of Freedom* in Danbury, November 5, 1834, after which my brother-in-law, John W. Amerman, issued the paper for me at Norwalk till the following year, when the *Herald* was sold to Mr. George Taylor.

Meanwhile, I had taken Horace Fairchild into partnership in my mercantile business, in 1831, and I had sold out to him and to a Mr. Toucey, in 1833, they forming a partnership under the firm of Fairchild & Co. So far as I was concerned my store was not a success. Ordinary trade was too slow for me. I bought largely and in order to sell I was compelled to give extensive credits. Hence I had an accumulation of bad debts; and my old ledger presents a long series of accounts balanced by "death," by "running away," by "failing," and by other similarly remunerative returns. I had expended money as freely as I had gained it, for I had already learned that I could make money rapidly and in large sums, when I set about it with a will, and hence I did not realize the worth of what I seemed to gain so readily. I looked forward to a future of saving when I should see the need of accumulation.

There was nothing more for me to do in Bethel; and in the winter of 1834–5, I removed my family to New York, where I hired a house in Hudson Street. I had no pecuniary resources, excepting such as might be derived from debts left for collection with my agent at Bethel, and I went to the metropolis literally to seek my fortune. I hoped to secure a situation in some mercantile house, not at a fixed salary, but so as to derive such portion of the profits as might be due to my individual tact, energy, and perseverance in the interests of the business. But I could find no such position; my resources began to fail; my family were in ill health; I must do something for a living; and so I acted as "drummer" to several concerns which allowed me a small commission on sales to customers of my introduction.

Every morning I used to look at the "wants" in the *Sun* for something that would suit me; and I had many a wildgoose chase in following up those "wants." In some instances success depended upon my advancing from three hundred to five hundred dollars; in other cases a new patent life-pill, or a self-acting mouse trap was to make my fortune. An advertisement announcing "An immense speculation on a small capital! $10,000 easily made in one year!" turned out to be an offer of Professor Somebody at Scudder's American Museum to sell a hydro-oxygen microscope, offered to me at two thousand dollars—one thousand in cash and the balance in sixty and ninety days, on good security,—and warranted to secure an independence after a short public exhibition through the country. If I had the desire to undertake this exhibition and experiment, I had not the capital. Other and many similar temptations were extended, but none of them seemed to open the door of fortune to me.

The advertisement in the *Sun,* of Mr. William Niblo, of Niblo's Garden, for a barkeeper first brought me in contact with that gentlemanly and justly-popular proprietor. He wanted a well-recommended, well-behaved, trustworthy man to fill a vacant situation, but as he wished him to bind himself to remain three years, I, who was only seeking the means of temporary support, was precluded from accepting the position.

Nor did all my efforts secure a situation for me during the whole winter; but, in the spring, I received several hundred dollars from my agent in Bethel, and finding no better business, May 1, 1835, I opened a small private boarding-house at No. 52 Frankfort Street. We soon had a very good run of custom from our Connecticut acquaintances who had occasion to visit New York, and as

this business did not sufficiently occupy my time, I
bought an interest with Mr. John Moody in a grocery
store, No. 156 South Street.

Although the years of manhood brought cares, anxi-
eties, and struggles for a livelihood, they did not change
my nature and the jocose element was still an essential
ingredient of my being. I loved fun, practical fun, for itself and for the enjoyment which it brought. During the
year, I occasionally visited Bridgeport where I almost always found at the hotel a noted joker, named Darrow,
who spared neither friend nor foe in his tricks. He was
the life of the bar-room and would always try to entrap
some stranger in a bet and so win a treat for the company.
He made several ineffectual attempts upon me, and at
last, one evening, Darrow, who stuttered, made a final
trial as follows: "Come, Barnum, I'll make you another
proposition; I'll bet you hain't got a whole shirt on your
back." The catch consists in the fact that generally only
one-half of that convenient garment is on the back; but I
had anticipated the proposition—in fact I had induced a
friend, Mr. Hough, to put Darrow up to the trick,—and
had folded a shirt nicely upon my back, securing it there
with my suspenders. The barroom was crowded with customers who thought that if I made the bet I should be
nicely caught, and I made pretence of playing off and at
the same time stimulated Darrow·to press the bet by
saying:

"That is a foolish bet to make; I am sure my shirt is
whole because it is nearly new; but I don't like to bet on
such a subject."

"A good reason why," said Darrow, in great glee; "it's
ragged. Come, I'll bet you a treat for the whole company
you hain't got a whole shirt on your b-b-b-back!"

"I'll bet my shirt is cleaner than yours," I replied.

"That's nothing to do w-w-with the case; it's ragged,
and y-y-you know it."

"I know it is not," I replied, with pretended anger,
which caused the crowd to laugh heartily.

"You poor ragged f-f-fellow, come down here from D-D-Danbury, I'm sorry for you," said Darrow tantalizingly.

"You would not pay if you lost," I remarked.

"Here's f-f-five dollars I'll put in Captain Hinman's (the landlord's) hands. Now b-b-bet if you dare, you ragged c-c-creature, you."

I put five dollars in Captain Hinman's hands, and told him to treat the company from it if I lost the bet.

"Remember," said Darrow, "I b-b-bet you hain't got a whole shirt on your b-b-back!"

"All right," said I, taking off my coat and commencing to unbutton my vest. The whole company, feeling sure that I was caught, began to laugh heartily. Old Darrow fairly danced with delight, and as I laid my coat on a chair he came running up in front of me, and slapping his hands together, exclaimed:

"You needn't t-t-take off any more c-c-c-clothes, for if it ain't all on your b-b-back, you've lost it."

"If it is, I suppose you have!" I replied, pulling the whole shirt from off my back!

Such a shriek of laughter as burst forth from the crowd I scarcely ever heard, and certainly such a blank countenance as old Darrow exhibited it would be hard to conceive. Seeing that he was most incontinently "done for," and perceiving that his neighbor Hough had helped to do it, he ran up to him in great anger, and shaking his fist in his face, exclaimed:

"H-H-Hough, you infernal r-r-rascal, to go against your own n-n-neighbor in favor of a D-D-Danbury man. I'll pay you for that some time, you see if I d-d-don't."

All hands went up to the bar and drank with a hearty good will, for it was seldom that Darrow got taken in, and he was such an inveterate joker they liked to see him paid in his own coin. Never till the day of his death did he hear the last of the "whole shirt."

CHAPTER V.

My Start as a
Showman.

B y this time it was clear to my mind that my proper
position in this busy world was not yet reached. I
had displayed the faculty of getting money, as well as
getting rid of it; but the business for which I was destined,
and, I believe, made, had not yet come to me; or rather, I
had not found that I was to cater for that insatiate want of
human nature—the love of amusement; that I was to
make a sensation on two continents; and that fame and
fortune awaited me so soon as I should appear before the
public in the character of a showman. These things I had
not foreseen. I did not seek the position or the character.
The business finally came in my way; I fell into the occupation, and far beyond any of my predecessors on this
continent, I have succeeded.

The show business has all phases and grades of dignity,
from the exhibition of a monkey to the exposition of that
highest art in music or the drama, which entrances em-
pires and secures for the gifted artist a world-wide fame
which princes well might envy. Such art is merchantable,
and so with the whole range of amusements, from the
highest to the lowest. The old word "trade" as it applies
to buying cheap and selling at a profit, is as manifest here
as it is in the dealings at a street-corner stand or in
Stewart's store covering a whole square. This is a trading
world, and men, women and children, who cannot live on
gravity alone, need something to satisfy their gayer,

lighter moods and hours, and he who ministers to this
want is in a business established by the Author of our
nature. If he worthily fulfils his mission, and amuses
without corrupting, he need never feel that he has lived in
vain.

Whether I may claim a pre-eminence of grandeur in
my career as a dispenser of entertainment for mankind, I
may not say. I have sometimes been weak enough to
think so, but let others judge; and whether I may assume
that on the whole, I have sought to make amusement
harmless, and have succeeded to a very great degree, in
eliminating from public entertainments certain corrup-
tions which have made so many theatrical "sensations"
positively shameful, may safely be left, I think, to the
thousands upon thousands who have known me and the
character of my amusement so long and so well.

But I shall by no means claim entire faultlessness in my
history as a showman. I confess that I have not always
been strong enough to rise out of the exceptional ways
which characterize the art of amusing—not more, however, than any other art of trade. When, in beginning
business under my own name in Bethel, in 1831, I advertised that I would sell goods "25 per cent cheaper"
than any of my neighbors, I was guilty of a trick of trade,
but so common a trick, that very few who saw my promise were struck with a sense of any particular enormity
therein, while, doubtless, a good many, who claim to be
specially exemplary, thought they were reading one of
their own advertisements. And in the show business I was
never guilty of a greater sin than this against truthfulness
and fair dealing.

The least deserving of all my efforts in the show line
was the one which introduced me to the business; a
scheme in no sense of my own devising; one which had
been sometime before the public and which had so many
vouchers for its genuineness that at the time of taking
possession of it I honestly believed it to be genuine; something, too, which, as I have said, I did not seek, but which

by accident came in my way and seemed almost to compel my agency—such was the "Joice Heth" exhibition which first brought me forward as a showman.

In the summer of 1835, Mr. Coley Bartram, of Reading, Connecticut, informed me that he had owned an interest in a remarkable negro woman whom he believed to be one hundred and sixty-one years old, and whom he also believed to have been the nurse of General Washington. He then showed me a copy of the following advertisement in the *Pennsylvania Inquirer*, of July 15, 1835:

CURIOSITY.—The citizens of Philadelphia and its vicinity have an opportunity of witnessing at the Masonic Hall, one of the greatest natural curiosities ever witnessed, viz: JOICE HETH, a negress, aged 161 years, who formerly belonged to the father of General Washington. She has been a member of the Baptist Church one hundred and sixteen years, and can rehearse many hymns, and sing them according to former custom. She was born near the old Potomac River in Virginia, and has for ninety or one hundred years lived in Paris, Kentucky, with the Bowling family.

All who have seen this extraordinary woman are satisfied of the truth of the account of her age. The evidence of the Bowling family, which is respectable, is strong, but the original bill of sale of Augustine Washington, in his own hand-writing, and other evidences which the proprietor has in his possession, will satisfy even the most incredulous.

A lady will attend at the hall during the afternoon and evening for the accommodation of those ladies who may call.

Mr. Bartram further stated that he had sold out his interest to his partner, R. W. Lindsay, of Jefferson County, Kentucky, who was then exhibiting Joice Heth in Philadelphia, but was anxious to sell out and go home—the alleged reason being that he had very little tact as a showman. As the New York papers had also contained

some account of Joice Heth, I went on to Philadelphia to
see Mr. Lindsay and his exhibition.

Joice Heth was certainly a remarkable curiosity, and
she looked as if she might have been far older than her
age as advertised. She was apparently in good health and
spirits, but from age or disease, or both, was unable to
change her position; she could move one arm at will, but
her lower limbs could not be straightened; her left arm
lay across her breast and she could not remove it; the fingers of her left hand were drawn down so as nearly to
close it, and were fixed; the nails on that hand were almost four inches long and extended above her wrist; the
nails on her large toes had grown to the thickness of a
quarter of an inch; her head was covered with a thick
bush of grey hair; but she was toothless and totally blind
and her eyes had sunk so deeply in the sockets as to have
disappeared altogether.

Nevertheless she was pert and sociable, and would talk
as long as people would converse with her. She was quite
garrulous about her *protege* "dear little George," at
whose birth she declared she was present, having been at
the time a slave of Elizabeth Atwood, a half-sister of
Augustine Washington, the father of George Washington. As nurse she put the first clothes on the infant and
she claimed to have "raised him." She professed to be a
member of the Baptist church, talking much in her way
on religious subjects, and she sang a variety of ancient
hymns.

In proof of her extraordinary age and pretensions, Mr.
Lindsay exhibited a bill of sale, dated February 5, 1727,
from Augustine Washington, County of Westmoreland,
Virginia, to Elizabeth Atwood, a half-sister and neighbor
of Mr. Washington, conveying "one negro woman,
named Joice Heth, aged fifty-four years, for and in consideration of the sum of thirty-three pounds lawful
money of Virginia." It was further claimed that as she
had long been a nurse in the Washington family she was
called in at the birth of George and clothed the new-born

infant. The evidence seemed authentic and in answer to the inquiry why so remarkable a discovery had not been made before, a satisfactory explanation was given in the statement that she had been carried from Virginia to Kentucky, had been on the plantation of John S. Bowling so long that no one knew or cared how old she was, and only recently the accidental discovery by Mr. Bowling's son of the old bill of sale in the Record Office in Virginia had led to the identification of this negro woman as "the nurse of Washington."

Everything seemed so straightforward that I was anxious to become proprietor of this novel exhibition, which was offered to me at one thousand dollars, though the price first demanded was three thousand. I had five hundred dollars, borrowed five hundred dollars more, sold out my interest in the grocery business to my partner, and began life as a showman. At the outset of my career I saw that everything depended upon getting people to think, and talk, and become curious and excited over and about the "rare spectacle." Accordingly, posters, transparencies, advertisements, newspaper paragraphs—all calculated to extort attention—were employed, regardless of expense. My exhibition rooms in New York, Boston, Philadelphia, Albany and in other large and small cities, were continually thronged and much money was made. In the following February, Joice Heth died, literally of old age, and her remains received a respectable burial in the town of Bethel.

At a post-mortem examination of Joice Heth by Dr. David L. Rogers, in the presence of some medical students, it was thought that the absence of ossification indicated considerably less age than had been assumed for her; but the doctors disagreed, and this "dark subject" will probably always continue to be shrouded in mystery.

I had at last found my true vocation. Indeed, soon after I began to exhibit Joice Heth, I had entrusted her to an agent and had entered upon my second step in the show line. The next venture, whatever it may have been in other respects, had the merit of being, in every essential, unmistakably genuine. I engaged from the Albany Museum an Italian who called himself "Signor Antonio" and who performed certain remarkable feats of balancing, stilt-walking, plate-spinning, etc. He had gone from England to Canada, and thence to Albany, and had performed in other American cities. I made terms with him for one year to exhibit anywhere in the United States at twelve dollars a week and expenses, and induced him to change his stage name to "Signor Vivalla." I then wrote a notice of his wonderful qualities and performances, printed it in one of the Albany papers as news, sent copies to the theatrical managers in New York and in other cities, and went with Vivalla to the metropolis.

Manager William Dinneford, of the Franklin Theatre, had seen so many performances of the kind that he declined to engage my "eminent Italian artist"; but I persuaded him to try Vivalla one night for nothing and by the potent aid of printer's ink the house was crammed. I appeared as a supernumerary to assist Vivalla in arranging his plates and other "properties"; and to hand him his gun to fire while he was hopping on one stilt ten feet high. This was "my first appearance on any stage." The applause which followed Vivalla's feats was tremendous, and Manager Dinneford was so delighted that he engaged him for the remainder of the week at fifty dollars. At the close of the performance, in response to a call from the house, I made a speech for Vivalla, thanking the audience for their appreciation and announcing a repetition of the exhibition every evening during the week.

Vivalla remained a second week at the Franklin Theatre, for which I received $150. I realized the same sum for a week in Boston. We then went to Washington to fulfil an engagement which was far from successful, since my remuneration depended upon the receipts, and it snowed continually during the week. I was a loser to such an extent that I had not funds enough to return to Philadelphia. I pawned my watch and chain for thirty-five dollars, when fortunately Manager Wemyss arrived on Saturday morning and loaned me the money to redeem my property.

As this was my first visit to Washington I was much interested in visiting the capitol and other public buildings. I also satisfied my curiosity in seeing Clay, Calhoun, Benton, John Quincy Adams, Richard M. Johnson, Polk, and other leading statesmen of the time. I was also greatly gratified in calling upon Anne Royall, author of the Black Book, publisher of a little paper called "Paul Pry," and quite a celebrated personage in her day. I had exchanged *The Herald of Freedom* with her journal and she strongly sympathized with me in my persecutions. She was delighted to see me and although she was the most garrulous old woman I ever saw, I passed a very amusing and pleasant time with her. Before leaving her, I manifested my showman propensity by trying to hire her to give a dozen or more lectures on "Government," in the Atlantic cities, but I could not engage her at any price, although I am sure the speculation would have been a very profitable one. I never saw this eccentric woman again; she died at a very advanced age, October 1, 1854, at her residence in Washington.

I went with Vivalla to Philadelphia and opened at the Walnut Street Theatre. Though his performances were very meritorious and were well received, theatricals were dull and houses were slim. It was evident that something must be done to stimulate the public.

And now that instinct—I think it must be—which can arouse a community and make it patronize, provided the article offered is worthy of patronage—an instinct which served me strangely in later years, astonishing the public and surprising me, came to my relief, and the help, curiously enough, appeared in the shape of an emphatic hiss from the pit!

This hiss, I discovered, came from one Roberts, a circus performer, and I had an interview with him. He was a professional balancer and juggler, who boasted that he could do all Vivalla had done and something more. I at once published a card in Vivalla's name, offering $1,000 to any one who would publicly perform Vivalla's feats at such place as should be designated, and Roberts issued a counter card, accepting the offer. I then contracted with Mr. Warren, treasurer of the Walnut St. Theatre, for one-third of the proceeds, if I should bring the receipts up to $400 a night—an agreement he could well afford to make as his receipts the night before had been but seventy-five dollars. From him I went to Roberts, who seemed disposed to "back down," but I told him I should not insist upon the terms of his published card, and asked him if he was under any engagement? Learning that he was not, I offered him thirty dollars to perform under my direction one night at the Walnut, and he accepted. A great trial of skill between Roberts and Vivalla was duly announced by posters and through the press. Meanwhile, they rehearsed privately to see what tricks each could perform, and the "business" was completely arranged.

Public excitement was at fever heat, and on the night of the trial the pit and upper boxes were crowded to the full; indeed sales of tickets to these localities were soon stopped, for there were no seats to sell. The "contest" between the performers, was eager and each had his party in the house. So far as I could learn, no one complained that he did not get all he paid for on that occasion. I engaged Roberts for a month and his subsequent "contests" with Vivalla amused the public and put money in my purse.

Vivalla continued to perform for me in various places, including Peale's Museum, in New York, and I took him to different towns in Connecticut and in New Jersey, with poor success sometimes, as frequently the expenses exceeded the receipts.

In April, 1836, I connected myself with Aaron Turner's travelling circus company as ticket-seller, secretary and treasurer, at thirty dollars a month and one-fifth of the entire profits, while Vivalla was to receive a salary of fifty dollars. As I was already paying him eighty dollars a month, our joint salaries reimbursed me and left me the chance of twenty per cent of the net receipts. We started from Danbury for West Springfield, Massachusetts, April 26th, and on the first day, instead of halting to dine, as I expected, Mr. Turner regaled the whole company with three loaves of rye bread and a pound of butter, bought at a farm house at a cost of fifty cents, and, after watering the horses, we went on our way.

We began our performances at West Springfield, April 28th, and as our expected band of music had not arrived from Providence, I made a prefatory speech announcing our disappointment, and our intention to please our patrons, nevertheless. The two Turner boys, sons of the proprietor, rode finely. Joe Pentland, one of the wittiest, best, and most original of clowns, with Vivalla's tricks and other performances in the ring, more than made up for the lack of music. In a day or two our band arrived and our "houses" improved. My diary is full of incidents of our summer tour through numerous villages, towns, and cities in New England, New York, New Jersey, Pennsylvania, Delaware, Maryland, District of Columbia, Virginia, and North Carolina.

While we were at Cabotville, Massachusetts, on going to bed one night one of my room-mates threw a lighted stump of a cigar into a spit-box filled with sawdust and the result was that about one o'clock T. V. Turner, who slept in the room, awoke in the midst of a dense smoke and barely managed to crawl to the window to open it, and to awaken us in time to save us from suffocation.

At Lenox, Massachusetts, one Sunday I attended church as usual, and the preacher denounced our circus and all connected with it as immoral, and was very abusive; whereupon when he had read the closing hymn I walked up the pulpit stairs and handed him a written request, signed "P. T. Barnum, connected with the circus, June 5, 1836," to be permitted to reply to him. He declined to notice it, and after the benediction I lectured him for not giving me an opportunity to vindicate myself and those with whom I was connected. The affair created considerable excitement and some of the members of the church apologized to me for their clergyman's ill-behavior. A similar affair happened afterwards at Port Deposit, on the lower Susquehanna, and in this instance I addressed the audience for half an hour, defending the circus company against the attacks of the clergyman, and the people listened, though their pastor repeatedly implored them to go home. Often have I collected our company on Sunday and read to them the Bible or a printed sermon, and one or more of the men frequently accompanied me to church. We made no pretence of religion, but we were not the worst people in the world, and we thought ourselves entitled to at least decent treatment when we went to hear the preaching of the gospel. . . .

CHAPTER VII.

At the Foot of
the Ladder.

I have said that the show business has as many grades of dignity as trade, which ranges all the way from the mammoth wholesale establishment down to the corner stand. The itinerant amusement business is at the bottom of the ladder. I had begun there, but I had no wish to stay there; in fact, I was thoroughly disgusted with the trade of a travelling showman, and although I felt that I could succeed in that line, yet I always regarded it, not as an end, but as a means to something better.

Longing now for some permanent respectable business, I advertised for a partner, stating that I had $2,500 to invest and would add my unremitting personal attention to the capital and the business. This advertisement gave me an altogether new insight into human nature. Whoever wishes to know how some people live, or want to live, let him advertise for a partner, at the same time stating that he has a large or small capital to invest. I was flooded with answers to my advertisements and received no less than ninety-three different propositions for the use of my capital. Of these, at least one-third were from the porter-house keepers. Brokers, pawnbrokers, lottery-policy dealers, patent medicine men, inventors, and others also made application. Some of my correspondents declined to specifically state the nature of their business, but they promised to open the door to untold wealth.

I had interviews with some of these mysterious million-makers. One of them was a counterfeiter, who, after much hesitation and pledges of secrecy showed me some counterfeit coin and bank notes; he wanted $2,500 to purchase paper and ink and to prepare new dies, and he actually proposed that I should join him in the business which promised, he declared, a safe and rich harvest. Another sedate individual, dressed in Quaker costume, wanted me to join him in an oat speculation. By buying a horse and wagon and by selling oats, bought at wholesale, in bags, he thought a good business could be done, especially as people would not be particular to measure after a Quaker.

"Do you mean to cheat in measuring your oats?" I asked.

"O, I should probably make them hold out," he answered, with a leer.

One application came from a Pearl street wool merchant, who failed a month afterwards. Then came a "perpetual motion" man who had a fortune-making machine, in which I discovered a main-spring slyly hid in a hollow post, the spring making perpetual motion—till it ran down. Finally, I went into partnership with a German, named Proler, who was a manufacturer of pasteblacking, water-proof paste for leather, Cologne water and bear's grease. We took the store No. 101½ Bowery, at a rent (including the dwelling) of $600 per annum, and opened a large manufactory of the above articles. Proler manufactured and sold the goods at wholesale in Boston, Charleston, Cleveland, and various other parts of the country. I kept the accounts, and attended to sales in the store, wholesale and retail. For a while the business seemed to prosper—at least till my capital was absorbed and notes for stock began to fall due, with nothing to meet them, since we had sold our goods on long credits. In January, 1840, I dissolved partnership with Proler, he buying the entire interest for $2,600 on credit, and then running away to Rotterdam without paying his note, and leaving me nothing but a few recipes. Proler was a good-looking, plausible, promising— scamp.

During my connection with Proler, I became acquainted with a remarkable young dancer named John Diamond. He was one of the first and best of the numerous negro and "break-down" dancers who have since surprised and amused the public, and I entered into an engagement with his father for his services, putting Diamond in the hands of an agent, as I did not wish to appear in the transaction. In the spring of 1840, I hired and opened the Vauxhall Garden saloon, in New York, and gave a variety of performances, including singing, dancing, Yankee stories, etc. In this saloon Miss Mary Taylor, afterwards so celebrated as an actress and singer, made her first appearance on the stage. The enterprise, however, did not meet my expectation and I relinquished it in August.

What was to be done next? I dreaded resuming the life of an itinerant showman, but funds were low, I had a family to care for, and as nothing better presented I made up my mind to endure the vexations and uncertainties of a tour in the West and South. I collected a company, consisting of Mr. C. D. Jenkins, an excellent singer and delineator of Yankee and other characters; Master John Diamond, the dancer; Francis Lynch, an orphan vagabond, fourteen years old, whom I picked up at Troy, and a fiddler. My brother-in-law, Mr. John Hallett, preceded us as agent and advertiser, and our route passed through Buffalo, Toronto, Detroit, Chicago, Ottawa, Springfield, the intermediate places, and St. Louis, where I took the steamboat for New Orleans with a company reduced by desertions to Master Diamond and the fiddler.

Arriving in New Orleans, January 2, 1841, I had but $100 in my purse, and I had started from New York four months before with quite as much in my pocket. Excepting some small remittances to my family I had made nothing more than current expenses; and, when I had been in New Orleans a fortnight, funds were so low that I was obliged to pledge my watch as security for my board bill. But on the 16th, I received from the St. Charles Theatre $500 as my half share of Diamond's benefit; the next night I had $50; and the third night $479 was my share of the proceeds of a grand dancing match at the theatre between Diamond and a negro dancer from Kentucky. Subsequent engagements at Vicksburg and Jackson were not so successful, but returning to New Orleans we again succeeded admirably and afterwards at Mobile. Diamond, however, after extorting considerable sums of money from me, finally ran away, and, March 12th, I started homeward by way of the Mississippi and the Ohio.

While I was in New Orleans I made the acquaintance of that genial man Tyrone Power, who was just concluding an engagement at the St. Charles Theatre. In bidding me farewell, he wished me every success and hoped we should meet again. Alas, poor Power! All the world knows how he set sail from our shores, and he and his ship were never seen again. Fanny Ellsler was also in New Orleans, and when I saw seats in the dress circle sold at an average of four dollars and one-half, I gave her agent, Chevalier Henry Wyckoff, great credit for exciting public enthusiasm to the highest pitch and I thought the prices enormous. I did not dream then that, within twelve years, I should be selling tickets in the same city for full five times that sum.

At Pittsburg, where I arrived March 30th, I learned that Jenkins, who had enticed Francis Lynch away from me at St. Louis, was exhibiting him at the Museum under the name of "Master Diamond," and visiting the performance, the next day I wrote Jenkins an ironical review for which he threatened suit and he actually instigated R. W. Lindsay, from whom I hired Joice Heth in Philadelphia in 1835, and whom I had not seen since, though he was then residing in Pittsburg, to sue me for a pipe of brandy which, it was pretended, was promised in addition to the money paid him. I was required to give bonds of $500, which, as I was among strangers, I could not immediately procure, and I was accordingly thrown into jail till four o'clock in the afternoon, when I was liberated. The next day I caused the arrest of Jenkins for trespass in assuming Master Diamond's name and reputation for Master Lynch, and he was sent to jail till four o'clock in the afternoon. Each having had his turn at this amusement, we adjourned our controversy to New York where I beat him. As for Lindsay, I heard nothing more of his claim or him till twelve years afterwards when he called on me in Boston with an apology. He was very poor and I was highly prosperous, and I may add that Lindsay did not lack a friend.

I arrived in New York, April 23rd, 1841, after an absence of eight months; finding my family in good health, I resolved once more that I would never again be an itinerant showman. Three days afterwards I contracted with Robert Sears, the publisher, for five hundred copies of "Sears' Pictorial Illustrations of the Bible," at $500, and accepting the United States agency, I opened an office, May 10th, at the corner of Beekman and Nassau Streets, the site of the present Nassau Bank. I had had a limited experience with that book in this way: When I was in Pittsburg, an acquaintance, Mr. C. D. Harker, was complaining that he had nothing to do, when I picked up a New York paper and saw the advertisement of "Sears's Pictorial Illustrations of the Bible, price $2 a copy." Mr. Harker thought he could get subscribers, and I bought him a specimen copy, agreeing to furnish him with as many as he wanted at $1.37½ a copy, though I had never before seen the work and did not know the wholesale price. The result was that he obtained eighty subscribers in two days, and made $50. My own venture in the work was not so successful; I advertised largely, had plenty of agents, and, in six months, sold thousands of copies; but irresponsible agents used up all my profits and my capital.

While engaged in this business I once more leased Vauxhall saloon, opening it June 14th, 1841, employing Mr. John Hallett, my brother-in-law, as manager under my direction, and at the close of the season, September 25th, we had cleared about two hundred dollars. This sum was soon exhausted, and with my family on my hands and no employment I was glad to do anything that would keep the wolf from my door. I wrote advertisements and notices for the Bowery Amphitheatre, receiving for the service four dollars a week, which I was very glad to get, and I also wrote articles for the Sunday papers, deriving a fair remuneration and managing to get a living. But I was at the bottom round of fortune's ladder, and it was necessary to make an effort which would raise me above want.

I was specially stimulated to this effort by a letter which I received, about this time, from my esteemed friend, Hon. Thomas T. Whittlesey, of Danbury. He held a mortgage of five hundred dollars on a piece of property I owned in that place, and, as he was convinced that I would never lay up anything, he wrote me that I might as well pay him then as ever. This letter made me resolve to live no longer from hand to mouth, but to concentrate my energies upon laying up something for the future.

While I was forming this practical determination I was much nearer to its realization than my most sanguine hopes could have predicted. The road to fortune was close by. Without suspecting it, I was about to enter upon an enterprise, which, while giving full scope for whatever tact, industry and pluck I might possess, was to take me from the foot of the ladder and place me many rounds above.

As outside clerk for the Bowery Amphitheatre I had casually learned that the collection of curiosities comprising Scudder's American Museum, at the corner of Broadway and Ann Street, was for sale. It belonged to the daughters of Mr. Scudder, and was conducted for their benefit by John Furzman, under the authority of Mr. John Heath, administrator. The price asked for the entire collection was fifteen thousand dollars. It had cost its founder, Mr. Scudder, probably fifty thousand dollars, and from the profits of the establishment he had been able to leave a large competency to his children. The Museum, however, had been for several years a losing concern, and the heirs were anxious to sell it. Looking at this property, I thought I saw that energy, tact and liberality, were only needed to make it a paying institution, and I determined to purchase it if possible.

"You buy the American Museum!" said a friend, who knew the state of my funds, "what do you intend buying it with?"

"Brass," I replied, "for silver and gold have I none."

The Museum building belonged to Mr. Francis W. Olmsted, a retired merchant, to whom I wrote stating my desire to buy the collection, and that although I had no means, if it could be purchased upon reasonable credit, I was confident that my tact and experience, added to a determined devotion to business, would enable me to make the payments when due. I therefore asked him to purchase the collection in his own name; to give me a writing securing it to me provided I made the payments punctually, including the rent of his building; to allow me twelve dollars and a half a week on which to support my family; and if at any time I failed to meet the instalment due, I would vacate the premises and forfeit all that might have been paid to that date.

"In fact, Mr. Olmsted," I continued in my earnestness, "you may bind me in any way, and as tightly as you please—only give me a chance to dig out, or scratch out, and I will do so or forfeit all the labor and trouble I may have incurred."

In reply to this letter, which I took to his house myself, he named an hour when I could call on him, and as I was there at the exact moment, he expressed himself pleased with my punctuality. He inquired closely as to my habits and antecedents, and I frankly narrated my experiences as a caterer for the public, mentioning my amusement ventures in Vauxhall Garden, the circus, and the exhibitions I had managed at the South and West.

"Who are your references?" he inquired.

"Any man in my line," I replied, "from Edmund Simpson, manager of the Park Theatre, or William Niblo, to Messrs. Welch, June, Titus, Turner, Angevine, or other circus or menagerie proprietors; also Moses Y. Beach, of the New York *Sun*.

"Can you get any of them to call on me?" he continued.

I told him that I could, and the next day my friend Niblo rode down and had an interview with Mr. Olmsted, while Mr. Beach and several other gentlemen also called, and the following morning I waited upon him for his decision.

"I don't like your references, Mr. Barnum," said Mr. Olmsted, abruptly, as soon as I entered the room.

I was confused, and said "I regretted to hear it."

"They all speak too well of you," he added, laughing; "in fact they all talk as if they were partners of yours, and intended to share the profits."

Nothing could have pleased me better. He then asked me what security I could offer in case he concluded to make the purchase for me, and it was finally agreed that, if he should do so, he should retain the property till it was entirely paid for, and should also appoint a ticket-taker and accountant (at my expense), who should render him a weekly statement. I was further to take an apartment hitherto used as a billiard room in an adjoining building, allowing therefor, $500 a year, making a total rent of $3,000 per annum, on a lease of ten years. He then told me to see the administrator and heirs of the estate, to get their best terms, and to meet him on his return to town a week from that time.

I at once saw Mr. John Heath, the administrator, and

his price was $15,000. I offered $10,000, payable in seven annual instalments, with good security. After several interviews, it was finally agreed that I should have it for $12,000, payable as above—possession to be given on the 15th November. Mr. Olmsted assented to this, and a morning was appointed to draw and sign the writings. Mr. Heath appeared, but said he must decline proceeding any farther in my case, as he had sold the collection to the directors of Peale's Museum (an incorporated institution), for $15,000, and had received $1,000 in advance.

I was shocked, and appealed to Mr. Heath's honor. He said that he had signed no writing with me; was in no way legally bound, and that it was his duty to do the best he could for the heirs. Mr. Olmsted was sorry, but could not help me; the new tenants would not require him to incur any risk, and my matter was at an end.

Of course, I immediately informed myself as to the character of Peale's Museum company. It proved to be a band of speculators who had bought Peale's collection for a few thousand dollars, expecting to join the American Museum with it, issue and sell stock to the amount of $50,000, pocket $30,000 profits, and permit the stockholders to look out for themselves.

I went immediately to several of the editors, including Major M. M. Noah, M. Y. Beach, my good friends West, Herrick and Ropes, of the *Atlas*, and others, and stated my grievances. "Now," said I, "if you will grant me the use of your columns, I'll blow that speculation sky-high." They all consented, and I wrote a large number of squibs, cautioning the public against buying the Museum stock, ridiculing the idea of a board of broken-down bank directors engaging in the exhibition of stuffed monkey and gander skins; appealing to the case of the Zoological Institute, which had failed by adopting such a plan as the one now proposed; and finally I told the public that such a speculation would be infinitely more ridiculous than Dickens's "Grand United Metropolitan Hot Muffin and Crumpet-baking and Punctual Delivery Company."

The stock was as "dead as a herring!" I then went to Mr. Heath and asked him when the directors were to pay the other $14,000. "On the 26th day of December, or forfeit the $1,000 already paid," was the reply. I assured him that they would never pay it, that they could not raise it, and that he would ultimately find himself with the Museum collection on his hands, and if once I started off with an exhibition for the South, I would not touch the Museum at *any* price. "Now," said I, "if you will agree with me confidentially, that in case these gentlemen do not pay you on the 26th of December, I may have it on the 27th for $12,000, I will run the risk, and wait in this city until that date." He readily agreed to the proposition, but said he was sure they would not forfeit their $1,000.

"Very well," said I; "all I ask of you is, that this arrangement shall not be mentioned." He assented. "On the 27th day of December, at ten o'clock A.M., I wish you to meet me in Mr. Olmsted's apartments, prepared to sign the writings, provided this incorporated company do not pay you $14,000 on the 26th." He agreed to this, and by my request put it in writing.

From that moment I felt that the Museum was mine. I saw Mr. Olmsted, and told him so. He promised secrecy, and agreed to sign the documents if the other parties did not meet their engagement.

This was about November 15th, and I continued my shower of newspaper squibs at the new company, which could not sell a dollar's worth of its stock. Meanwhile, if any one spoke to me about the Museum, I simply replied that I had lost it.

CHAPTER VIII.

The American Museum.

M y newspaper squib war against the Peale combination was vigorously kept up; when one morning, about the first of December, I received a letter from the Secretary of that company (now calling itself the "New York Museum Company,") requesting me to meet the directors at the Museum on the following Monday morning. I went, and found the directors in session. The venerable president of the board, who was also the expresident of a broken bank, blandly proposed to hire me to manage the united museums, and though I saw that he merely meant to buy my silence, I professed to entertain the proposition, and in reply to an inquiry as to what salary I should expect, I specified the sum of $3,000 a year. This was at once acceded to, the salary to begin January 1, 1842, and after complimenting me on my ability, the president remarked: "Of course, Mr. Barnum, we shall have no more of your squibs through the newspapers"—to which I replied that I should "ever try to serve the interests of my employers," and I took my leave.

It was as clear to me as noonday that after buying my silence so as to appreciate their stock, these directors meant to sell out to whom they could, leaving me to look to future stockholders for my salary. They thought, no doubt, that they had nicely entrapped me, but I knew I had caught them.

For, supposing me to be out of the way, and having no

other rival purchaser, these directors postponed the advertisement of their stock to give people time to forget the attacks I had made on it, and they also took their own time for paying the money promised to Mr. Heath, December 26th—indeed, they did not even call on him at the appointed time. But on the following morning, as agreed, I was promptly and hopefully at Mr. Olmsted's apartments with my legal adviser, at half-past nine o'clock; Mr. Heath came with his lawyer at ten, and before two o'clock that day I was in formal possession of the American Museum. My first managerial act was to write and despatch the following complimentary note:

AMERICAN MUSEUM, NEW YORK, Dec. 27, 1841.
To the President and Directors of the New York Museum:
GENTLEMEN:—It gives me great pleasure to inform you that you are placed upon the Free List of this establishment until further notice.

P. T. BARNUM, *Proprietor.*

It is unnecessary to say that the "President of the New York Museum" was astounded, and when he called upon Mr. Heath, and learned that I had bought and was really in possession of the American Museum, he was indignant. He talked of prosecution, and demanded the $1,-000 paid on his agreement, but he did not prosecute, and he justly forfeited his deposit money.

And now that I was proprietor and manager of the American Museum I had reached a new epoch in my career which I felt was the beginning of better days, though the full significance of this important step I did not see. I was still in the show business, but in a settled, substantial phase of it, that invited industry and enterprise, and called for ever earnest and ever heroic endeavor. Whether I should sink or swim depended wholly upon my own energy. I must pay for the establishment within a stipulated time, or forfeit it with whatever I had paid on account. I meant to make it my own, and brains, hands and every effort were devoted to the interests of the Museum.

The nucleus of this establishment, Scudder's Museum, was formed in 1810, the year in which I was born. It was begun in Chatham Street, and was afterwards transferred to the old City Hall, and from small beginnings, by purchases, and to a considerable degree by presents, it had grown to be a large and valuable collection. People in all parts of the country had sent in relics and rare curiosities; sea captains, for years, had brought and deposited strange things from foreign lands; and besides all these gifts, I have no doubt that the previous proprietor had actually expended, as was stated, $50,000 in making the collection. No one could go through the halls, as they were when they came under my proprietorship, and see one-half there was worth seeing in a single day; and then, as I always justly boasted afterwards, no one could visit my Museum and go away without feeling that he had received the full worth of his money. In looking over the immense collection, the accumulation of so many years, I saw that it was only necessary to properly present its merits to the public, to make it the most attractive and popular place of resort and entertainment in the United States.

Valuable as the collection was when I bought it, it was only the beginning of the American Museum as I made it. In my long proprietorship I considerably more than doubled the permanent attractions and curiosities of the establishment. In 1842, I bought and added to my collection the entire contents of Peale's Museum; in 1850, I purchased the large Peale collection in Philadelphia; and year after year, I bought genuine curiosities, regardless of cost, wherever I could find them, in Europe or America.

At the very outset, I was determined to deserve success. My plan of economy included the intention to support my family in New York on $600 a year, and my treasure of a wife not only gladly assented, but was willing to reduce the sum to $400, if necessary. Some six months after I had bought the Museum, Mr. Olmsted happened in at my ticket-office at noon and found me eating a frugal dinner of cold corned beef and bread, which I had brought from home.

"Is this the way you eat your dinner?" he asked.

"I have not eaten a warm dinner, except on Sundays," I replied, "since I bought the Museum, and I never intend to, on a week day, till I am out of debt."

"Ah!" said he, clapping me on the shoulder, "you are safe, and will pay for the Museum before the year is out."

And he was right, for within twelve months I was in full possession of the property as my own and it was entirely paid for from the profits of the business.

In 1865, the space occupied for my Museum purposes was more than double what it was in 1842. The Lecture Room, originally narrow, ill-contrived and inconvenient, was so enlarged and improved that it became one of the most commodious and beautiful amusement halls in the City of New York. At first, my attractions and inducements were merely the collection of curiosities by day, and an evening entertainment, consisting of such variety performances as were current in ordinary shows. Then Saturday afternoons, and, soon afterwards, Wednesday afternoons were devoted to entertainments and the popularity of the Museum grew so rapidly that I presently found it expedient and profitable to open the great Lecture Room every afternoon, as well as every evening, on every week-day in the year. The first experiments in this direction, more than justified my expectations, for the day exhibitions were always more thronged than those of the evening. Of course I made the most of the holidays, advertising extensively and presenting extra inducements; nor did attractions elsewhere seem to keep the crowd from coming to the Museum. On great holidays, I gave as many as twelve performances to as many different audiences.

By degrees the character of the stage performances

was changed. The transient attractions of the Museum were constantly diversified, and educated dogs, industrious fleas, automatons, jugglers, ventriloquists, living statuary, tableaux, gipsies, Albinoes, fat boys, giants, dwarfs, rope-dancers, live "Yankees," pantomime, instrumental music, singing and dancing in great variety, dioramas, panoramas, models of Niagara, Dublin, Paris, and Jerusalem; Hannington's dioramas of the Creation, the Deluge, Fairy Grotto, Storm at Sea; the first English Punch and Judy in this country, Italian Fantoccini, mechanical figures, fancy glass-blowing, knitting machines and other triumphs in the mechanical arts; dissolving views, American Indians, who enacted their warlike and religious ceremonies on the stage,—these, among others, were all exceedingly successful.

I thoroughly understood the art of advertising, not merely by means of printer's ink, which I have always used freely, and to which I confess myself so much indebted for my success, but by turning every possible circumstance to my account. It was my monomania to make the Museum the town wonder and town talk. I often seized upon an opportunity by instinct, even before I had a very definite conception as to how it should be used, and it seemed, somehow, to mature itself and serve my purpose. As an illustration, one morning a stout, hearty-looking man, came into my ticket-office and begged some money. I asked him why he did not work and earn his living? He replied that he could get nothing to do and that he would be glad of any job at a dollar a day. I handed him a quarter of a dollar, told him to go and get his breakfast and return, and I would employ him at light labor at a dollar and a half a day. When he returned I gave him five common bricks.

"Now," said I, "go and lay a brick on the sidewalk at the corner of Broadway and Ann Street; another close by the Museum; a third diagonally across the way at the corner of Broadway and Vesey Street, by the Astor House; put down the fourth on the sidewalk in front of St. Paul's

Church, opposite; then, with the fifth brick in hand, take up a rapid march from one point to the other, making the circuit, exchanging your brick at every point, and say nothing to any one."

"What is the object of this?" inquired the man.

"No matter," I replied; "all you need to know is that it brings you fifteen cents wages per hour. It is a bit of my fun, and to assist me properly you must seem to be as deaf as a post; wear a serious countenance; answer no questions; pay no attention to any one; but attend faithfully to the work and at the end of every hour by St. Paul's clock show this ticket at the Museum door; enter, walking solemnly through every hall in the building; pass out, and resume your work."

With the remark that it was "all one to him, so long as he could earn his living," the man placed his bricks and began his round. Half an hour afterwards, at least five hundred people were watching his mysterious movements. He had assumed a military step and bearing, and looking as sober as a judge, he made no response whatever to the constant inquiries as to the object of his singular conduct. At the end of the first hour, the sidewalks in the vicinity were packed with people all anxious to solve the mystery. The man, as directed, then went into the Museum, devoting fifteen minutes to a solemn survey of the halls, and afterwards returning to his round. This was repeated every hour till sundown and whenever the man went into the Museum a dozen or more persons would buy tickets and follow him, hoping to gratify their curiosity in regard to the purpose of his movements. This was continued for several days—the curious people who followed the man into the Museum considerably more than paying his wages—till finally the policeman, to whom I had imparted my object, complained that the obstruction of the sidewalk by crowds had become so serious that I must call in my "brick man." This trivial incident excited considerable talk and amusement; it advertised me; and it materially advanced my purpose of making a lively corner near the Museum.

I am tempted to relate some of the incidents and anecdotes which attended my career as owner and manager of the Museum. The stories illustrating merely my introduction of novelties would more than fill this book, but I must make room for a few of them.

An actor, named La Rue, presented himself as an imitator of celebrated histrionic personages, including Macready, Forrest, Kemble, the elder Booth, Kean, Hamblin, and others. Taking him into the green-room for a private rehearsal, and finding his imitations excellent, I engaged him. For three nights he gave great satisfaction, but early in the fourth evening he staggered into the Museum so drunk that he could hardly stand, and in half an hour he must be on the stage! Calling an assistant, we took La Rue between us, and marched him up Broadway as far as Chambers Street, and back to the lower end of the Park, hoping to sober him. At this point we put his head under a pump, and gave him a good ducking, with visible beneficial effect,—then a walk around the Park, and another ducking,—when he assured me that he should be able to give his imitations "to a charm."

"You drunken brute," said I, "if you fail, and disappoint my audience, I will throw you out of the window."

He declared that he was "all right," and I led him behind the scenes, where I waited with considerable trepidation to watch his movements on the stage. He began by saying:

"Ladies and gentlemen: I will now give you an imitation of Mr. Booth, the eminent tragedian."

His tongue was thick, his language somewhat incoherent, and I had great misgivings as he proceeded; but as no token of disapprobation came from the audience, I began to hope he would go through with his parts without exciting suspicion of his condition. But before he had half finished his representation of Booth, in the soliloquy in the opening act of Richard III., the house discovered that he was very drunk, and began to hiss. This only seemed to stimulate him to make an effort to appear sober, which, as is usual in such cases, only made matters worse, and the hissing increased. I lost all patience, and going on the stage and taking the drunken fellow by the collar, I apologized to the audience, assuring them that he should not appear before them again. I was about to march him off, when he stepped to the front, and said:

"Ladies and gentlemen: Mr. Booth often appeared on the stage in a state of inebriety, and I was simply giving you a truthful representation of him on such occasions. I beg to be permitted to proceed with my imitations."

The audience at once supposed it was all right, and cried out, "go on, go on"; which he did, and at every imitation of Booth, whether as Richard, Shylock, or Sir Giles Overreach, he received a hearty round of applause. I was quite delighted with his success; but when he came to imitate Forrest and Hamblin, necessarily representing them as drunk also, the audience could be no longer deluded; the hissing was almost deafening, and I was forced to lead the actor off. It was his last appearance on my stage.

From the first, it was my study to give my patrons a superfluity of novelties, and for this I make no special claim to generosity, for it was strictly a business transaction. To send away my visitors more than doubly satisfied, was to induce them to come again and to bring their friends. I meant to make people talk about my Museum; to exclaim over its wonders; to have men and women all over the country say: "There is not another place in the United States where so much can be seen for twenty-five cents as in Barnum's American Museum." It was the best advertisement I could possibly have, and one for which I could afford to pay. I knew, too, that it was an honorable advertisement, because it was as deserved as it was spontaneous. And so, in addition to the permanent collection and the ordinary attractions of the stage, I labored to keep the Museum well supplied with transient novelties; I exhibited such living curiosities as a rhinoceros, giraffes, grizzly bears, ourang-outangs, great serpents, and whatever else of the kind money would buy or enterprise secure.

Knowing that a visit to my varied attractions and genuine curiosities was well worth to any one three times the amount asked as an entrance fee, I confess that I was not so scrupulous, as possibly I should have been, about the methods used to call public attention to my establishment. The one end aimed at was to make men and women think and talk and wonder, and, as a practical result, go to the Museum. This was my constant study and occupation.

It was the world's way then, as it is now, to excite the community with flaming posters, promising almost everything for next to nothing. I confess that I took no pains to set my enterprising fellow-citizens a better example. I fell in with the world's way; and if my "puffing" was more persistent, my advertising more audacious, my posters more glaring, my pictures more exaggerated, my flags more patriotic and my transparencies more brilliant than they would have been under the management of my neighbors, it was not because I had less scruple than they, but more energy, far more ingenuity, and a better foundation for such promises. In all this, if I cannot be justified, I at least find palliation in the fact that I presented a wilderness of wonderful, instructive and amusing realities of such evident and marked merit that I have yet to learn of a single instance where a visitor went away from the Museum complaining that he had been defrauded of his money. Surely this is an offset to any eccentricities to which I may have resorted to make my establishment widely known.

Very soon after introducing my extra exhibitions, I purchased for $200, a curiosity which had much merit and some absurdity. It was a model of Niagara Falls, in which the merit was that the proportions of the great cataract, the trees, rocks, and buildings in the vicinity were mathematically given, while the absurdity was in introducing "real water" to represent the falls. Yet the model served a purpose in making "a good line in the bill"—an end in view which was never neglected—and it helped to give the Museum notoriety. One day I was summoned to appear before the Board of Croton Water Commissioners, and was informed that as I paid only $25 per annum for water at the Museum, I must pay a large extra compensation for the supply for my Niagara Falls. I begged the board not to believe all that appeared in the papers, nor to interpret my show-bills too literally, and assured them that a single barrel of water, if my pump was in good order, would furnish my falls for a month.

It was even so, for the water flowed into a reservoir behind the scenes, and was forced back with a pump over the falls. On one occasion, Mr. Louis Gaylord Clark, the editor of the *Knickerbocker*, came to view my museum, and introduced himself to me. As I was quite anxious that my establishment should receive a first-rate notice at his hands, I took pains to show him everything of interest, except the Niagara Falls, which I feared would prejudice him against my entire show. But as we passed the room the pump was at work, warning me that the great cataract was in full operation, and Clark, to my dismay, insisted upon seeing it.

"Well, Barnum, I declare, this is quite a new idea; I never saw the like before."

"No?" I faintly inquired, with something like reviving hope.

"No," said Clark, "and I hope, with all my heart, I never shall again."

But the *Knickerbocker* spoke kindly of me, and refrained from all allusions to "the Cataract of Niagara, with real water." Some months after, Clark came in breathless one day, and asked me if I had the club with which Captain Cook was killed? As I had a lot of Indian war clubs in the collection of aboriginal curiosities, and owing Clark something on the old Niagara Falls account, I told him I had the veritable club with documents which placed its identity beyond question, and I showed him the warlike weapon.

"Poor Cook! poor Cook!" said Clark, musingly. "Well, Mr. Barnum," he continued, with great gravity, at the same time extending his hand and giving mine a hearty shake, "I am really very much obliged to you for your kindness. I had an irrepressible desire to see the club that killed Captain Cook, and I felt quite confident you could accommodate me. I have been in half a dozen smaller museums, and as they all had it, I was sure a large establishment like yours would not be without it."

A few weeks afterwards, I wrote to Clark that if he would come to my office I was anxious to consult him on a matter of great importance. He came, and I said:

"Now, I don't want any of your nonsense, but I want your sober advice."

He assured me that he would serve me in any way in his power, and I proceeded to tell him about a wonderful fish from the Nile, offered to me for exhibition at $100 a week, the owner of which was willing to forfeit $5,000, if, within six weeks, this fish did not pass through a transformation in which the tail would disappear and the fish would then have legs.

"Is it possible!" asked the astonished Clark.

I assured him that there was no doubt of it.

Thereupon he advised me to engage the wonder at any price; that it would startle the naturalists, wake up the whole scientific world, draw in the masses, and make $20,000 for the Museum. I told him that I thought well of the speculation, only I did not like the name of the fish.

"That makes no difference whatever," said Clark; "what is the name of the fish?"

"Tadpole," I replied with becoming gravity, "but it is vulgarly called 'pollywog.' "

"Sold, by thunder!" exclaimed Clark, and he left.

A curiosity, which in an extraordinary degree served my ever-present object of extending the notoriety of the Museum was the so-called "Fejee Mermaid." It has been supposed that this mermaid was manufactured by my order, but such is not the fact. I was known as a successful showman, and strange things of every sort were brought to me from all quarters for sale or exhibition. In the summer of 1842, Mr. Moses Kimball, of the Boston Museum, came to New York and showed me what purported to be a mermaid. He had bought it from a sailor whose father, a sea captain, had purchased it in Calcutta, in 1822, from some Japanese sailors. I may mention here that this identical preserved specimen was exhibited in London in 1822, as I fully verified in my visit to that city in 1858, for I found an advertisement of it in an old file of the London *Times,* and a friend gave me a copy of the *Mirror,* published by J. Limbird, 335 Strand, November 9, 1822, containing a cut of this same creature and two pages of letter-press describing it, together with an account of other mermaids said to have been captured in different parts of the world. The *Mirror* stated that this specimen was "the great source of attraction in the British metropolis, and three to four hundred people every day pay their shilling to see it."

This was the curiosity which had fallen into Mr. Kimball's hands. I requested my naturalist's opinion of the genuineness of the animal and he said he could not conceive how it could have been manufactured, for he never saw a monkey with such peculiar teeth, arms, hands, etc., and he never saw a fish with such peculiar fins; but he did not believe in mermaids. Nevertheless, I concluded to hire this curiosity and to modify the general incredulity as to the possibility of the existence of mermaids, and to awaken curiosity to see and examine the specimen, I invoked the potent power of printer's ink.

Since Japan has been opened to the outer world it has been discovered that certain "artists" in that country manufacture a great variety of fabulous animals, with an ingenuity and mechanical perfection well calculated to deceive. No doubt my mermaid was a specimen of this curious manufacture. I used it mainly to advertise the regular business of the Museum, and this effective indirect advertising is the only feature I can commend, in a special show of which, I confess, I am not proud. I might have published columns in the newspapers, presenting and praising the great collection of genuine specimens of natural history in my exhibition, and they would not have attracted nearly so much attention as did a few paragraphs about the mermaid which was only a small part of my show. Newpapers throughout the country copied the mermaid notices, for they were novel and caught the attention of readers. Thus was the fame of the Museum, as well as the mermaid, wafted from one end of the land to the other. I was careful to keep up the excitement, for I knew that every dollar sown in advertising would return in tens, and perhaps hundreds, in a future harvest, and after obtaining all the notoriety possible by advertising and by exhibiting the mermaid at the Museum, I sent the curiosity throughout the country, directing my agent to everywhere advertise it as "From Barnum's Great American Museum, New York." The effect was immediately felt; money flowed in rapidly and was readily expended in more advertising.

While I expended money liberally for attractions for the inside of my Museum, and bought or hired everything curious or rare which was offered or could be found, I was prodigal in my outlays to arrest or arouse public attention. When I became proprietor of the establishment, there were only the words: "American Museum," to indicate the character of the concern; there was no bustle or activity about the place; no posters to announce what was to be seen;—the whole exterior was as dead as the skeletons and stuffed skins within. My experiences had taught me the advantages of advertising. I printed whole columns in the papers, setting forth the wonders of my establishment. Old "fogies" opened their eyes in amazement at a man who could expend hundreds of dollars in announcing a show of "stuffed monkey skins"; but these same old fogies paid their quarters, nevertheless, and when they saw the curiosities and novelties in the Museum halls, they, like all other visitors, were astonished as well as pleased, and went home and told their families and neighbors and thus assisted in advertising my business.

For other and not less effective advertising,—flags and banners, began to adorn the exterior of the building. I kept a band of music on the front balcony and announced "Free Music for the Million." People said, "Well, that Barnum is a liberal fellow to give us music for nothing," and they flocked down to hear my outdoor free concerts. But I took pains to select and maintain the poorest band I could find—one whose discordant notes would drive the crowd into the Museum, out of earshot of my outside orchestra. Of course, the music was poor. When people expect to get "something for nothing" they are sure to be cheated, and generally deserve to be, and so, no doubt, some of my out-door patrons were sorely disappointed; but when they came inside and paid to be amused and instructed, I took care to see that they not only received the full worth of their money, but were more than satisfied. Powerful Drummond lights were placed at the top of the Museum, which, in the darkest night, threw a flood of light up and down Broadway, from the Battery to Niblo's, that would enable one to read a newspaper in the street. These were the first Drummond lights ever seen in New York, and they made people talk, and so advertise my Museum.

CHAPTER IX.

The Road to Riches.

The American Museum was the ladder by which I rose to fortune. Whenever I cross Broadway at the head of Vesey Street, and see the *Herald* building and that gorgeous pile, the Park Bank, my mind's eye recalls that less solid, more showy edifice which once occupied the site and was covered with pictures of all manner of beasts, birds and creeping things, and in which were treasures that brought treasures and notoriety and pleasant hours to me. The Jenny Lind enterprise was more audacious, more immediately remunerative, and I remember it with a pride which I do not attempt to conceal; but instinctively I often go back and live over again the old days of my struggles and triumphs in the American Museum.

The Museum was always open at sunrise, and this was so well known throughout the country that strangers coming to the city would often take a tour through my halls before going to breakfast or to their hotels. I do not believe there was ever a more truly popular place of amusement. I frequently compared the annual number of visitors with the number officially reported as visiting (free of charge), the British Museum in London, and my list was invariably the larger. Nor do I believe that any man or manager ever labored more industriously to please his patrons. I furnished the most attractive exhibitions which money could procure; I abolished all vulgarity and profanity from the stage, and I prided myself upon the fact that parents and children could attend the dramatic performances in the so-called Lecture Room, and not be shocked or offended by anything they might see or hear; I introduced the "Moral Drama," producing such plays as "The Drunkard," "Uncle Tom's Cabin," "Moses in Egypt," "Joseph and His Brethren," and occasional spectacular melodramas produced with great care and at considerable outlay.

Mr. Sothern, who has since attained such wide-spread celebrity at home and abroad as a character actor, was a member of my dramatic company for one or two seasons. Mr. Barney Williams also began his theatrical career at the Museum, occupying, at first, quite a subordinate position, at a salary of ten dollars a week. During the past twelve or fifteen years, I presume his weekly receipts, when he has acted, have been nearly $3,000. The late Miss Mary Gannon also commenced at the Museum, and many more actors and actresses of celebrity have been, from time to time, engaged there. What was once the small Lecture Room was converted into a spacious and beautiful theatre, extending over the lots adjoining the Museum, and capable of holding about three thousand persons. The saloons were greatly multiplied and enlarged, and the "egress" have been made to work to perfection, on holidays I advertised Lecture Room performances every hour through the afternoon and evening, and consequently the actors and actresses were dressed for the stage as early as eleven o'clock in the morning and did not resume their ordinary clothes till ten o'clock at night. In these busy days the meals for the company were brought in and served in the dressing-rooms and green-rooms, and the company always received extra pay.

Leaving nothing undone that would bring Barnum and his Museum before the public, I often engaged some exhibition, knowing that it would directly bring no extra dollars to the treasury, but hoping that it would incite a newspaper paragraph which would float through the columns of the American press and be copied, perhaps, abroad, and my hopes in this respect were often gratified.

I confess that I liked the Museum mainly for the opportunities it afforded for rapidly making money. Before I bought it, I weighed the matter well in my mind, and was convinced that I could present to the American public such a variety, quantity and quality of amusement, blended with instruction, "all for twenty-five cents, children half price," that my attractions would be irresistible, and my fortune certain. I myself relished a higher grade of amusement, and I was a frequent attendant at the opera, first-class concerts, lectures, and the like; but I worked for the million, and I knew the only way to make a million from my patrons was to give them abundant and wholesome attractions for a small sum of money.

About the first of July, 1842, I began to make arrangements for extra novelties, additional performances, a large amount of extra advertising, and an out-door display for the "Glorious Fourth." Large parti-colored bills were ordered, transparencies were prepared, the free band of music was augmented by a trumpeter, and columns of advertisements, headed with large capitals, were written and put on file.

I wanted to run out a string of American flags across the street on that day, for I knew there would be thousands of people passing the Museum with leisure and pocket-money, and I felt confident that an unusual display of national flags would arrest their patriotic attention, and bring many of them within my walls. Unfortunately for my purpose, St. Paul's Church stood directly opposite, and there was nothing to which I could attach my flag-rope, unless it might be one of the trees in the church-yard. I went to the vestrymen for permission to so attach my flag rope on the Fourth of July, and they were indignant at what they called my "insulting proposition"; such a concession would be "sacrilege." I plied them with arguments, and appealed to their patriotism, but in vain.

Returning to the Museum I gave orders to have the string of flags made ready, with directions at daylight on the Fourth of July to attach one end of the rope to one of the third story windows of the Museum, and the other end to a tree in St. Paul's churchyard. The great day arrived, and my orders were strictly followed. The flags attracted great attention, and before nine o'clock I have no doubt that hundreds of additional visitors were drawn by this display into the Museum. By half-past nine Broadway was thronged, and about that time two gentlemen in a high state of excitement rushed into my office, announcing themselves as injured and insulted vestrymen of St. Paul's Church.

"Keep cool, gentlemen," said I; "I guess it is all right."

"Right!" indignantly exclaimed one of them, "do you think it is right to attach your Museum to our Church? We will show you what is 'right' and what is law, if we live till to-morrow; those flags must come down instantly."

"Thank you," I said, "but let us not be in a hurry. I will go out with you and look at them, and I guess we can make it all right."

Going into the street, I remarked: "Really, gentlemen, these flags look very beautiful; they do not injure your tree; I always stop my balcony music for your accommodation whenever you hold week-day services, and it is but fair that you should return the favor."

"We could indict your 'music,' as you call it, as a nuisance, if we chose," answered one vestryman, "and now I tell you that if these flags are not taken down in ten minutes, *I* will cut them down."

His indignation was at the boiling point. The crowd in the street was dense, and the angry gesticulation of the vestryman attracted their attention. I saw there was no use in trying to parley with him or coax him, and so, assuming an angry air, I rolled up my sleeves, and exclaimed, in a loud tone,—

"Well, Mister, I should just like to see you dare to cut down the American flag on the Fourth of July; you must be a 'Britisher' to make such a threat as that; but I'll show you a thousand pairs of Yankee hands in two minutes, if you dare to attempt to take down the stars and stripes on this great birth-day of American freedom!"

"What's that John Bull a-saying," asked a brawny fellow, placing himself in front of the irate vestryman; "Look here, old fellow," he continued, "if you want to save a whole bone in your body, you had better slope, and never dare to talk again about hauling down the American flag in the city of New York."

Throngs of excited, exasperated men crowded around, and the vestryman, seeing the effect of my ruse, smiled faintly and said, "Oh, of course it is all right," and he and his companion quietly edged out of the crowd. The flags remained up all day and all night. The next morning I sought the vanquished vestrymen and obtained formal permission to make this use of the tree on following holidays, in consideration of my willingness to arrest the doleful strains of my discordant balcony band whenever services were held on week days in the church.

On that Fourth of July, at one o'clock, P.M., my Museum was so densely crowded that we could admit no more visitors, and we were compelled to stop the sale of tickets. I pushed through the throng until I reached the roof of the building, hoping to find room for a few more, but it was in vain. Looking down into the street it was a sad sight to see the thousands of people who stood ready with their money to enter the Museum, but who were actually turned away. It was exceedingly harrowing to my feelings. Rushing down stairs, I told my carpenter and his assistants to cut through the partition and floor in the rear and to put in a temporary flight of stairs so as to let out people by that egress into Ann Street. By three o'clock the egress was opened and a few people were passed down the new stairs, while a corresponding number came in at the front. But I lost a large amount of money that day by not having sufficiently estimated the value of my own advertising, and consequently not having provided for the thousands who had read my announcements and seen my outside show, and had taken the first leisure day to visit the Museum. I had learned one lesson, however, and that was to have the egress ready on future holidays.

Early in the following March, I received notice from some of the Irish population that they meant to visit me in great numbers on "St. Patrick's day in the morning." "All right," said I to my carpenter, "get your egress ready for March 17"; and I added, to my assistant manager: "If there is much of a crowd, don't let a single person pass out at the front, even if it were St. Patrick himself; put every man out through the egress in the rear." The day came, and before noon we were caught in the same dilemma as we were on the Fourth of July; the Museum was jammed and the sale of tickets was stopped. I went to the egress and asked the sentinel how many hundreds had passed out?

"Hundreds," he replied, "why only three persons have gone out by this way and they came back, saying that it was a mistake and begging to be let in again."

"What does this mean?" I inquired; "surely thousands of people have been all over the Museum since they came in."

"Certainly," was the reply, "but after they have gone from one saloon to another and have been on every floor, even to the roof, they come down and travel the same route over again."

At this time I espied a tall Irish woman with two good-sized children whom I had happened to notice when they came in early in the morning.

"Step this way, madam," said I politely, "you will never be able to get into the street by the front door without crushing these dear children. We have opened a large egress here and you can pass by these rear stairs into Ann Street and thus avoid all danger."

"Sure," replied the woman, indignantly, "an' I'm not going out at all, at all, nor the children aither, for we've brought our dinners and we are going to stay all day."

Further investigation showed that pretty much all of my visitors had brought their dinners with the evident intention of literally "making a day of it." No one expected to go home till night; the building was overcrowded, and meanwhile hundreds were waiting at the front entrance to get in when they could. In despair I sauntered upon the stage behind the scenes, biting my lips with vexation, when I happened to see the scene-painter at work and a happy thought struck me: "Here," I exclaimed, "take a piece of canvas four feet square, and paint on it as soon as you can, in large letters—

TO THE EGRESS.''

Seizing his brush he finished the sign in fifteen minutes, and I directed the carpenter to nail it over the door leading to the back stairs. He did so, and as the crowd, after making the entire tour of the establishment, came pouring down the main stairs from the third story, they stopped and looked at the new sign, while some of them read audibly: "To the Aigress."

"The Aigress," said others, "sure that's an animal we haven't seen," and the throng began to pour down the back stairs only to find that the "Aigress" was the elephant, and the elephant was all out o'doors, or so much of it as began with Ann Street. Meanwhile, I began to accommodate those who had long been waiting with their money at the Broadway entrance.

Notwithstanding my continual outlays for additional novelties and attractions, or rather I might say, because of these outlays, money poured in upon me so rapidly that I was sometimes actually embarrassed to devise means to carry out my original plan for laying out the entire profits of the first year in advertising. I meant to sow first and reap afterwards. I finally hit upon a plan which cost a large sum, and that was to prepare large oval oil paintings to be placed between the windows of the entire building, representing nearly every important animal known in zoology. These paintings were put on the building in a single night, and so complete a transformation in the appearance of an edifice is seldom witnessed. When the living stream rolled down Broadway the next morning and reached the Astor House corner, opposite the Museum, it seemed to meet with a sudden check. I never before saw so many open mouths and astonished eyes. Some people were puzzled to know what it all meant; some looked as if they thought it was an enchanted palace that had suddenly sprung up; others exclaimed, "Well, the animals all seem to have 'broken out' last night," and hundreds came in to see how the establishment survived the sudden eruption. At all events, from that morning the Museum receipts took a jump forward of nearly a hundred dollars a day, and they never fell back again. Strangers would look at this great pictorial magazine and argue that an establishment with so many animals on the outside must have something on the inside, and in they would go to see. Inside, I took particular pains to please and astonish those strangers, and when they went back to the country, they carried plenty of pictorial bills and lithographs, which I always lavishly furnished, and thus the fame of Barnum's Museum became so widespread, that people scarcely thought of visiting the city without going to my establishment.

In fact, the Museum has become an established institution in the land. Now and then some one would cry out "humbug" and "charlatan," but so much the better for me. It helped to advertise me, and I was willing to bear the reputation—and I engaged queer curiosities, and even monstrosities, simply to add to the notoriety of the Museum.

Dr. Valentine will be remembered by many as a man who gave imitations and delineations of eccentric characters. He was quite a card at the Museum when I first purchased that establishment, and before I introduced dramatic representations into the "Lecture Room." His representations were usually given as follows: A small table was placed in about the centre of the stage; a curtain reaching to the floor covered the front and two ends of the table; under this table, on little shelves and hooks, were placed caps, hats, coats, wigs, moustaches, curls, cravats, and shirt collars, and all sorts of gear for changing the appearance of the upper portion of the person. Dr. Valentine would seat himself in a chair behind the table, and addressing his audience, would state his intention to represent different peculiar characters, male and female, including the Yankee tin peddler; "Tabitha Twist," a maiden lady; "Sam Slick, Jr.," the precocious author; "Solomon Jenkins," a crusty old bachelor, with a song; the down-east school-teacher with his refractory pupils, with many other characters; and he simply asked the indulgence of the audience for a few seconds between each imitation, to enable him to stoop down behind the table and "dress" each character appropriately.

The Doctor himself was a most eccentric character. He was very nervous, and was always fretting lest his audience should be composed of persons who would not appreciate his "imitations." During one of his engagements the Lecture Room performances consisted of negro minstrelsy and Dr. Valentine's imitations. As the minstrels gave the entire first half of the entertainment, the Doctor would post himself at the entrance to the Museum to study the character of the visitors from their appearance. He fancied that he was a great reader of character in this way, and as most of my visitors were from the country, the Doctor, after closely perusing their faces, would decide that they were not the kind of persons who would appreciate his efforts, and this made him extremely nervous. When this idea was once in his head, it took complete possession of the poor Doctor, and worked him up into a nervous excitement which it was often painful to behold. Every country-looking face was a dagger to the Doctor, for he had a perfect horror of exhibiting to an unappreciative audience. When so much excited that he could stand at the door no longer, the disgusted Doctor would come into my office and pour out his lamentations in this wise:

"There, Barnum, I never saw such a stupid lot of country bumpkins in my life. I shan't be able to get a smile out of them. I had rather be horse-whipped than attempt to satisfy an audience who have not got the brains to appreciate me. Sir, mine is a highly intellectual entertainment, and none but refined and educated persons can comprehend it."

"Oh, I think you will make them laugh some, Doctor," I replied.

"Laugh, sir, laugh! why, sir, they have no laugh in them, sir; and if they had, your devilish nigger minstrels would get it all out of them before I commenced."

"Don't get excited, Doctor," I said; "you will please the people."

"Impossible, sir! I was a fool to ever permit my entertainment to be mixed up with that of nigger singers."

"But you could not give an entire entertainment satisfactorily to the public; they want more variety."

"Then you should have got something more refined, sir. Why, one of those cursed nigger breakdowns excites your audience so they don't want to hear a word from me. At all events, I ought to commence the entertainment and let the niggers finish up. I tell you, Mr. Barnum, I won't stand it! I would rather go to the poor-house. I won't stay here over a fortnight longer! It is killing me!"

In this excited state the Doctor would go upon the stage, dressed very neatly in a suit of black. Addressing a few pleasant words to the audience, he would then take a seat behind his little table, and with a broad smile covering his countenance would ask the audience to excuse him a few seconds, and he would appear as "Tabitha Twist," a literary spinster of fifty-five. On these occasions I was usually behind the scenes, standing at one of the wings opposite the Doctor's table, where I could see and hear all that occurred "behind the curtain." The moment the Doctor was down behind the table, a wonderful change came over that smiling countenance.

"Blast this infernal, stupid audience! they would not laugh to save the city of New York!" said the Doctor, while he rapidly slipped on a lady's cap and a pair of long curls. Then, while arranging a lace handkerchief around his shoulders, he would grate his teeth and curse the Museum, its manager, the audience and everybody else. The instant the handkerchief was pinned, the broad smile would come upon his face, and up would go his head and shoulders showing to the audience a rollicking specimen of a good-natured old maid.

"How do you do, ladies and gentlemen? You all know me, Tabitha Twist, the happiest maiden in the village; always laughing. Now, I'll sing you one of my prettiest songs."

The mock maiden would then sing a lively, funny ditty, followed by faint applause, and down would bob the head behind the table to prepare for a presentation of "Sam Slick, junior."

"Curse such a set of fools" (off goes the cap, followed by the curls). "They think it's a country Sunday school" (taking off the lace handkerchief). "I expect they will hiss me next, the donkeys" (on goes a light wig of long, flowing hair). "I wish the old Museum was sunk in the Atlantic" (puts on a Yankee round-jacket, and broad-brimmed hat). "I never will be caught in this infernal place, curse it;" up jump head and shoulders of the Yankee, and Sam Slick, junior, sings out a merry—

"Ha! ha! why, folks, how de dew. Darn glad to see you, by hokey; I came down here to have lots of fun, for you know I always believe we must laugh and grow fat."

After five minutes of similar rollicking nonsense, down would bob the head again, and the cursing, swearing, tearing, and teeth-grating would commence, and continue till the next character appeared to the audience, bedecked with smiles and good-humor.

On several occasions I got up "Baby shows," at which I paid liberal prizes for the finest baby, the fattest baby, the handsomest twins, for triplets, and so on. I always gave several months' notice of these intended shows and limited the number of babies at each exhibition to one hundred. Long before the appointed time, the list would be full and I have known many a fond mother to weep bitterly because the time for application was closed and she could not have the opportunity to exhibit her beautiful baby. These shows were as popular as they were unique, and while they paid in a financial point of view, my chief object in getting them up was to set the newspapers to talking about me, thus giving another blast on the trumpet which I always tried to keep blowing for the Museum. Flower shows, dog shows, poultry shows and bird shows, were held at intervals in my establishment and in each instance the same end was attained as by the baby shows. I gave prizes in the shape of medals, money and diplomas and the whole came back to me four-fold in the shape of advertising.

There was great difficulty, however, in awarding the principal prize of $100 at the baby shows. Every mother thought her own baby the brightest and best, and confidently expected the capital prize.

> For where was ever seen the mother
> Would give her baby for another?

Not foreseeing this when I first stepped into the expectant circle and announced in a matter of fact way that a committee of ladies had decided upon the baby of Mrs. So and So as entitled to the leading prize, I was ill-prepared for the storm of indignation that arose on every side. Ninety-nine disappointed, and as they thought, deeply injured, mothers made common cause and pronounced the successful little one the meanest, homeliest baby in the lot, and roundly abused me and my committee for our stupidity and partiality. "Very well, ladies," said I in the first instance, "select a committee of your own and I will give another $100 prize to the baby you shall pronounce to be the best specimen." This was only throwing oil upon flame; the ninety-nine confederates were deadly enemies from the moment and no new babies were presented in competition for the second prize. Thereafter, I took good care to send in a written report and did not attempt to announce the prize in person.

At the first exhibition of the kind, there was a vague, yet very current rumor, that in the haste of departure from the Museum several young mothers had exchanged babies (for the babies were nearly all of the same age and were generally dressed alike) and did not discover the mistake till they arrived home and some such conversation as this occurred between husband and wife:

"Did our baby take the prize?"

"No! the darling was cheated out of it."

"Well, why didn't you bring home the same baby you carried to the Museum?"

I am glad to say that I could not trace this cruel rumor to an authentic source.

In June 1843, a herd of yearling buffaloes was on exhibition in Boston. I bought the lot, brought them to New Jersey, hired the race course at Hoboken, chartered the ferry-boats for one day, and advertised that a hunter had arrived with a herd of buffaloes—I was careful not to state their age—and that August 31st there would be a "Grand Buffalo Hunt" on the Hoboken race course—all persons to be admitted free of charge.

The appointed day was warm and delightful, and no less than twenty-four thousand people crossed the North River in the ferry-boats to enjoy the cooling breeze and to see the "Grand Buffalo Hunt." The hunter was dressed as an Indian, and mounted on horseback; he proceeded to show how the wild buffalo is captured with a lasso, but unfortunately the yearlings would not run till the crowd gave a great shout, expressive at once of derision and delight at the harmless humbug. This shout started the young animals into a weak gallop and the lasso was duly thrown over the head of the largest calf. The crowd roared with laughter, listened to my balcony band, which I also furnished "free," and then started for New York, little dreaming who was the author of this sensation, or what was its object.

Mr. N. P. Willis, then editor of the *Home Journal,* wrote an article illustrating the perfect good nature with which the American public submit to a clever humbug. He said that he went to Hoboken to witness the Buffalo Hunt. It was nearly four o'clock when the boat left the foot of Barclay Street, and it was so densely crowded that many persons were obliged to stand on the railings and hold on to the awning posts. When they reached the Hoboken side a boat equally crowded was coming out of the slip. The passengers just arriving cried out to those who were coming away, "Is the Buffalo Hunt over?" To which came the reply, "Yes, and it was the biggest humbug you ever heard of!" Willis added that passengers on the boat with him instantly gave three cheers for the author of the humbug, whoever he might be.

After the public had enjoyed a laugh for several days over the Hoboken "Free Grand Buffalo Hunt," I permitted it to be announced that the proprietor of the American Museum was responsible for the joke, thus using the buffalo hunt as a sky-rocket to attract public attention to my Museum. The object was accomplished and although some people cried out "humbug," I had added to the notoriety which I so much wanted and I was satisfied. As for the cry of "humbug," it never harmed me, and I was in the position of the actor who had much rather be roundly abused than not to be noticed at all. I ought to add, that the forty-eight thousand sixpences— the usual fare—received for ferry fares, less what I paid for the charter of the boats on that one day, more than remunerated me for the cost of the buffaloes and the expenses of the "hunt," and the enormous gratuitous advertising of the Museum must also be placed to my credit.

With the same object—that is, advertising my Museum,—I purchased, for $500, in Cincinnati, Ohio, a "Woolly Horse" I found on exhibition in that city. It was a well formed, small sized horse, with no mane, and not a particle of hair on his tail, while his entire body and legs were covered with thick, fine hair or wool, which curled tight to his skin. This horse was foaled in Indiana, and was a remarkable freak of nature, and certainly a very curious looking animal.

I had not the remotest idea, when I bought this horse, what I should do with him; but when the news came that Colonel John C. Fremont (who was supposed to have been lost in the snows of the Rocky Mountains) was in safety, the "Woolly Horse" was exhibited in New York, and was widely advertised as a most remarkable animal that had been captured by the great explorer's party in the passes of the Rocky Mountains. The exhibition met with only moderate success in New York, and in several Northern provincial towns, and the show would have fallen flat in Washington, had it not been for the over-zeal of Colonel Thomas H. Benton, then a United States Senator from Missouri. He went to the show, and then caused the arrest of my agent for obtaining twenty-five cents from him under "false pretences." No mention had been made of this curious animal in any letter he had received from his son-in-law, Colonel John C. Fremont, and therefore the Woolly Horse had not been captured by any of Fremont's party. The reasoning was hardly as sound as were most of the arguments of "Old Bullion," and the case was dismissed. After a few days of merriment, public curiosity no longer turned in that direction, and the old horse was permitted to retire to private life. My object in the exhibition, however, was fully attained. When it was generally known that the proprietor of the American Museum was also the owner of the famous "Woolly Horse," it caused yet more talk about me and my establishment, and visitors began to say that they would give more to see the proprietor of the Museum than to view the entire collection of curiosities. As for my ruse in advertising the "Woolly Horse" as having been captured by Fremont's exploring party, of course the announcement neither added to nor took from the interest of the exhibition; but it arrested public attention, and it was the only feature of the show that I now care to forget.

It will be seen that very much of the success which attended my many years proprietorship of the American Museum was due to advertising, and especially to my odd methods of advertising. Always claiming that I had curiosities worth showing and worth seeing, and exhibited "dog cheap" at "twenty-five cents admission, children half price"—I studied ways to arrest public attention; to startle, to make people talk and wonder; in short, to let the world know that I had a Museum.

About this time, I engaged a band of Indians from Iowa. They had never seen a railroad or steamboat until they saw them on the route from Iowa to New York. Of course they were wild and had but faint ideas of civilization. The party comprised large and noble specimens of the untutored savage, as well as several very beautiful squaws, with two or three interesting "papooses." They lived and lodged in a large room on the top floor of the Museum, and cooked their own victuals in their own way. They gave their war-dances on the stage in the Lecture Room with great vigor and enthusiasm, much to the satisfaction of the audiences. But these wild Indians seemed to consider their dances as realities. Hence when they gave a real War Dance, it was dangerous for any parties, except their manager and interpreter, to be on the stage, for the moment they had finished their war dance, they began to leap and peer about behind the scenes in search of victims for their tomahawks and scalping knives! Indeed, lest in these frenzied moments they might make a dash at the orchestra or the audience, we had a high rope barrier placed between them and the savages on the front of the stage.

After they had been a week in the Museum, I proposed a change of performance for the week following, by introducing new dances. Among these was the Indian Wedding Dance. At that time I printed but one set of posters (large bills) per week, so that whatever was announced for Monday, was repeated every day and evening during that week. Before the Wedding Dance came off on Monday afternoon, I was informed that I was to provide a large new red woollen blanket, at a cost of ten dollars, for the bridegroom to present to the father of the bride. I ordered the purchase to be made; but was considerably taken aback, when I was informed that I must have another new blanket for the evening, inasmuch as the savage old Indian Chief, father-in-law to the bridegroom, would not consent to his daughter's being approached with the Wedding Dance unless he had his blanket present.

I undertook to explain to the chief, through the interpreter, that this was only a "make believe" wedding; but the old savage shrugged his shoulders, and gave such a terrific "Ugh!" that I was glad to make my peace by ordering another blanket. As we gave two performances per day, I was out of pocket $120 for twelve "wedding blankets," that week.

One of the beautiful squaws named Do-humme died in the Museum. She had been a great favorite with many ladies,—among whom I can especially name Mrs. C. M. Sawyer, wife of the Rev. Dr. T. J. Sawyer. Do-humme was buried on the border of Sylvan Water, at Greenwood Cemetery, where a small monument, erected by her friends, designates her last resting place.

The poor Indians were very sorrowful for many days, and desired to get back again to their western wilds. The father and the betrothed of Do-humme cooked various dishes of food and placed them upon the roof of the Museum, where they believed the spirit of their departed friend came daily for its supply; and these dishes were renewed every morning during the stay of the Indians at the Museum.

It was sometimes very amusing to hear the remarks of strangers who came to visit my Museum. One afternoon a prim maiden lady from Portland, Maine, walked into my private office, where I was busily engaged in writing, and taking a seat on the sofa she asked:

"Is this Mr. Barnum?"

"It is," I replied.

"Is this Mr. P. T. Barnum, the proprietor of the Museum?" she asked.

"The same," was my answer.

"Why, really, Mr. Barnum," she continued, "you look much like other common folks, after all."

I remarked that I presumed I did; but I could not help it, and I hoped she was not disappointed at my appearance.

"Oh, no," she said; "I suppose I have no right to be disappointed, but I have read and heard so much about you and your Museum that I was quite prepared to be astonished."

I asked her if she had been through the establishment.

"I have," she replied; "I came in immediately after breakfast; I have been here ever since, and, I can say I think with the Queen of Sheba, that 'the half had not been told me.' But, Mr. Barnum," she continued, "I have long felt a desire to see you; I wanted to attend when you lectured on temperance in Portland, but I had a severe cold and could not go out."

"Do you like my collection as well as you do the one in the Boston Museum?" I asked.

"Dear me! Mr. Barnum," said she, "I never went to any Museum before, nor to any place of amusement or public entertainment, excepting our school exhibitions;

and I have sometimes felt that they even may be wicked, for some parts of the dialogues seemed frivolous; but I have heard so much of your 'moral drama' and the great good you are doing for the rising generation that I thought I must come here and see for myself."

"We represent the pathetic story of 'Charlotte Temple' in the Lecture Room to-day," I remarked, with an inward chuckle at the peculiarities of my singular visitor, who, although she was nearly fifty years of age, had probably never been in an audience of a hundred persons, unless it might be at a school exhibition, or in Sunday school, or in church.

"Indeed! I am quite familiar with the sad history of Miss Temple, and I think I can derive great consolation from witnessing the representation of the touching story."

At this moment the gong sounded to announce the opening of the Lecture Room, and the crowd passed on in haste to secure seats. My spinster visitor sprang to her feet and anxiously inquired:

"Are the services about to commence?"

"Yes," I replied, "the congregation is now going up."

She marched along with the crowd as demurely as if she was going to a funeral. After she was seated, I watched her, and in the course of the play I noticed that she was several times so much overcome as to be moved to tears. She was very much affected, and when the "services" were over, without seeking another interview with me, she went silently and tearfully away.

One day, two city boys who had thoroughly explored the wonders of the Museum, on their way out passed the open door of my private office, and seeing me sitting there, one of them exclaimed to his companion:

"There! That's Mr. Barnum."

"No! is it?" asked the other, and then with his mind full of the glories of the stuffed gander-skins, and other wealth which had been displayed to his wondering eyes in the establishment, he summed up his views of the vastness and value of the whole collection, and its fortunate proprietor in a single sentence:

"Well, he's an awful rich old cuss, ain't he!"

Those boys evidently took a strictly financial view of the establishment.

CHAPTER X.

Another Successful Speculation.

The president and directors of the "New York Museum Company" not only failed to buy the American Museum as they confidently expected to do, but, after my newspaper squib war and my purchase of the Museum, they found it utterly impossible to sell their stock. By some arrangement, the particulars of which I do not remember, if, indeed, I ever cared to know them, Mr. Peale was conducting Peale's Museum which he claimed was a more "scientific" establishment than mine, and he pretended to appeal to a higher class of patrons. Mesmerism was one of his scientific attractions, and he had a subject upon whom he operated at times with the greatest seeming success, and fairly astonished his audiences. But there were times when the subject was wholly unimpressible and then those who had paid their money to see the woman put into the mesmeric state cried out "humbug," and the reputation of the establishment seriously suffered.

It devolved upon me to open a rival mesmeric performance, and accordingly I engaged a bright little girl who was exceedingly susceptible to such mesmeric influences as I could induce. That is, she learned her lesson thoroughly, and when I had apparently put her to sleep with a few passes and stood behind her, she seemed to be duly "impressed" as I desired; raised her hands as I willed; fell from her chair to the floor; and if I put candy or tobacco into my mouth, she was duly delighted or disgusted. She never failed in these routine performances. Strange to say, believers in mesmerism used to witness her performances with the greatest pleasure and adduce them as positive proofs that there was something in mesmerism, and they applauded tremendously—up to a certain point.

That point was reached, when leaving the girl "asleep," I called up some one in the audience, promising to put him "in the same state" within five minutes, or forfeit fifty dollars. Of course, all my "passes" would not put any man in the mesmeric state; at the end of three minutes he was as wide awake as ever.

"Never mind," I would say, looking at my watch; "I have two minutes more, and meantime, to show that a person in this state is utterly insensible to pain, I propose to cut off one of the fingers of the little girl who is still asleep." I would then take out my knife and feel of the edge, and when I turned around to the girl whom I left on the chair she had fled behind the scenes to the intense amusement of the greater part of the audience and to the amazement of the mesmerists who were present.

"Why! where's my little girl?" I asked with feigned astonishment.

"Oh! she ran away when you began to talk about cutting off fingers."

"Then she was wide awake, was she?"

"Of course she was, all the time."

"I suppose so; and, my dear sir, I promised that you should be 'in the same state' at the end of five minutes, and as I believe you are so, I do not forfeit fifty dollars."

I kept up this performance for several weeks, till I quite killed Peale's "genuine" mesmerism in the rival establishment. After Peale, "Yankee" Hill undertook the management of that Museum, but in a little while he failed. It was then let to Henry Bennett, who reduced the entrance price to one shilling,—a half price which led me to characterize his concern as "cheap and nasty,"—and he began a serious rivalry with my Museum. His main reliances were burlesques and caricatures of whatever novelties I was exhibiting; thus, when I advertised an able company of vocalists, well-known as the Orphean Family, Bennett announced the "Orphan Family;" my Fejee Mermaid he offset with a figure made of a monkey and codfish joined together and called the "Fudg-ee Mermaid." These things created some laughter at my expense, but they also served to advertise my Museum.

When the novelty of this opposition died away, Bennett did a decidedly losing business. I used to send a man with a shilling to his place every night and I knew exactly how much he was doing and what were his receipts. The holidays were coming and might tide him over a day or two, but he was at the very bottom and I said to him, one day:

"Bennett, if you can keep open one week after New Year's I will give you a hundred dollars."

He made every effort to win the money, and even went to the landlord and offered him the entire receipts for a week if he would only let him stay there; but he would not do it, and the day after New Year's, January 2, 1843, Bennett shut up shop, having lost his last dollar and even failing to secure the handsome premium I offered him.

The entire collection fell into the hands of the landlord for arrearages of rent, and I privately purchased it for $7,000 cash, hired the building, and secretly engaged Bennett as my agent. We ran a very spirited opposition for a long time and abused each other terribly in public. It was very amusing when actors and performers failed to make terms with one of us and went to the other, carrying from one to the other the price each was willing to pay for an engagement. We thus used to hear extraordinary stories about each other's "liberal terms," but between the two we managed to secure such persons as we wanted at about the rates at which their services were really worth. While these people were thus running from one manager to the other, supposing we were rivals, Bennett said to me one day:

"You and I are like a pair of shears; we seem to cut each other, but we only cut what comes between."

I ran my opposition long enough to beat myself. It answered every purpose, however, in awakening public attention to my Museum, and was an advantage in preventing others from starting a genuine opposition. At the end of six months, the whole establishment, including the splendid gallery of American portraits, was removed to the American Museum and I immediately advertised the great card of a "Double attraction" and "Two Museums in One," without extra charge.

A Museum proper obviously depends for patronage largely upon country people who visit the city with a worthy curiosity to see the novelties of the town. As I had opened a dramatic entertainment in connection with my curiosities, it was clear that I must adapt my stage to the wants of my country customers. While I was disposed to amuse my provincial patrons, I was determined that there should be nothing in my establishment, where many of my visitors would derive their first impressions of city life, that could contaminate or corrupt them. At this period, it was customary to tolerate very considerable license on the stage. Things were said and done and permitted in theatres that elsewhere would have been pronounced highly improper. The public seemed to demand these things, and it is an axiom in political economy, that the demand must regulate the supply. But I determined, at the start, that, let the demand be what it might, the Museum dramatic entertainments should be unexceptionable on the score of morality.

I have already mentioned some of the immediate reforms I made in the abuses of the stage. I went farther, and, at the risk of some pecuniary sacrifice, I abolished what was common enough in other theatres, even the most "respectable," and was generally known as the "third tier." Nor was a bar permitted on my premises. To be sure, I had no power to prevent my patrons from going out between the acts and getting liquor if they chose to do so, and I gave checks, as is done in other theatres, and some of my city customers availed themselves of the opportunity to go out for drinks and return again. Practically, then, it was much the same as if I had kept a bar in the Museum, and so I abolished the check business. There was great reason to apprehend that such a course would rob me of the patronage of a considerable class of play-goers, but I rigidly adhered to the new rule, and what I may have lost in money, I more than gained in the greater decorum which characterized my audiences.

The Museum became a mania with me and I made everything possible subservient to it. On the eve of elections, rival politicians would ask me for whom I was going to vote, and my answer invariably was, "I vote for the American Museum." In fact, at that time, I cared very little about politics, and a great deal about my business. Meanwhile the Museum prospered wonderfully, and everything I attempted or engaged in seemed at the outset an assured success.

The giants whom I exhibited from time to time were always literally great features in my establishment, and they oftentimes afforded me, as well as my patrons, food for much amusement as well as wonder. The Quaker giant, Hales, was quite a wag in his way. He went once to see the new house of an acquaintance who had suddenly become rich, but who was a very ignorant man. When he came back he described the wonders of the mansion and said that the proud proprietor showed him everything from basement to attic; parlors, bed-rooms, dining room, and," said Hales, "what he called his 'study'— meaning, I suppose, the place where he intends to study his spelling-book!"

I had at one time two famous men, the French giant, M. Bihin, a very slim man, and the Arabian giant, Colonel Goshen. These men generally got on together very well, though, of course, each was jealous of the other, and of the attention the rival received, or the notice he attracted. One day they quarrelled, and a lively interchange of compliments ensued, the Arabian calling the Frenchman a "Shanghai," and receiving in return the epithet of "Nigger." From words both were eager to proceed to blows, and both ran to my collection of arms, one seizing the club with which Captain Cook or any other man might have been killed, if it were judiciously wielded, and the other laying hands on a sword of the terrific size which is supposed to have been conventional in the days of the Crusades. The preparations for a deadly encounter, and the high words of the contending parties brought a dozen of the Museum *attaches* to the spot, and these men threw themselves between the gigantic combatants. Hearing the disturbance, I ran from my private office to the duelling ground, and said:

"Look here! This is all right; if you want to fight each other, maiming and perhaps killing one or both of you, that is your affair; but my interest lies here—you are both under engagement to me, and if this duel is to come off, I and the public have a right to participate. It must be duly advertised, and must take place on the stage of the Lecture Room. No performance of yours would be a greater attraction, and if you kill each other, our engagement can end with your duel."

This proposition, made in apparent earnest, so delighted the giants that they at once burst into a laugh, shook hands, and quarrelled no more.

I now come to the details of one of the most interesting, as well as successful, of all the show enterprises in which I have engaged—one which not only taxed all my ingenuity and industry, but which gave unqualified delight to thousands of people on two continents and put enormous sums of money into many pockets besides my own.

In November, 1842, I was in Albany on business, and as the Hudson River was frozen over, I returned to New

York by the Housatonic Railroad, stopping one night at Bridgeport, Connecticut, with my brother, Philo F. Barnum, who at that time kept the Franklin Hotel. I had heard of a remarkably small child in Bridgeport, and, at my request, my brother brought him to the hotel. He was not two feet high; he weighed less than sixteen pounds, and was the smallest child I ever saw that could walk alone; but he was a perfectly formed, bright-eyed little fellow, with light hair and ruddy cheeks and he enjoyed the best of health. He was exceedingly bashful, but after some coaxing he was induced to talk with me, and he told me that he was the son of Sherwood E. Stratton, and that his own name was Charles S. Stratton. After seeing him and talking with him, I at once determined to secure his services from his parents and to exhibit him in public.

But as he was only five years of age, to exhibit him as a "dwarf" might provoke the inquiry "How do you know he is a dwarf?" Some liberty might be taken with the facts, but even with this license, I felt that the venture was only an experiment, and I engaged him for four weeks at three dollars a week, with all travelling and boarding charges for himself and his mother at my expense. They came to New York, Thanksgiving day, December 8, 1842, and Mrs. Stratton was greatly surprised to see her son announced on my Museum bills as "General Tom Thumb."

I took the greatest pains to educate and train my diminutive prodigy, devoting many hours to the task by day and by night, and I was very successful, for he was an apt pupil with a great deal of native talent, and a keen sense of the ludicrous. He made rapid progress in preparing himself for such performances as I wished him to undertake and he became very much attached to his teacher.

When the four weeks expired, I re-engaged him for one year at seven dollars a week, with a gratuity of fifty dollars at the end of the engagement, and the privilege of exhibiting him anywhere in the United States, in which event his parents were to accompany him and I was to pay all travelling expenses. He speedily became a public favorite, and, long before the year was out, I voluntarily increased his weekly salary to twenty-five dollars, and he fairly earned it. Sometimes I exhibited him for several weeks in succession at the Museum, and when I wished to introduce other novelties I sent him to different towns and cities, accompanied by my friend, Mr. Fordyce Hitchcock, and the fame of General Tom Thumb soon spread throughout the country.

Two years had now elapsed since I bought the Museum and I had long since paid for the entire establishment from the profits; I had bought out my only rival; I was free from debt, and had a handsome surplus in the treasury. The business had long ceased to be an experiment; it was an established success and was in such perfect running order, that it could safely be committed to the management of trustworthy and tried agents.

Accordingly, looking for a new field for my individual efforts, I entered into an agreement for General Tom Thumb's services for another year, at fifty dollars a week and all expenses, with the privilege of exhibiting him in Europe. I proposed to test the curiosity of men and women on the other side of the Atlantic. Much as I hoped for success, in my most sanguine moods, I could not anticipate the half of what was in store for me; I did not foresee nor dream that I was shortly to be brought in close contact with kings, queens, lords, and illustrious commoners, and that such association, by means of my exhibition, would afterwards introduce me to the great public and the public's money, which was to fill my coffers. Or, if I saw some such future, it was dreamily, dimly, and with half-opened eyes, as the man saw the "trees walking."

After arranging my business affairs for a long absence, and making every preparation for an extended foreign tour, on Thursday, January 18, 1844, I went on board the new and fine sailing ship "Yorkshire," Captain D. G.

Bailey, bound for Liverpool. Our party included General Tom Thumb, his parents, his tutor, and Professor Guillaudeu, the French naturalist. We were accompanied by several personal friends, and the City Brass Band kindly volunteered to escort us to Sandy Hook.

My name has been so long associated with mirthful incidents that I presume many persons do not suppose I am susceptible of sorrowful, or even sentimental emotions; but when the bell of the steamer that towed our ship down the bay announced the hour of separation, and then followed the hastily-spoken words of farewell, and the parting grasp of friendly hands, I confess that I was very much in the "melting mood," and when the band played "Home, Sweet Home," I was moved to tears.

A voyage to Liverpool is now an old, familiar story, and I abstain from entering into details, though I have abundant material respecting my own experiences of my first sea-voyage in the first two of a series of one hundred letters which I wrote in Europe as correspondent of the New York *Atlas*. But some of the incidents and adventures of my voyage on the "Yorkshire" are worth transcribing in these pages of my personal history.

Occasional calms and adverse winds protracted our passage to nineteen days, but a better ship and a more competent captain never sailed. I was entirely exempt from sea-sickness, and enjoyed the voyage very much. Good fellowship prevailed among the passengers, the time passed rapidly, and we had a good deal of fun on board.

Several of the passengers were English merchants from Canada and one of the number, who reckoned himself "A, No. 1," and often hinted that he was too 'cute for any Yankee, boasted so much of his shrewdness that a Yankee friend of mine confederated with me to test it. I thought of an old trick and arranged with my friend to try it on the boastful John Bull. Coming out of my state-room, with my hand to my face, and apparently in great pain, I asked my fellow passengers what was good for the tooth-ache. My friend and confederate recommended heating tobacco, and holding it to my face. I therefore borrowed a little tobacco, and putting it in a paper of a peculiar color, placed it on the stove to warm. I then retired for a few minutes, during which time the Yankee proposed playing a trick on me by emptying the tobacco, and filling the paper with ashes, which our smart Englishman thought would be a very fine joke, and he himself made the substitution, putting ashes into the paper and throwing the tobacco into the fire.

I soon reappeared and gravely placed the paper to my face to the great amusement of the passengers and walked up and down the cabin as if I was suffering terribly. At the further end of the cabin I slyly exchanged the paper for another in my pocket of the same color and containing tobacco and then walked back again a picture of misery. Whereupon, the Merry Englishman cried out:

"Mr. Barnum, what have you got in that paper?"

"Tobacco," I replied.

"What will you bet it is tobacco?" said the Englishman.

"Oh, don't bother me," said I; "my tooth pains me sadly; I know it is tobacco, for I put it there myself."

"I'll bet you a dozen of champagne that it is not tobacco," said the Englishman.

"Nonsense," I replied, "I will not bet, for it would not be fair; I know it is tobacco."

"I'll bet you fifty dollars it is not," said John Bull, and he counted ten sovereigns upon the table.

"I'll not bet the money," I replied, "for I tell you I *know* it is tobacco; I placed it there myself."

"You dare not bet!" he rejoined.

At last, merely to accommodate him, I bet a dozen of champagne. The Englishman fairly jumped with delight, and roared out:

"Open the paper! open the paper!"

The passengers crowded round the table in great glee to see me open the paper, for all but the Yankee thought I was taken in. I quietly opened the paper, and remarked:

"There, I told you it was tobacco—how foolish you were to suppose it was not—for, as I told you, I put it there myself."

The passengers, my confederate excepted, were amazed and the Englishman was absolutely astounded. It was the biter bitten. But he told the steward to bring the champagne, and turning to my confederate who had so effectually assisted in "selling" him, he pronounced the affair "a contemptible Yankee trick." It was several days before he recovered his good humor, but he joined at last with the rest of us in laughing at the joke, and we heard no more about his extraordinary shrewdness.

On our arrival at Liverpool, quite a crowd had assembled at the dock to see Tom Thumb, for it had been previously announced that he would arrive in the "Yorkshire," but his mother managed to smuggle him ashore unnoticed, for she carried him, as if he was an infant, in her arms. We went to the Waterloo Hotel, and, after an excellent dinner, walked out to take a look at the town. While I was viewing the Nelson monument a venerable looking, well-dressed old gentleman volunteered to explain to me the different devices and inscriptions. I looked upon him as a disinterested and attentive man of means who was anxious to assist a stranger and to show his courtesy; but when I gave him a parting bow of thanks, half ashamed that I had so trespassed on his kindness, he put out the hand of a beggar and said that he would be thankful for any remuneration I saw fit to bestow upon him for his trouble. I was certainly astonished, and I thrust a shilling into his hand and walked rapidly away.

In the evening of the same day, a tall, raw-boned man came to the hotel and introduced himself to me as a brother Yankee, who would be happy in pointing out the many wonders in Liverpool that a stranger would be pleased to see.

I asked him how long he had been in Liverpool, and he replied, "Nearly a week." I declined his proffered services abruptly, remarking that if he had been there only a week, I probably knew as much about England as he did.

"Oh," said he, "you are mistaken. I have been in England before, though never till recently in Liverpool."

"What part of England?" I inquired.

"Opposite Niagara Falls," he replied; "I spent several days there with the British soldiers."

I laughed in his face, and reminded him that England did·not lie opposite Niagara Falls. The impudent fellow was confused for a moment, and then triumphantly exclaimed:

"I didn't mean England. I know what country it is as well as you do."

"Well, what country is it?" I asked, quite assured that he did not know.

"Great Britain, of course," he replied.

It is needless to add that the honor of his company as a guide in Liverpool was declined, and he went off apparently in a huff because his abilities were not appreciated.

Later in the evening, the proprietor of a cheap waxworks show, at three ha' pence admission, called upon me. He had heard of the arrival of the great American curiosity, and he seized the earliest opportunity to make the General and myself the magnificent offer of ten dollars a week if we would join ourselves to his already remarkable and attractive exhibition. I could not but think, that dwarfs must be literally at a "low figure" in England, and my prospects were gloomy indeed. I was a stranger in the land; my letters of introduction had not been delivered; beyond my own little circle, I had not seen a friendly face, nor heard a familiar voice. I was "blue," homesick, almost in despair. Next morning, there came a ray of sunshine in the following note:

> "Madame CELESTE presents her compliments to Mr. Barnum, and begs to say that her private box is quite at his service, any night, for himself and friends.
> "Theatre Royal, Williamson Square."

This polite invitation was thankfully accepted, and we went to the theatre that evening. Our party, including the General, who was partly concealed by his tutor's cloak, occupied Celeste's box, and in the box adjoining sat an English lady and gentleman whose appearance indicated respectability, intelligence and wealth. The General's interest in the performance attracted their attention, and the lady remarked to me:

"What an intelligent-looking child you have! He appears to take quite an interest in the stage."

"Pardon me, madam," said I, "this is not a child. This is General Tom Thumb."

"Indeed!" they exclaimed. They had seen the announcements of our visit and were greatly gratified at an interview with the pigmy prodigy. They at once advised me in the most complimentary and urgent manner to take the General to Manchester, where they resided, assuring me that an exhibition in that place would be highly remunerative. I thanked my new friends for their counsel and encouragement, and ventured to ask them what price they would recommend me to charge for admission.

"The General is so decidedly a curiosity," said the lady, "that I think you might put it as high as tuppence!" (two-pence.)

She was, however, promptly interrupted by her husband, who was evidently the economist of the family: "I am sure you would not succeed at that price," said he; "you should put admission at one penny, for that is the usual price for seeing giants and dwarfs in England."

This was worse than the ten dollars a week offer of the wax-works proprietor, but I promptly answered "Never shall the price be less than one shilling sterling and some of the nobility and gentry of England will yet pay gold to see General Tom Thumb."

My letters of introduction speedily brought me into friendly relations with many excellent families and I was induced to hire a hall and present the General to the public, for a short season, in Liverpool. I had intended to proceed directly to London and begin operations at "head-quarters," that is, in Buckingham Palace, if possible; but I had been advised that the royal family was in mourning for the death of Prince Albert's father, and would not permit the approach of any entertainments.

Meanwhile confidential letters from London informed me that Mr. Maddox, Manager of Princess's Theatre, was coming down to witness my exhibition, with a view to making an engagement. He came privately, but I was fully informed as to his presence and object. A friend pointed him out to me in the hall, and when I stepped up to him, and called him by name, he was "taken all aback," and avowed his purpose in visiting Liverpool. An interview resulted in an engagement of the General for three nights at Princess's Theatre. I was unwilling to contract for a longer period, and even this short engagement, though on liberal terms, was acceded to only as a means of advertisement. So soon, therefore, as I could bring my short, but highly successful season in Liverpool to a close, we went to London.

CHAPTER XI.

General Tom Thumb
in England.

Immediately after our arrival in London, the General came out at the Princess's Theatre, and made so decided a "hit" that it was difficult to decide who was best pleased, the spectators, the manager, or myself. The spectators were delighted because they could not well help it; the manager was satisfied because he had coined money by the engagement; and I was greatly pleased because I now had a visible guaranty of success in London. I was offered far higher terms for a re-engagement, but my purpose had been already answered; the news was spread everywhere that General Tom Thumb, an unparalleled curiosity, was in the city; and it only remained for me to bring him before the public, on my own account and in my own time and way.

I took a furnished mansion in Grafton Street, Bond Street, West End, in the very centre of the most fashionable locality. The house had previously been occupied for several years by Lord Talbot, and Lord Brougham and half a dozen families of the aristocracy and many of the gentry were my neighbors. From this magnificent mansion, I sent letters of invitation to the editors and several of the nobility, to visit the General. Most of them called, and were highly gratified. The word of approval was indeed so passed around in high circles, that uninvited parties drove to my door in crested carriages, and were not admitted.

147

This procedure, though in some measure a stroke of policy, was neither singular nor hazardous, under the circumstances. I had not yet announced a public exhibition, and as a private American gentleman, it became me to maintain the dignity of my position. I therefore instructed my liveried servant to deny admission to see my "ward," excepting to persons who brought cards of invitation. He did it in a proper manner, and no offence could be taken, though I was always particular to send an invitation immediately to such as had not been admitted.

During our first week in London, the Hon. Edward Everett, the American Minister, to whom I had letters of introduction, called and was highly pleased with his diminutive though renowned countryman. We dined with him the next day, by invitation, and his family loaded the young American with presents. Mr. Everett kindly promised to use influence at the Palace in person, with a view to having Tom Thumb introduced to Her Majesty Queen Victoria.

A few evenings afterwards the Baroness Rothschild sent her carriage for us. Her mansion is a noble structure in Piccadilly, surrounded by a high wall, through the gate of which our carriage was driven, and brought up in front of the main entrance. Here we were received by half a dozen servants, and were ushered up the broad flight of marble stairs to the drawing-room, where we met the Baroness and a party of twenty or more ladies and gentlemen. In this sumptuous mansion of the richest banker in the world, we spent about two hours, and when we took our leave a well-filled purse was quietly slipped into my hand. The golden shower had begun to fall, and that it was no dream was manifest from the fact that, very shortly afterwards, a visit to the mansion of Mr. Drummond, another eminent banker, came to the same golden conclusion.

I now engaged the "Egyptian Hall," in Piccadilly, and the announcement of my unique exhibition was promptly

answered by a rush of visitors, in which the wealth and
fashion of London were liberally represented. I made
these arrangements because I had little hope of being
soon brought to the Queen's presence, (for the reason
before mentioned,) but Mr. Everett's generous influence
secured my object. I breakfasted at his house one morning, by invitation, in company with Mr. Charles Murray,
an author of creditable repute, who held the office of
Master of the Queen's Household. In the course of conversation, Mr. Murray inquired as to my plans, and I
informed him that I intended going to the Continent
shortly, though I should be glad to remain if the General
could have an interview with the Queen—adding that
such an event would be of great consequence to me.

Mr. Murray kindly offered his good offices in the case,
and the next day one of the Life Guards, a tall, noble-
looking fellow, bedecked as became his station, brought
me a note, conveying the Queen's invitation to General
Tom Thumb and his guardian, Mr. Barnum, to appear at
Buckingham Palace on an evening specified. Special instructions were the same day orally given me by Mr.
Murray, by Her Majesty's command, to suffer the General to appear before her, as he would appear anywhere
else, without any training in the use of titles of royalty, as
the Queen desired to see him act naturally and without
restraint.

Determined to make the most of the occasion, I put a
placard on the door of the Egyptian Hall: "Closed this
evening, General Tom Thumb being at Buckingham
Palace by command of Her Majesty."

On arriving at the Palace, the Lord in Waiting put me
"under drill" as to the manner and form in which I should
conduct myself in the presence of royalty. I was to answer
all questions by Her Majesty through him, and in no
event to speak directly to the Queen. In leaving the royal
presence I was to "back out," keeping my face always towards Her Majesty, and the illustrious lord kindly gave

me a specimen of that sort of backward locomotion. How far I profited by his instructions and example, will presently appear.

We were conducted through a long corridor to a broad flight of marble steps, which led to the Queen's magnificent picture gallery, where Her Majesty and Prince Albert, the Duchess of Kent, and twenty or thirty of the nobility were awaiting our arrival. They were standing at the farther end of the room when the doors were thrown open, and the General walked in, looking like a wax doll gifted with the power of locomotion. Surprise and pleasure were depicted on the countenances of the royal circle at beholding this remarkable specimen of humanity so much smaller than they had evidently expected to find him.

The General advanced with a firm step, and as he came within hailing distance made a very graceful bow, and exclaimed, "Good evening, Ladies and Gentlemen!"

A burst of laughter followed this salutation. The Queen then took him by the hand, led him about the gallery, and asked him many questions, the answers to which kept the party in an uninterrupted strain of merriment. The General familiarly informed the Queen that her picture gallery was "first-rate," and told her he should like to see the Prince of Wales. The Queen replied that the Prince had retired to rest, but that he should see him on some future occasion. The General then gave his songs, dances, and imitations, and after a conversation with Prince Albert and all present, which continued for more than an hour, we were permitted to depart.

Before describing the process and incidents of "backing out," I must acknowledge how sadly I broke through the counsel of the Lord in Waiting. While Prince Albert and others were engaged with the General, the Queen was gathering information from me in regard to his history, etc. Two or three questions were put and answered through the process indicated in my drill. It was a round-about way of doing business not at all to my liking, and I suppose the Lord in Waiting was seriously shocked, if not outraged, when I entered directly into conversation with Her Majesty. She, however, seemed not disposed to check my boldness, for she immediately spoke directly to me in obtaining the information which she sought. I felt entirely at ease in her presence, and could not avoid contrasting her sensible and amiable manners with the stiffness and formality of upstart gentility at home or abroad.

The Queen was modestly attired in plain black, and wore no ornaments. Indeed, surrounded as she was by ladies arrayed in the highest style of magnificence, their dresses sparkling with diamonds, she was the last person whom a stranger would have pointed out in that circle as the Queen of England.

The Lord in Waiting was perhaps mollified toward me when he saw me following his illustrious example in retiring from the royal presence. He was accustomed to the process, and therefore was able to keep somewhat ahead (or rather aback) of me, but even *I* stepped rather fast for the other member of the retiring party. We had a considerable distance to travel in that long gallery before reaching the door, and whenever the General found he was losing ground, he turned around and ran a few steps, then resumed the position of "backing out," then turned around and ran, and so continued to alternate his methods of getting to the door, until the gallery fairly rang with the merriment of the royal spectators. It was really one of the richest scenes I ever saw; running, under the circumstances, was an offence sufficiently heinous to excite the indignation of the Queen's favorite poodle-dog, and he vented his displeasure by barking so sharply as to startle the General from his propriety. He, however, recovered immediately, and with his little cane commenced an attack on the poodle, and a funny fight ensued, which renewed and increased the merriment of the royal party.

This was near the door of exit. We had scarcely passed

into the ante-room, when one of the Queen's attendants came to us with the expressed hope of Her Majesty that the General had sustained no damage—to which the Lord in Waiting playfully added, that in case of injury to so renowned a personage, he should fear a declaration of war by the United States!

The courtesies of the Palace were not yet exhausted, for we were escorted to an apartment in which refreshments had been provided for us. We did ample justice to the viands, though my mind was rather looking into the future than enjoying the present. I was anxious that the "Court Journal" of the ensuing day should contain more than a mere line in relation to the General's interview with the Queen, and, on inquiry, I learned that the gentleman who had charge of that feature in the daily papers was then in the Palace. He was sent for by my solicitation, and promptly acceded to my request for such a notice as would attract attention. He even generously desired me to give him an outline of what I sought, and I was pleased to see afterwards, that he had inserted my notice *verbatim*.

This notice of my visit to the Queen wonderfully increased the attraction of my exhibition and compelled me to obtain a more commodious hall for my exhibition. I accordingly removed to the larger room in the same building, for some time previously occupied by our countryman, Mr. Catlin, for his great Gallery of Portraits of American Indians and Indian Curiosities, all of which remained as an adornment.

On our second visit to the Queen, we were received in what is called the "Yellow Drawing-Room," a magnificent apartment, surpassing in splendor and gorgeousness anything of the kind I had ever seen. It is on the north side of the gallery, and is entered from that apartment. It was hung with drapery of rich yellow satin damask, the couches, sofas and chairs being covered with the same material. The vases, urns and ornaments were all of modern patterns, and the most exquisite workmanship. The room was panelled in gold, and the heavy cornices beautifully carved and gilt. The tables, pianos, etc., were mounted with gold, inlaid with pearl of various hues, and of the most elegant designs.

We were ushered into this gorgeous drawing-room before the Queen and royal circle had left the dining-room, and, as they approached, the General bowed respectfully, and remarked to Her Majesty "that he had seen her before," adding, "I think this is a prettier room than the picture gallery; that chandelier is very fine."

The Queen smilingly took him by the hand, and said she hoped he was very well.

"Yes, ma'am," he replied, "I am first rate."

"General," continued the Queen, "this is the Prince of Wales."

"How are you, Prince?" said the General, shaking him by the hand; and then standing beside the Prince, he remarked, "the Prince is taller than I am, but I feel as big as anybody"—upon which he strutted up and down the room as proud as a peacock, amid shouts of laughter from all present.

The Queen then introduced the Princess Royal, and the General immediately led her to his elegant little sofa, which we took with us, and with much politeness sat himself down beside her. Then, rising from his seat, he went through his various performances, and the Queen handed him an elegant and costly souvenir, which had been expressly made for him by her order—for which, he told her, "he was very much obliged, and would keep it as long as he lived." The Queen of the Belgians, (daughter of Louis Philippe) was present on this occasion. She asked the General where he was going when he left London?

"To Paris," he replied.

"Whom do you expect to see there?" she continued.

Of course all expected he would answer, "the King of the French," but the little fellow replied:

"I shall see Monsieur Guillaudeu in Paris."

The two Queens looked inquiringly to me, and when I

informed them that M. Guillaudeu was my French naturalist, who had preceded me to Paris, they laughed most heartily.

On our third visit to Buckingham Palace, Leopold, King of the Belgians, was also present. He· was highly pleased, and asked a multitude of questions. Queen Victoria desired the General to sing a song, and asked him what song he preferred to sing.

"Yankee Doodle," was the prompt reply.

This answer was as unexpected to me as it was to the royal party. When the merriment it occasioned somewhat subsided, the Queen good-humoredly remarked, "That is a very pretty song, General. Sing it if you please." The General complied, and soon afterwards we retired. I ought to add, that after each of our three visits to Buckingham Palace, a very handsome sum was sent to me, of course by the Queen's command. This, however, was the smallest part of the advantage derived from these interviews, as will be at once apparent to all who consider the force of Court example in England.

The British public were now fairly excited. Not to have seen General Tom Thumb was decidedly unfashionable, and from March 20th until July 20th, the levees of the little General at the Egyptian Hall were continually crowded, the receipts averaging during the whole period about five hundred dollars per day, and sometimes going considerably beyond that sum. At the fashionable hour, between fifty and sixty carriages of the nobility have been counted at one time standing in front of our exhibition rooms in Piccadilly.

Portraits of the little General were published in all the pictorial papers of the time. Polkas and quadrilles were named after him, and songs were sung in his praise. He was an almost constant theme for the London *Punch*, which served up the General and myself so daintily that it no doubt added vastly to our receipts.

Besides his three public performances per day, the little General attended from three to four private parties per week, for which we were paid eight to ten guineas each. Frequently we would visit two parties in the same evening, and the demand in that line was much greater than the supply. The Queen Dowager Adelaide requested the General's attendance at Marlborough House one afternoon. He went in his court dress, consisting of a richly embroidered brown silk-velvet coat and short breeches, white satin vest with fancy-colored embroidery, white silk stockings and pumps, wig, bag-wig, cocked hat, and a dress sword.

"Why, General," said the Queen Dowager, "I think you look very smart to-day."

"I guess I do," said the General complacently.

A large party of the nobility were present. The old Duke of Cambridge offered the little General a pinch of snuff, which he declined. The General sang his songs, performed his dances, and cracked his jokes, to the great amusement and delight of the distinguished circle of visitors.

"Dear little General," said the kind-hearted Queen, taking him upon her lap, "I see you have got no watch. Will you permit me to present you with a watch and chain?"

"I would like them very much," replied the General, his eyes glistening with joy as he spoke.

"I will have them made expressly for you," responded the Queen Dowager; and at the same moment she called a friend and desired him to see that the proper order was executed. A few weeks thereafter we were called again to Marlborough House. A number of the children of the nobility were present, as well as some of their parents. After passing a few compliments with the General, Queen Adelaide presented him with a beautiful little gold watch, placing the chain around his neck with her own hands. The little fellow was delighted, and scarcely knew how sufficiently to express his thanks. The good Queen gave him some excellent advice in regard to his morals, which he strictly promised to obey.

After giving his performances, we withdrew from the royal presence, and the elegant little watch presented by the hands of Her Majesty the Queen Dowager was not only duly heralded, but was also placed upon a pedestal in the hall of exhibition, together with the presents from Queen Victoria, and covered with a glass vase. These presents, to which were soon added an elegant gold snuff-box mounted with turquoise, presented by his Grace the Duke of Devonshire, and many other costly gifts of the nobility and gentry, added greatly to the attractions of the exhibition. The Duke of Wellington called frequently to see the little General at his public levees. The first time he called, the General was personating Napoleon Bonaparte, marching up and down the platform, apparently taking snuff in deep meditation. He was dressed in the well-known uniform of the Emperor. I introduced him to the "Iron Duke," who inquired the subject of his meditations. "I was thinking of the loss of the battle of Waterloo," was the little General's immediate reply. This display of wit was chronicled throughout the country, and was of itself worth thousands of pounds to the exhibition.

While we were in London the Emperor Nicholas, of Russia, visited Queen Victoria, and I saw him on several public occasions. I was present at the grand review of troops in Windsor Park in honor of and before the Emperor of Russia and the King of Saxony.

General Tom Thumb had visited the King of Saxony and also Ibrahim Pacha who was then in London. At the different parties we attended, we met, in the course of the season, nearly all of the nobility. I do not believe that a single nobleman in England failed to see General Tom Thumb at his own house, at the house of a friend, or at the public levees at Egyptian Hall. The General was a decided pet with some of the first personages in the land, among whom may be mentioned Sir Robert and Lady Peel, the Duke and Duchess of Buckingham, Duke of Bedford, Duke of Devonshire, Count d'Orsay, Lady

Blessington, Daniel O'Connell, Lord Adolphus Fitz-
clarence, Lord Chesterfield, Mr. and Mrs. Joshua Bates,
of the firm of Baring Brothers & Co., and many other
persons of distinction. We had the free entrée to all
the theatres, public gardens, and places of entertainment, and frequently met the principal artists, editors,
poets, and authors of the country. Albert Smith was a
particular friend of mine. He wrote a play for the General
entitled "Hop o' my Thumb," which was presented with
great success at the Lyceum Theatre, London, and in
several of the provincial theatres. Our visit in London
and tour through the provinces were enormously successful. . . .

CHAPTER XVI.

At Home.

One of my main objects in returning home at this time, was to obtain a longer lease of the premises occupied by the American Museum. My lease had still three years to run, but Mr. Olmsted, the proprietor of the building, 'was dead, and I was anxious to make provision in time for the perpetuity of my establishment, for I meant to make the Museum a permanent institution in the city, and if I could not renew my lease, I intended to build an appropriate edifice on Broadway. I finally succeeded, however, in getting the lease of the entire building, covering fifty-six feet by one hundred, for twenty-five years, at an annual rent of $10,000 and the ordinary taxes and assessments. I had already hired in addition the upper stories of three adjoining buildings. My Museum receipts were more in one day, than they formerly were in an entire week, and the establishment had become so popular that it was thronged at all hours from early morning to closing time at night.

On my return, I promptly made use of General Tom Thumb's European reputation. He immediately appeared in the American Museum, and for four weeks drew such crowds of visitors as had never been seen there before. He afterwards spent a month in Bridgeport, with his kindred. To prevent being annoyed by the curious, who would be sure to throng the houses of his relatives, he exhibited two days at Bridgeport. The receipts, amounting to several hundred dollars, were presented to the Bridgeport Charitable Society. The Bridgeporters were much delighted to see their old friend, "little Charlie," again. They little thought, when they saw him playing about the streets a few years previously, that he was destined to create such a sensation among the crowned heads of the old world; and now, returning with his European reputation, he was, of course, a great curiosity to his former acquaintances, as well as to the public generally. His Bridgeport friends found that he had not increased in size during the four and a half years of his absence, but they discovered that he had become sharp and witty, "abounding in foreign airs and native graces"; in fact, that he was quite unlike the little, diffident country fellow whom they had formerly known.

"We never thought Charlie much of a phenomenon when he lived among us," said one of the first citizens of the place, "but now that he has become 'Barnumized,' he is a rare curiosity."

But there was really no mystery about it; the whole change made by training and travel, had appeared to me by degrees, and it came to the citizens of Bridgeport suddenly. The terms upon which I first engaged the lad showed that I had no over-sanguine expectations of his success as a "speculation." When I saw, however, that he was wonderfully popular, I took the greatest pains to engraft upon his native talent all the instruction he was capable of receiving. He was an apt pupil, and I provided for him the best of teachers. Travel and attrition with so many people in so many lands did the rest. The General left America three years before, a diffident, uncultivated little boy; he came back an educated, accomplished little man. He had seen much, and had profited much. He went abroad poor, and he came home rich.

On January 1, 1845, my engagement with the General at a salary ceased, and we made a new arrangement by which we were equal partners, the General, or his father for him, taking one-half of the profits. A reservation, however, was made of the first four weeks after our arrival in New York, during which he was to exhibit at my Museum for two hundred dollars. When we returned to America, the General's father had acquired a handsome fortune, and settling a large sum upon the little General personally, he placed the balance at interest, secured by bond and mortgage, excepting thirty thousand dollars, with which he purchased land near the city limits of Bridgeport, and erected a large and substantial mansion, where he resided till the day of his death, and in which his only two daughters were married, one in 1850, the other in 1853. His only son, besides the General, was born in 1851. All the family, except "little Charlie," are of the usual size.

After spending a month in visiting his friends, it was determined that the General and his parents should travel through the United States. I agreed to accompany them, with occasional intervals of rest at home, for one year, sharing the profits equally, as in England. We proceeded to Washington city, where the General held his levees in April, 1847, visiting President Polk and lady at the White House—thence to Richmond, returning to Baltimore and Philadelphia. Our receipts in Philadelphia in twelve days were $5,594.91. The tour for the entire year realized about the same average. The expenses were from twenty-five dollars to thirty dollars per day. From Philadelphia we went to Boston, Lowell, and Providence. Our receipts on one day in the latter city were $976.97. We then visited New Bedford, Fall River, Salem, Worcester, Springfield, Albany, Troy, Niagara Falls, Buffalo, and intermediate places, and in returning to New York we stopped at the principal towns on the Hudson River. After this we visited New Haven, Hartford, Portland, Me., and intermediate towns.

I was surprised to find that, during my long absence abroad, I had become almost as much of a curiosity to my patrons as I was to the spinster from Maine who once came to see me and to attend the "services" in my Lecture Room. If I showed myself about the Museum or wherever else I was known, I found eyes peering and fingers pointing at me, and could frequently overhear the remark, "There's Barnum." On one occasion soon after my return, I was sitting in the ticket-office reading a newspaper. A man came and purchased a ticket of admission. "Is Mr. Barnum in the Museum?" he asked. The ticket-seller, pointing to me, answered, "This is Mr. Barnum." Supposing the gentleman had business with me, I looked up from the paper. "Is this Mr. Barnum?" he asked. "It is," I replied. He stared at me for a moment, and then, throwing down his ticket, exclaimed, "It's all right; I have got the worth of my money"; and away he went, without going into the Museum at all!

In November, 1847, we started for Havana, taking the steamer from New York to Charleston, where the General exhibited, as well as at Columbia, Augusta, Savannah, Milledgeville, Macon, Columbus, Montgomery, Mobile and New Orleans. At this latter city we remained three weeks, including Christmas and New Year's. We arrived in Havana by the schooner Adams Gray, in January, 1848, and were introduced to the Captain-General and the Spanish nobility. We remained a month in Havana and Matanzas, the General proving an immense favorite. In Havana he was the especial pet of Count Santovania. In Matanzas we were very much indebted to the kindness of a princely American merchant, Mr. Brinckerhoff. Mr. J. S. Thrasher, the American patriot and gentleman, was also of great assistance to us, and placed me under deep obligations.

The hotels in Havana are not good. An American who is accustomed to substantial living, finds it difficult to get enough to eat. We stopped at the Washington House, which at that time was "first-rate bad." It was filthy, and kept by a woman who was drunk most of the time. Several Americans boarded there who were regular gormandizers. One of them, seeing a live turkey on a New Orleans vessel, purchased and presented it to the landlady. It was a small one, and when it was carved, there was not enough of it to "go round." An American, (a large six-footer and a tremendous eater,) who resided on a sugar plantation near Havana, happened to sit near the carver, and seeing an American turkey so near him, and feeling that it was a rare dish for that latitude, kept helping himself, so that when the carving was finished, he had eaten about one half of the turkey. Unfortunately the man who bought it was sitting at the further end of the table, and did not get a taste of the coveted bird. He was indignant, especially against the innocent gormandizer from the sugar plantation, who, of course, was not acquainted with the history of the turkey. When they arose from the table, the planter smacked his lips, and patting his stomach, remarked, "That was a glorious turkey. I have not tasted one before these two years. I am very fond of them, and when I go back to my plantation I mean to commence raising turkeys."

"If you don't raise one before you leave town, you'll be a dead man," said the disappointed poultry purchaser.

From Havana we went to New Orleans, where we remained several days, and from New Orleans we proceeded to St. Louis, stopping at the principal towns on the Mississippi river, and returning *via* Louisville, Cincinnati, and Pittsburgh. We reached the latter city early in May, 1848. From this point it was agreed between Mr. Stratton and myself, that I should go home and henceforth travel no more with the little General. I had competent agents who could exhibit him without my personal assistance, and I preferred to relinquish a portion of the profits, rather than continue to be a travelling showman. I had now been a straggler from home most of the time for thirteen years, and I cannot describe the feelings of gratitude with which I reflected, that having by the most arduous toil and deprivations succeeded in securing a satisfactory competence, I should henceforth spend my days in the bosom of my family. I was fully determined that no pecuniary temptation should again induce me to forego the enjoyments to be secured only in the circle of home. I reached my residence in Bridgeport, Connecticut, in the latter part of May, rejoiced to find my family and friends in good health, and delighted to find myself once more at home.

My new home, which was then nearly ready for occupancy, was the well-known Iranistan. More than two years had been employed in building this beautiful residence. In 1846, finding that fortune was continuing to favor me, I began to look forward eagerly to the time when I could withdraw from the whirlpool of business excitement and settle down permanently with my family, to pass the remainder of my days in comparative rest.

I wished to reside within a few hours of New York. I had never seen more delightful locations than there are upon the borders of Long Island Sound, between New Rochelle, New York, and New Haven, Connecticut; and my attention was therefore turned in that direction. Bridgeport seemed to be about the proper distance from the great metropolis. It is pleasantly situated at the terminus of two railroads, which traverse the fertile valleys of the Naugatuck and Housatonic rivers. The New York and New Haven Railroad runs through the city, and there is also daily steamboat communication with New York. The enterprise which characterized the city, seemed to mark it as destined to become the first in the State in size and opulence; and I was not long in deciding, with the concurrence of my wife, to fix our future residence in that vicinity.

I accordingly purchased seventeen acres of land, less than a mile west of the city, and fronting with a good view upon the Sound. Although nominally in Bridgeport, my property was really in Fairfield, a few rods west of the Bridgeport line. In deciding upon the kind of house to be erected, I determined, first and foremost, to consult convenience and comfort. I cared little for style, and my wife cared still less; but as we meant to have a good house, it might as well, at the same time, be unique. In this, I confess, I had "an eye to business," for I thought that a pile of buildings of a novel order might indirectly serve as an advertisement of my Museum.

In visiting Brighton, in England, I had been greatly pleased with the Pavilion erected by George IV. It was the only specimen of Oriental architecture in England, and the style had not been introduced into America. I concluded to adopt it, and engaged a London architect to furnish me a set of drawings after the general plan of the Pavilion, differing sufficiently to be adapted to the spot of ground selected for my homestead. On my second return visit to the United States, I brought these drawings with me and engaged a competent architect and builder, giving him instructions to proceed with the work, not "by the job" but "by the day," and to spare neither time nor expense in erecting a comfortable, convenient, and tasteful residence. The work was thus begun and continued while I was still abroad, and during the time when I was making my tour with General Tom Thumb through the United States and Cuba. New and magnificent avenues were opened in the vicinity of my property. The building progressed slowly, but surely and substantially. Elegant and appropriate furniture was made expressly for every room in the house. I erected expensive water works to supply the premises. The stables, conservatories and out-buildings were perfect in their kind. There was a profusion of trees set out on the grounds. The whole was built and established literally "regardless of expense," for I had no desire even to ascertain the entire cost. All I cared to know was that it suited me, and that would have been a small consideration with me if it had not also suited my family.

The whole was finally completed to my satisfaction. My family removed into the premises, and, on the fourteenth of November, 1848, nearly one thousand invited guests, including the poor and the rich, helped us in the old-fashioned custom of "house-warming."

When the name "Iranistan" was announced, a wag-

gish New York editor syllabled it, I-ran-i-stan, and gave
as the interpretation, that "I ran a long time before I
could stan'!" Literally, however, the name signifies,
"Eastern Country Place," or, more poetically, "Oriental
Villa."

The plot of ground upon which Iranistan was erected,
was at the date of my purchase, in March 1846, a bare
field. But I transplanted many hundreds of fruit and forest trees, some of the latter of very large growth when
they were moved, and thus in a few years my premises
were adorned with what, in the ordinary process of
growth, would have required a whole generation. I have
never waited for my trees to grow, if money would
transplant them of nearly full growth at the start.

The years 1848 and 1849 were mainly spent with my
family, though I went every week to New York to look
after the interests of the American Museum. While I was
in Europe, in 1845, my agent, Mr. Fordyce Hitchcock,
had bought out for me the Baltimore Museum, a fully-
supplied establishment, in full operation, and I placed it
under the charge of my uncle, Alanson Taylor. He died
in 1846, and I then sold the Baltimore Museum to the
"Orphean Family," by whom it was subsequently transferred to Mr. John E. Owens, the celebrated comedian.
After my return from Europe, I opened, in 1849, a Museum in Dr. Swain's fine building, at the corner of
Chestnut and Seventh streets, in Philadelphia.

This was in all respects a first-class establishment. It
was elegantly fitted up, and contained, among other
things, a dozen fine large paintings, such as "The Deluge," "Cain and his Family," and other similar subjects
which I had ordered copied, when I was in Paris, from
paintings in the gallery of the Louvre. There was also a
complete and valuable collection of curiosities and I sent
from New York, from time to time, my transient novelties in the way of giants, dwarfs, fat boys, animals and
other attractions. There was a lecture room and stage for
dramatic entertainments; but I was catering for a Quaker

population, and was careful to introduce or permit nothing which could possibly be objectionable. While the Museum contained such wax-works as "The Temperate Family," "The Intemperate Family," and Mrs. Pelby's representation of "The Last Supper," the theatre presented "The Drunkard" and other moral dramas. The most respectable people in the city patronized the museum and attended the theatre. "The Drunkard" was exceedingly well played and it made a great impression. There was a temperance pledge in the box-office, which was signed by thousands during the run of the piece. Almost every hour during the day and evening, women could be seen bringing their husbands to the Museum to sign the pledge.

I stayed in Philadelphia long enough to identify myself with this Museum and to successfully start the enterprise and then left it in the hands of different managers who profitably conducted it till 1851, when, finding that it occupied too much of my time and attention, I sold it to Mr. Clapp Spooner for $40,000. At the end of that year, the building and contents were destroyed by fire. The loss was a serious one to Philadelphia, and the people were very desirous that Mr. Spooner should rebuild the establishment; but a highly profitable business connection with the Adams Express Company prevented him from doing so.

While my Philadelphia Museum was in full operation, Peale's Museum ran me a strong opposition at the Masonic Hall. That enterprise proved disastrous, and I purchased the collection at sheriff's sale, for five or six thousand dollars, on joint account of my friend Moses Kimball and myself. The curiosities were equally divided, one-half going to his Boston Museum and the other half to my American Museum in New York.

In 1848 I was elected President of the Fairfield County Agricultural Society in Connecticut. Although not practically a farmer, I had purchased about one hundred acres of land in the vicinity of my residence, and felt and still feel a deep interest in the cause of agriculture. I had begun by importing some blood stock for Iranistan, and, as I was at one time attacked by the "hen fever," I erected several splendid poultry-houses on my grounds. These were built for me by a carpenter who wrote an application for a situation, sending me a frightfully misspelled letter, in which he said that he was "youste" to hard work. I thought if his work was as strong as his spelling, he was the man I wanted, and I employed him. When the time came to prepare for our agricultural fair in the fall, he made a series of gorgeous cages in which to exhibit my shanghaes, bantams, and other fancy fowls. I went out to see them before they were sent away, and was horrified to find that he had marked the cages in his own peculiar style, describing my "Jersey Blues," for instance, in startling capitals as "Gersy Blews." I called for a jack-plane to remove every mark on the cages and told the astonished carpenter that he might do anything in the world for me, except to spell.

In 1849 it was determined by the Society that I should deliver the annual address. I begged to be excused on the ground of incompetency, but my excuses were of no avail, and as I could not instruct my auditors in farming, I gave them the benefit of several mistakes which I had committed. Among other things, I told them that in the fall of 1848 my head gardener reported that I had fifty bushels of potatoes to spare. I thereupon directed him to barrel them up and ship them to New York for sale. He did so, and received two dollars per barrel, or about sixty-seven cents per bushel. But, unfortunately, after the potatoes had been shipped, I found that my gardener had selected all the largest for market, and left my family nothing but "small potatoes" to live on during the winter. But the worst is still to come. My potatoes were all gone before March, and I was obliged to buy, during the spring, over fifty bushels of potatoes, at $1.25 per bushel! I also related my first experiment in the arboricultural line, when I cut from two thrifty rows of young cherry-trees any quantity of what I supposed to be "suckers" or "sprouts," and was thereafter informed by my gardener that I had cut off all his grafts!

A friend of mine, Mr. James D. Johnson, lived in a fine house a quarter of a mile west of Iranistan, and as I owned several acres of land at the corner of two streets directly adjoining his homestead, I surrounded the ground with high pickets, and introducing a number of Rocky Mountain elk, reindeer, and American deer, I converted it into a deer park. Strangers passing by would naturally suppose that it belonged to Johnson's estate, and to render the illusion more complete, his son-in-law, Mr. S. H. Wales, of the *Scientific American,* placed a sign in the park, fronting on the street, and reading:

"All persons are forbid trespassing on these grounds, or disturbing the deer.   J. D. JOHNSON."

I "acknowledged the corn," and was much pleased with the joke. Johnson was delighted, and bragged considerably of having got ahead of Barnum, and the sign remained undisturbed for several days. It happened at length that a party of friends came to visit him from New York, arriving in the evening. Johnson told them he had got a capital joke on Barnum; he would not explain, but said they should see it for themselves the next morning. Bright and early he led them into the street, and after conducting them a proper distance, wheeled them around in front of the sign. To his dismay he discovered that I had added directly under his name the words, *"Game-keeper to P. T. Barnum."* His friends, as soon as they understood the joke, enjoyed it mightily, but it was said that neighbor Johnson laughed out of "the wrong side of his mouth."

Thereafter, Mr. Johnson was known among his friends and acquaintances as "Barnum's game-keeper." Sometime afterwards when I was President of the Pequonnock Bank, it was my custom every year to give a grand dinner at Iranistan to the directors, and in making preparations I used to send to certain friends in the West for prairie chickens and other game. On one occasion a large box, marked "P. T. Barnum, Bridgeport; Game," was lying in the express office, when Johnson seeing it, and espying the word "game," said:

"Look here! I am 'Barnum's game-keeper,' and I'll take charge of this box."

And "take charge" of it he did, carrying it home and notifying me that it was in his possession, and that as he was my game-keeper he would "keep" this, unless I sent him an order for a new hat. He knew very well that I would give fifty dollars rather than be deprived of the box, and as he also threatened to give a game dinner at his own house, I speedily sent the order for the hat, acknowledged the good joke, and my own guests enjoyed the double "game."

During the year 1848, Mr. Frank Leslie, since so widely known as the publisher of several illustrated journals, came to me with letters of introduction from London, and I employed him to get up for me an illustrated catalogue of my Museum. This he did in a splendid manner, and hundreds of thousands of copies were sold and distributed far and near, thus adding greatly to the renown of the establishment.

I count these two years—1848 and 1849—among the happiest of my life. I had enough to do in the management of my business, and yet I seemed to have plenty of leisure hours to pass with my family and friends in my beautiful home of Iranistan.

CHAPTER XVII.

The Jenny Lind
Enterprise.

Many of my most fortunate enterprises have fairly startled me by the magnitude of their success. When my sanguine hopes predicted a steady flow of fortune, I have been inundated; when I calculated upon making a curious public pay me liberally for a meritorious article, I have often found the same public eager to deluge me with compensation. Yet, I never believed in mere luck and I always pitied the simpleton who relies on luck for his success. Luck is in no sense the foundation of my fortune; from the beginning of my career I planned and worked for my success. To be sure, my schemes often amazed me with the affluence of their results, and, arriving at the very best, I sometimes "builded better than" I "knew."

For a long time I had been incubating a plan for an extraordinary exhibition which I was sure would be a success and would excite universal attention and commendation in America and abroad. This was nothing less than a "Congress of Nations"—an assemblage of representatives of all the nations that could be reached by land or sea. I meant to secure a man and woman, as perfect as could be procured, from every accessible people, civilized and barbarous, on the face of the globe. I had actually contracted with an agent to go to Europe to make arrangements to secure "specimens" for such a show. Even now, I can conceive of no exhibition which would be more interesting and which would appeal more generally to all classes of patrons. As it was, and while positively preparing for such a congress, it occurred to me that another great enterprise could be undertaken at less risk, with far less real trouble, and with more remunerative results.

And now I come to speak of an undertaking which my worst enemy will admit was bold in its conception, complete in its development, and astounding in its success. It was an enterprise never before or since equalled in managerial annals. As I recall it now, I almost tremble at the seeming temerity of the attempt. That I am proud of it I freely confess. It placed me before the world in a new light; it gained me many warm friends in new circles; it was in itself a fortune to me—I risked much but I made more.

It was in October 1849, that I conceived the idea of bringing Jenny Lind to this country. I had never heard her sing, inasmuch as she arrived in London a few weeks after I left that city with General Tom Thumb. Her reputation, however, was sufficient for me. I usually jump at conclusions, and almost invariably find that my first impressions are correct. It struck me, when I first thought of this speculation, that if properly managed it must prove immensely profitable, provided I could engage the "Swedish Nightingale" on any terms within the range of reason. As it was a great undertaking, I considered the matter seriously for several days, and all my "cipherings" and calculations gave but one result—immense success.

Reflecting that very much would depend upon the manner in which she should be brought before the public, I saw that my task would be an exceedingly arduous one. It was possible, I knew, that circumstances might occur which would make the enterprise disastrous. "The public" is a very strange animal, and although a good knowledge of human nature will generally lead a caterer of amusements to hit the people, they are fickle, and ofttimes perverse. A slight misstep in the management of a public entertainment, frequently wrecks the most promising enterprise. But I had marked the "divine Jenny" as a sure card, and to secure the prize I began to cast about for a competent agent.

I found in Mr. John Hall Wilton, an Englishman who had visited this country with the Sax-Horn Players, the best man whom I knew for that purpose. A few minutes sufficed to make the arrangement with him, by which I was to pay but little more than his expenses if he failed in his mission, but by which also he was to be paid a large sum if he succeeded in bringing Jenny Lind to our shores, on any terms within a liberal schedule which I set forth to him in writing.

On the 6th of November, 1849, I furnished Wilton with the necessary documents, including a letter of general instructions which he was at liberty to exhibit to Jenny Lind and to any other musical notables whom he thought proper, and a private letter, containing hints and suggestions not embodied in the former. I also gave him letters of introduction to my bankers, Messrs. Baring Brothers & Co., of London, as well as to many friends in England and France.

The sum of all my instructions, public and private, to Wilton amounted to this: He was to engage her on shares, if possible. I, however, authorized him to engage her at any rate, not exceeding one thousand dollars a night, for any number of nights up to one hundred and fifty, with all her expenses, including servants, carriages, secretary, etc., besides also engaging such musical assistants, not exceeding three in number, as she should select, let the terms be what they might. If necessary, I should place the entire amount of money named in the engagement in the hands of London bankers before she sailed. Wilton's compensation was arranged on a kind of sliding scale, to be governed by the terms which he made for me—so that the farther he kept below my utmost limits, the better he should be paid for making the engagements. He proceeded to London, and opened a correspondence with Miss Lind, who was then on the Continent. He learned from the tenor of her letters, that if she could be induced to visit America at all, she must be accompanied by Mr. Julius Benedict, the accomplished composer, pianist, and musical director, and also she was impressed with the belief that Signor Belletti, the fine baritone, would be of essential service. Wilton therefore at once called upon Mr. Benedict and also Signor Belletti, who were both then in London, and in numerous interviews was enabled to learn the terms on which they would consent to engage to visit this country with Miss Lind. Having obtained the information desired, he proceeded to Lubeck, in Germany, to seek an interview with Miss Lind herself. Upon arriving at her hotel, he sent his card, requesting her to specify an hour for an interview. She named the following morning, and he was punctual to the appointment.

In the course of the first conversation, she frankly told him that during the time occupied by their correspondence, she had written to friends in London, including my friend Mr. Joshua Bates, of the house of Baring Brothers, and had informed herself respecting my character, capacity, and responsibility, which she assured him were quite satisfactory. She informed him, however, that at that time there were four persons anxious to negotiate with her for an American tour. One of these gentlemen was a well-known opera manager in London; another, a theatrical manager in Manchester; a third, a musical composer and conductor of the orchestra of Her Majesty's Opera in London; and the fourth, Chevalier Wyckoff, a person who had conducted a successful speculation some years previously by visiting America in charge of the celebrated danseuse, Fanny Ellsler. Several of these parties had called upon her personally, and Wyckoff upon hearing my name, attempted to deter her from making any engagement with me, by assuring her that I was a mere showman, and that, for the sake of making money by the speculation, I would not scruple to put her into a box and exhibit her through the country at twenty-five cents a head.

This, she confessed, somewhat alarmed her, and she wrote to Mr. Bates on the subject. He entirely disabused her mind, by assuring her that he knew me personally, and that in treating with me she was not dealing with an "adventurer" who might make her remuneration depend entirely upon the success of the enterprise, but I was able to carry out all my engagements, let them prove never so unprofitable, and she could place the fullest reliance upon my honor and integrity.

"Now," said she to Mr. Wilton, "I am perfectly satisfied on that point, for I know the world pretty well, and am aware how far jealousy and envy will sometimes carry persons; and as those who are trying to treat with me are all anxious that I should participate in the profits or losses of the enterprise, I much prefer treating with you, since your principal is willing to assume all the responsibility, and take the entire management and chances of the result upon himself."

Several interviews ensued, during which she learned from Wilton that he had settled with Messrs. Benedict and Belletti, in regard to the amount of their salaries, provided the engagement was concluded, and in the course of a week, Mr. Wilton and Miss Lind had arranged the terms and conditions on which she was ready to conclude the negotiations. As these terms were within the limits fixed in my private letter of instructions, the following agreement was duly drawn in triplicate, and signed by herself and Wilton, at Lubeck, January 9, 1850; and the signatures of Messrs. Benedict and Belletti were affixed in London a few days afterwards:

MEMORANDUM of an agreement entered into this ninth day of January, in the year of our Lord one thousand eight hundred and fifty, between John Hall Wilton, as agent for PHINEAS T. BARNUM, of New York, in the United States of North America, of the one part, and

Mademoiselle JENNY LIND, Vocalist, of Stockholm in Sweden, of the other part, wherein the said Jenny Lind doth agree:

1st. To sing for the said Phineas T. Barnum in one hundred and fifty concerts, including oratorios, within (if possible) one year, or eighteen months from the date of her arrival in the City of New York—the said concerts to be given in the United States of North America and Havana. She, the said Jenny Lind, having full control as to the number of nights or concerts in each week, and the number of pieces in which she will sing in each concert, to be regulated conditionally with her health and safety of voice, but the former never less than one or two, nor the latter less than four; but in no case to appear in operas.

2d. In consideration of said services, the said John Hall Wilton, as agent for the said Phineas T. Barnum, of New York, agrees to furnish the said Jenny Lind with a servant as waiting-maid, and a male servant to and for the sole service of her and her party; to pay the travelling and hotel expenses of a friend to accompany her as a companion; to pay also a secretary to superintend her finances; to pay all her and her party's travelling expenses from Europe, and during the tour in the United States of North America and Havana; to pay all hotel expenses for board and lodging during the same period; to place at her disposal in each city a carriage and horses with their necessary attendants, and to give her in addition, the sum of two hundred pounds sterling, or one thousand dollars, for each concert or oratorio in which the said Jenny Lind shall sing.

3d. And the said John Hall Wilton, as agent for the said Phineas T. Barnum, doth further agree to give the said Jenny Lind the most satisfactory security and assurance for the full amount of her engagement, which shall be placed in the hands of Messrs. Baring Brothers, of London, previous to the departure and subject to the order of the said Jenny Lind, with its interest due on its current reduction, by her services in the concerts or oratorios.

4th. And the said John Hall Wilton, on the part of the said Phineas T. Barnum, further agrees, that should the said Phineas T. Barnum, after seventy-five concerts, have realized so much as shall, after paying all current expenses, have returned to him all the sums disbursed, either as deposits at interest, for securities of salaries, preliminary outlay, or moneys in any way expended consequent on this engagement, and in addition, have gained a clear profit of at least fifteen thousand pounds sterling, then the said Phineas T. Barnum will give the said Jenny Lind, in addition to the former sum of one thousand dollars current money of the United States of North America, nightly, one fifth part of the profits arising from the remaining seventy-five concerts or oratorios, after deducting every expense current and appertaining thereto; or the said Jenny Lind agrees to try with the said Phineas T. Barnum fifty concerts or oratorios on the aforesaid and first-named terms, and if then found to fall short of the expectations of the said Phineas T. Barnum, then the said Jenny Lind agrees to reorganize this agreement, on terms quoted in his first proposal, as set forth in the annexed copy of his letter; but should such be found unnecessary, then the engagement continues up to seventy-five concerts or oratorios, at the end of which, should the aforesaid profit of fifteen thousand pounds sterling have not been realized, then the engagement shall continue as at first—the sums herein, after expenses for Julius Benedict and Giovanni Belletti, to remain unaltered except for advancement.

5th. And the said John Hall Wilton, agent for the said Phineas T. Barnum, at the request of the said Jenny Lind, agrees to pay to Julius Benedict, of London, to accompany the said Jenny Lind as musical director, pianist, and superintendent of the musical department, also to assist the said Jenny Lind in one hundred and fifty concerts or oratorios, to be given in the United States of

North America and Havana, the sum of five thousand pounds (£5,000) sterling, to be satisfactorily secured to him with Messrs. Baring Brothers, of London, previous to his departure from Europe; and the said John Hall Wilton agrees further, for the said Phineas T. Barnum, to pay all his travelling expenses from Europe, together with his hotel and travelling expenses during the time occupied in giving the aforesaid one hundred and fifty concerts or oratorios—he, the said Julius Benedict, to superintend the organization of oratorios, if required.

6th. And the said John Hall Wilton, at the request, selection, and for the aid of the said Jenny Lind, agrees to pay to Giovanni Belletti, baritone vocalist, to accompany the said Jenny Lind during her tour and in one hundred and fifty concerts or oratorios in the United States of North America and Havana, and in conjunction with the aforesaid Julius Benedict, the sum of two thousand five hundred pounds (£2,500) sterling, to be satisfactorily secured to him previous to his departure from Europe, in addition to all his hotel and travelling expenses.

7th. And it is further agreed that the said Jenny Lind shall be at full liberty to sing at any time she may think fit for charitable institutions or purposes independent of the engagement with the said Phineas T. Barnum, she, the said Jenny Lind, consulting with the said Phineas T. Barnum with a view to mutually agreeing as to the time and its propriety, it being understood that in no case shall the first or second concert in any city selected for the tour be for such purpose, or where-ever it shall appear against the interests of the said Phineas T. Barnum.

8th. It is further agreed that should the said Jenny Lind by any act of God be incapacitated to fulfil the entire engagement before mentioned, that an equal proportion of the terms agreed upon shall be given to the said Jenny Lind, Julius Benedict, and Giovanni Belletti, for services rendered to that time.

9th. It is further agreed and understood, that the said Phineas T. Barnum shall pay every expense appertaining to the concerts or oratorios before mentioned, excepting those for charitable purposes, and that all accounts shall be settled and rendered by all parties weekly.

10th. And the said Jenny Lind further agrees that she will not engage to sing for any other person during the progress of this said engagement with the said Phineas T. Barnum, of New York, for one hundred and fifty concerts or oratorios, excepting for charitable purposes as before mentioned; and all travelling to be first and best class.

In witness hereof to the within written memorandum of agreement we set hereunto our hand and seal.

[L. S.] JOHN HALL WILTON, Agent for
         PHINEAS T. BARNUM, of New York, U. S.
[L. S.] JENNY LIND.
[L. S.] JULIUS BENEDICT.
[L. S.] GIOVANNI BELLETTI.

In the presence of C. ACHILLING, Consul of His Majesty the King of Sweden and Norway.

Extract from a Letter addressed to John Hall Wilton by PHINEAS T. BARNUM, *and referred to in paragraph No. 4 of the annexed agreement.*

NEW YORK, *November 6, 1849.*

MR. J. HALL WILTON:

SIR:—In reply to your proposal to attempt a negotiation with Mlle. Jenny Lind to visit the United States professionally, I propose to enter into an arrangement with her to the following effect: I will engage to pay all her expenses from Europe, provide for and pay for one principal tenor and one pianist, their salaries not exceeding together one hundred and fifty dollars per night; to support for her a carriage, two servants, and a friend to accompany her and superintend her finances. I will furthermore pay all and every expense appertaining to her appearance before the public, and give her half of the gross receipts arising from concerts or operas. I will engage to travel with her personally and attend to the arrangements, provided she will undertake to give not less than eighty nor more than one hundred and fifty concerts, or nights' performances.

PHINEAS T. BARNUM.

I certify the above to be a true extract from the letter.
J. H. WILTON.

I was at my Museum in Philadelphia when Wilton arrived in New York, February 19, 1850. He immediately telegraphed to me, in the cipher we had agreed upon, that he had signed an engagement with Jenny Lind, by which she was to commence her concerts in America in the following September. I was somewhat startled by this sudden announcement; and feeling that the time to elapse before her arrival was so long that it would be policy to keep the engagement private for a few months, I immediately telegraphed him not to mention it to any person, and that I would meet him the next day in New York.

When we reflect how thoroughly Jenny Lind, her musical powers, her character, and wonderful successes, were subsequently known by all classes in this country as well as throughout the civilized world, it is difficult to realize that, at the time this engagement was made, she was comparatively unknown on this side the water. We can hardly credit the fact, that millions of persons in America had never heard of her, that other millions had merely read her name, but had no distinct idea of who or what she was. Only a small portion of the public were really aware of her great musical triumphs in the Old World, and this portion was confined almost entirely to musical people, travellers who had visited the Old World, and the conductors of the press.

The next morning I started for New York. On arriving at Princeton we met the New York cars, and purchasing the morning papers, I was surprised to find in them a full account of my engagement with Jenny Lind. However, this premature announcement could not be recalled, and I put the best face on the matter. Anxious to learn how this communication would strike the public mind, I informed the conductor, whom I well knew, that I had made an engagement with Jenny Lind, and that she would surely visit this country in the following August.

"Jenny Lind! Is she a dancer?" asked the conductor.

I informed him who and what she was, but his question had chilled me as if his words were ice. Really, thought I, if this is all that a man in the capacity of a railroad conductor between Philadelphia and New York knows of the greatest songstress in the world, I am not sure that six months will be too long a time for me to occupy in enlightening the public in regard to her merits.

I had an interview with Wilton, and learned from him that, in accordance with the agreement, it would be requisite for me to place the entire amount stipulated, $187,500, in the hands of the London bankers. I at once resolved to ratify the agreement, and immediately sent the necessary documents to Miss Lind and Messrs. Benedict and Belletti.

I then began to prepare the public mind, through the newspapers, for the reception of the great songstress. How effectually this was done, is still within the remembrance of the American public. As a sample of the manner in which I accomplished my purpose, I present the following extract from my first letter, which appeared in the New York papers of February 22, 1850:

"Perhaps I may not make any money by this enterprise; but I assure you that if I knew I should not make a farthing profit, I would ratify the engagement, so anxious am I that the United States should be visited by a lady whose vocal powers have never been approached by any other human being, and whose character is charity, simplicity, and goodness personified.

"Miss Lind has great anxiety to visit America. She

speaks of this country and its institutions in the highest terms of praise. In her engagement with me (which includes Havana), she expressly reserves the right to give charitable concerts whenever she thinks proper.

"Since her *début* in England, she has given to the poor from her own private purse more than the whole amount which I have engaged to pay her, and the proceeds of concerts for charitable purposes in Great Britain, where she has sung gratuitously, have realized more than ten times that amount."

The people soon began to talk about Jenny Lind, and I was particularly anxious to obtain a good portrait of her. Fortunately, a fine opportunity occurred. One day, while I was sitting in the office of the Museum, a foreigner approached me with a small package under his arm. He informed me in broken English that he was a Swede, and said he was an artist, who had just arrived from Stockholm, where Jenny Lind had kindly given him a number of sittings, and he now had with him the portrait of her which he had painted upon copper. He unwrapped the package, and showed me a beautiful picture of the Swedish Nightingale, inclosed in an elegant gilt frame, about fourteen by twenty inches. It was just the thing I wanted; the price was fifty dollars, and I purchased it at once. Upon showing it to an artist friend the same day, he quietly assured me that it was a cheap lithograph pasted on a tin back, neatly varnished, and made to appear like a fine oil painting. The intrinsic value of the picture did not exceed thirty-seven and one half cents!

After getting together all my available funds for the purpose of transmitting them to London in the shape of United States bonds, I found a considerable sum still lacking to make up the amount. I had some second mortgages which were perfectly good, but I could not negotiate them in Wall Street. Nothing would answer there short of first mortgages on New York or Brooklyn city property.

I went to the president of the bank where I had done

all my business for eight years. I offered him, as security for a loan, my second mortgages, and as an additional inducement, I proposed to make over to him my contract with Jenny Lind, with a written guaranty that he should appoint a receiver, who, at my expense, should take charge of all the receipts over and above three thousand dollars per night, and appropriate them towards the payment of my loan. He laughed in my face, and said: "Mr. Barnum, it is generally believed in Wall Street, that your engagement with Jenny Lind will ruin you. I do not think you will ever receive so much as three thousand dollars at a single concert." I was indignant at his want of appreciation, and answered him that I would not at that moment take $150,000 for my contract; nor would I. I found, upon further inquiry, that it was useless in Wall Street to offer the "Nightingale" in exchange for Gold-finches. I finally was introduced to Mr. John L. Aspinwall, of the firm of Messrs. Howland & Aspinwall, and he gave me a letter of credit from his firm on Baring Brothers, for a large sum on collateral securities, which a spirit of genuine respect for my enterprise induced him to accept.

After disposing of several pieces of property for cash, I footed up the various amounts, and still discovered myself five thousand dollars short. I felt that it was indeed "the last feather that breaks the camel's back." Happening casually to state my desperate case to the Rev. Abel C. Thomas, of Philadelphia, for many years a friend of mine, he promptly placed the requisite amount at my disposal. I gladly accepted his proffered friendship, and felt that he had removed a mountain-weight from my shoulders.

CHAPTER XVIII.

The Nightingale in New York.

After the engagement with Miss Lind was consummated, she declined several liberal offers to sing in London, but, at my solicitation, gave two concerts in Liverpool, on the eve of her departure for America. My object in making this request was, to add the *éclat* of that side to the excitement on this side of the Atlantic, which was already nearly up to fever heat.

The first of the two Liverpool concerts was given the night previous to the departure of the Saturday steamer for America. My agent had procured the services of a musical critic from London, who finished his account of this concert at half past one o'clock the following morning, and at two o'clock my agent was overseeing its insertion in a Liverpool morning paper, numbers of which he forwarded to me by the steamer of the same day. The republication of the criticism in the American papers, including an account of the enthusiasm which attended and followed this concert,—her trans-Atlantic,—had the desired effect.

On Wednesday morning, August 21, 1850, Jenny Lind and Messrs. Benedict and Belletti, set sail from Liverpool in the steamship Atlantic, in which I had long before engaged the necessary accommodations, and on board of which I had shipped a piano for their use. They were accompanied by my agent, Mr. Wilton, and also by Miss Ahmansen and Mr. Max Hjortzberg, cousins of

Miss Lind, the latter being her Secretary; also by her two servants, and the valet of Messrs. Benedict and Belletti.

It was expected that the steamer would arrive on Sunday, September 1, but, determined to meet the song-stress on her arrival whenever it might be, I went to Staten Island on Saturday, and slept at the hospitable residence of my friend, Dr. A. Sidney Doane, who was at that time the Health Officer of the Port of New York. A few minutes before twelve o'clock, on Sunday morning, the Atlantic hove in sight, and immediately afterwards, through the kindness of my friend Doane, I was on board the ship, and had taken Jenny Lind by the hand.

After a few moments' conversation, she asked me when and where I had heard her sing.

"I never had the pleasure of seeing you before in my life," I replied.

"How is it possible that you dared risk so much money on a person whom you never heard sing?" she asked in surprise.

"I risked it on your reputation, which in musical matters I would much rather trust than my own judgment," I replied.

I may as well state, that although I relied prominently upon Jenny Lind's reputation as a great musical *artiste*, I also took largely into my estimate of her success with all classes of the American public, her character for extraordinary benevolence and generosity. Without this peculiarity in her disposition, I never would have dared make the engagement which I did, as I felt sure that there were multitudes of individuals in America who would be prompted to attend her concerts by this feeling alone.

Thousands of persons covered the shipping and piers, and other thousands had congregated on the wharf at Canal Street, to see her. The wildest enthusiasm prevailed as the steamer approached the dock. So great was the rush on a sloop near the steamer's berth, that one man, in his zeal to obtain a good view, accidentally tumbled overboard, amid the shouts of those near him. Miss

Lind witnessed this incident, and was much alarmed. He was, however, soon rescued, after taking to himself a cold duck instead of securing a view of the Nightingale. A bower of green trees, decorated with beautiful flags, was discovered on the wharf, together with two triumphal arches, on one of which was inscribed, "Welcome, Jenny Lind!" The second was surmounted by the American eagle, and bore the inscription, "Welcome to America!" These decorations were not produced by magic, and I do not know that I can reasonably find fault with those who suspected I had a hand in their erection. My private carriage was in waiting, and Jenny Lind was escorted to it by Captain West. The rest of the musical party entered the carriage, and mounting the box at the driver's side, I directed him to the Irving House. I took that seat as a legitimate advertisement, and my presence on the outside of the carriage aided those who filled the windows and side-walks along the whole route, in coming to the conclusion that Jenny Lind had arrived.

A reference to the journals of that day will show, that never before had there been such enthusiasm in the City of New York, or indeed in America. Within ten minutes after our arrival at the Irving House, not less than twenty thousand persons had congregated around the entrance in Broadway, nor was the number diminished before nine o'clock in the evening. At her request, I dined with her that afternoon, and when, according to European custom, she prepared to pledge me in a glass of wine, she was somewhat surprised at my saying, "Miss Lind, I do not think you can ask any other favor on earth which I would not gladly grant; but I am a teetotaler, and must beg to be permitted to drink your health and happiness in a glass of cold water."

At twelve o'clock that night, she was serenaded by the New York Musical Fund Society, numbering, on that occasion, two hundred musicians. They were escorted to the Irving House by about three hundred firemen, in their red shirts, bearing torches. There was a far greater throng in the streets than there was even during the day. The calls for Jenny Lind were so vehement that I led her through a window to the balcony. The loud cheers from the crowds lasted for several minutes, before the serenade was permitted to proceed again.

I have given the merest sketch of but a portion of the incidents of Jenny Lind's first day in America. For weeks afterwards the excitement was unabated. Her rooms were thronged by visitors, including the magnates of the land in both Church and State. The carriages of the wealthiest citizens could be seen in front of her hotel at nearly all hours of the day, and it was with some difficulty that I prevented the "fashionables" from monopolizing her altogether, and thus, as I believed, sadly marring my interests by cutting her off from the warm sympathies she had awakened among the masses. Presents of all sorts were showered upon her. Milliners, mantua-makers, and shopkeepers vied with each other in calling her attention to their wares, of which they sent her many valuable specimens, delighted if, in return, they could receive her autograph acknowledgment. Songs, quadrilles and polkas were dedicated to her, and poets sung in her praise. We had Jenny Lind gloves, Jenny Lind bonnets, Jenny Lind riding hats, Jenny Lind shawls, mantillas, robes, chairs, sofas, pianos—in fact, every thing was Jenny Lind. Her movements were constantly watched, and the moment her carriage appeared at the door, it was surrounded by multitudes, eager to catch a glimpse of the Swedish Nightingale.

In looking over my "scrap-books" of extracts from the New York papers of that day, in which all accessible details concerning her were duly chronicled, it seems almost incredible that such a degree of enthusiasm should have existed. An abstract of the "sayings and doings" in regard to the Jenny Lind mania for the first ten days after her arrival, appeared in the London *Times* on Sept. 23, 1850, and although it was an ironical "showing up" of the American enthusiasm, filling several columns, it was nevertheless a faithful condensation of facts which at this late day seem even to myself more like a dream than reality.

Before her arrival I had offered $200 for a prize ode, "Greeting to America," to be sung by Jenny Lind at her first concert. Several hundred "poems" were sent in from all parts of the United States and the Canadas. The duties of the Prize Committee, in reading these effusions and making choice of the one most worthy the prize, were truly arduous. The "offerings," with perhaps a dozen exceptions, were the merest doggerel trash. The prize was awarded to Bayard Taylor for the following ode:

GREETING TO AMERICA.
WORDS BY BAYARD TAYLOR—MUSIC BY JULIUS BENEDICT.

I greet with a full heart the Land of the West,
  Whose Banner of Stars o'er a world is unrolled;
Whose empire o'ershadows Atlantic's wide breast,
  And opens to sunset its gateway of gold!
The land of the mountain, the land of the lake,
  And rivers that roll in magnificent tide—
Where the souls of the mighty from slumber awake,
  And hallow the soil for whose freedom they died!

Thou Cradle of Empire! though wide be the foam
  That severs the land of my fathers and thee,
I hear, from thy bosom, the welcome of home,
  For Song has a home in the hearts of the Free!
And long as thy waters shall gleam in the sun,
  And long as thy heroes remember their scars,
Be the hands of thy children united as one,
  And Peace shed her light on thy Banner of Stars!

This award, although it gave general satisfaction, yet was met with disfavor by several disappointed poets, who, notwithstanding the decision of the committee, persisted in believing and declaring their own productions to be the best. This state of feeling was doubtless, in part, the cause which led to the publication, about this time, of a witty pamphlet entitled "Barnum's Parnassus; being Confidential Disclosures of the Prize Committee on the Jenny Lind song."

It gave some capital hits in which the committee, the enthusiastic public, the Nightingale, and myself, were roundly ridiculed. The following is a fair specimen from the work in question:

BARNUMOPSIS.
A RECITATIVE.

When to the common rest that crowns his days,
　　Dusty and worn the tired pedestrian goes,
What light is that whose wide o'erlooking blaze
　　A sudden glory on his pathway throws?

'Tis not the setting sun, whose drooping lid
　　Closed on the weary world at half-past six;
'Tis not the rising moon, whose rays are hid
　　Behind the city's sombre piles of bricks.

It is the Drummond Light, that from the top
　　Of Barnum's massive pile, sky-mingling there,
Darts its quick gleam o'er every shadowed shop,
　　And gilds Broadway with unaccustomed glare.

There o'er the sordid gloom, whose deep'ning tracks
　　Furrow the city's brow, the front of ages,
Thy loftier light descends on cabs and hacks,
　　And on two dozen different lines of stages!

O twilight Sun, with thy far darting ray,
　　Thou art a type of him whose tireless hands
Hung thee on high to guide the stranger's way,
　　Where, in its pride, his vast Museum stands.

Him, who in search of wonders new and strange,
　　Grasps the wide skirts of Nature's mystic robe
Explores the circles of eternal change,
　　And the dark chambers of the central globe.

He, from the reedy shores of fabled Nile,
　　Has brought, thick-ribbed and ancient as old iron,
That venerable beast the crocodile,
　　And many a skin of many a famous lion.

Go lose thyself in those continuous halls,
    Where strays the fond papa with son and daughter
And all that charms or startles or appals,
    Thou shalt behold, and for a single quarter!

Far from the Barcan deserts now withdrawn,
    There huge constrictors coil their scaly backs:
There, cased in glass, malignant and unshorn,
    Old murderers glare in sullenness and wax.

There many a varied form the sight beguiles,
    In rusty broadcloth decked and shocking hat,
And there the unwieldy Lambert sits and smiles,
    In the majestic plentitude of fat.

Or for thy gayer hours, the orang-outang
    Or ape salutes thee with his strange grimace,
And in their shapes, stuffed as on earth they sprang,
    Thine individual being thou canst trace!

And joys the youth in life's green spring, who goes
    With the sweet babe and the gray-headed nurse,
To see those Cosmoramic orbs disclose
    The varied beauties of the universe.

And last, not least, the marvellous Ethiope,
    Changing his skin by preternatural skill,
Whom every setting sun's diurnal slope
    Leaves whiter than the last, and whitening still.

All that of monstrous, scaly, strange and queer,
    Has come from out the womb of earliest time,
Thou hast, O Barnum, in thy keeping here,
    Nor is this all—for triumphs more sublime

Await thee yet! I, Jenny Lind, who reigned
    Sublimely throned, the imperial queen of song,
Wooed by thy golden harmonies, have deigned
    Captive to join the heterogeneous throng.

Sustained by an unfaltering trust in coin,
    Dealt from thy hand, O thou illustrious man,
Gladly I heard the summons come to join
    Myself the innumerable caravan.

Besides the foregoing, this pamphlet contained eleven poems, most of which abounded in wit. I have room for but a single stanza. The poet speaks of the various curiosities in the Museum, and representing me as still searching for further novelties, makes me address the Swedish Nightingale as follows:

"So Jenny, come along! you're just the card for me,
And quit these kings and queens, for the country of the free;
They'll welcome you with speeches, and serenades, and
   rockets,
And you will touch their hearts, and I will tap their pockets;
And if between us both the public isn't skinned,
Why, my name isn't Barnum, nor your name Jenny Lind!"

Various extracts from this brochure were copied in the papers daily, and my agents scattered the work as widely as possible, thus efficiently aiding and advertising my enterprise and serving to keep up the public excitement.

Among the many complimentary poems sent in, was the following, by Mrs. L. H. SIGOURNEY, which that distinguished writer enclosed in a letter to me, with the request that I should hand it to Miss Lind:

THE SWEDISH SONGSTRESS AND HER CHARITIES.
BY MRS. L. H. SIGOURNEY.

Blest must their vocation be
Who, with tones of melody,
Charm the discord and the strife
And the railroad rush of life,
And with Orphean magic move
Souls inert to life and love.
But there's one who doth inherit
Angel gift and angel spirit,
Bidding tides of gladness flow
Through the realms of want and woe;
'Mid lone age and misery's lot,
Kindling pleasures long forgot,
Seeking minds oppressed with night,

And on darkness shedding light.
She the seraph's speech doth know,
She hath done their deeds below:
So, when o'er this misty strand,
They will fold her to their breast,
More a sister than a guest.

Jenny Lind's first concert was fixed to come off at
Castle Garden, on Wednesday evening, September 11th,
and most of the tickets were sold at auction on the Saturday and Monday previous to the concert. John N. Genin,
the hatter, laid the foundation of his fortune by
purchasing the first ticket at $225. It has been exten-
sively reported that Mr. Genin and I are brothers-
in-law, but our only relations are those of business
and friendship. The proprietors of the Garden saw fit to
make the usual charge of one shilling to all persons who
entered the premises, yet three thousand people were
present at the auction. One thousand tickets were sold on
the first day for an aggregate sum of $10,141.

On the Tuesday after her arrival I informed Miss Lind
that I wished to make a slight alteration in our agreement. "What is it?" she asked in surprise.

"I am convinced," I replied, "that our enterprise will
be much more successful than either of us anticipated. I
wish, therefore, to stipulate that you shall receive not
only $1,000 for each concert, besides all the expenses, as
heretofore agreed on, but after taking $5,500 per night
for expenses and my services, the balance shall be equally
divided between us."

Jenny looked at me with astonishment. She could not
comprehend my proposition. After I had repeated it, and
she fully understood its import, she cordially grasped me
by the hand, and exclaimed, "Mr. Barnum, you are a
gentleman of honor: you are generous; it is just as Mr.
Bates told me; I will sing for you as long as you please; I
will sing for you in America—in Europe—anywhere!"

Upon drawing the new contract which was to include

this entirely voluntary and liberal advance on my part,
beyond the terms of the original agreement, Miss Lind's
lawyer, Mr. John Jay, who was present solely to put in
writing the new arrangement between Miss Lind and
myself, insisted upon intruding the suggestion that she
should have the right to terminate the engagement at the
end of the sixtieth concert, if she should choose to do so.
This proposition was so persistently and annoyingly
pressed that Miss Lind was finally induced to entertain it,
at the same time offering, if she did so, to refund to me all
moneys paid her up to that time, excepting the $1,000
per concert according to the original agreement. This
was agreed to, and it was also arranged that she might
terminate the engagement at the one-hundredth concert,
if she desired, upon paying me $25,000 for the loss of the
additional fifty nights.

After this new arrangement was completed, I said:
"Now, Miss Lind, as you are directly interested, you
must have an agent to assist in taking and counting the
tickets"; to which she replied, "Oh, no! Mr. Barnum; I
have every confidence in you and I must decline to act
upon your suggestion"; but I continued:

"I never allow myself, if it can be avoided, when I have
associates in the same interests, to be placed in a position
where I must assume the sole responsibility. I never even
permitted an actor to take a benefit at my Museum, unless he placed a ticket-taker of his own at the door."

Thus urged, Miss Lind engaged Mr. Seton to act as
her ticket-taker, and after we had satisfactorily arranged
the matter, Jay, knowing the whole affair, had the impudence to come to me with a package of blank printed
affidavits, which he demanded that I should fill out, from
day to day, with the receipts of each concert, and swear to
their correctness before a magistrate!

I told him that I would see him on the subject at Miss
Lind's hotel that afternoon, and going there a few moments before the appointed hour, I narrated the circumstances to Mr. Benedict and showed him an affidavit

which I had made that morning to the effect that I would
never directly or indirectly take any advantage whatever
of Miss Lind. This I had made oath to, for I thought if
there was any swearing of that kind to be done I would do
it "in a lump" rather than in detail. Mr. Benedict was
very much opposed to it, and arriving during the interview, Jay was made to see the matter in such a light that
he was thoroughly ashamed of his proposition, and, requesting that the affair might not be mentioned to Miss
Lind, he begged me to destroy the affidavit. I heard no
more about swearing to our receipts.

On Tuesday, September 10th, I informed Miss Lind
that, judging by present appearances, her portion of the
proceeds of the first concert would amount to $10,000.
She immediately resolved to devote every dollar of it to
charity; and, sending for Mayor Woodhull, she acted
under his and my advice in selecting the various institutions among which she wished the amount to be distributed.

My arrangements of the concert room were very
complete. The great *parterre* and gallery of Castle Garden were divided by imaginary lines into four compart-
ments, each of which was designated by a lamp of a
different color. The tickets were printed in colors corresponding with the location which the holders were to occupy, and one hundred ushers, with rosettes and bearing
wands tipped with ribbons of the several hues, enabled
every individual to find his or her seat without the
slightest difficulty. Every seat was of course numbered in
color to correspond with the check, which each person
retained after giving up an entrance ticket at the door.
Thus, tickets, checks, lamps, rosettes, wands, and even
the seat numbers were all in the appropriate colors to des-
ignate the different departments. These arrangements
were duly advertised, and every particular was also
printed upon each ticket. In order to prevent confusion,
the doors were opened at five o'clock, while the concert
did not commence until eight. The consequence was, that

although about five thousand persons were present at the first concert, their entrance was marked with as much order and quiet as was ever witnessed in the assembling of a congregation at church. These precautions were observed at all the concerts given throughout the country under my administration, and the good order which always prevailed was the subject of numberless encomiums from the public and the press.

The reception of Jenny Lind on her first appearance, in point of enthusiasm, was probably never before equalled in the world. As Mr. Benedict led her towards the foot-lights, the entire audience rose to their feet and welcomed her with three cheers, accompanied by the waving of thousands of hats and handkerchiefs. This was by far the largest audience to which Jenny Lind had ever sung. She was evidently much agitated, but the orchestra commenced, and before she had sung a dozen notes of "Casta Diva," she began to recover her self-possession, and long before the *scena* was concluded, she was as calm as if she was in her own drawing-room. Towards the last portion of the *cavatina,* the audience were so completely carried away by their feelings, that the remainder of the air was drowned in a perfect tempest of acclamation. Enthusiasm had been wrought to its highest pitch, but the musical powers of Jenny Lind exceeded all the brilliant anticipations which had been formed, and her triumph was complete. At the conclusion of the concert Jenny Lind was loudly called for, and was obliged to appear three times before the audience could be satisfied. They then called vociferously for "Barnum," and I reluctantly responded to their demand.

On this first night, Mr. Julius Benedict firmly established with the American people his European reputation, as a most accomplished conductor and musical composer; while Signor Belletti inspired an admiration which grew warmer and deeper in the minds of the American people, to the end of his career in this country.

It would seem as if the Jenny Lind mania had reached

its culminating point before she appeared, and I confess
that I feared the anticipations of the public were too high
to be realized, and hence that there would be a reaction
after the first concert; but I was happily disappointed.
The transcendent musical genius of the Swedish Nightingale was superior to all that fancy could paint, and the
furor did not attain its highest point until she had been
heard. The people were in ecstasies; the powers of editorial acumen, types and ink, were inadequate to sound her
praises. The Rubicon was passed. The successful issue of
the Jenny Lind enterprise was established. I think there
were a hundred men in New York, the day after her first
concert, who would have willingly paid me $200,000 for
my contract. I received repeated offers for an eighth, a
tenth, or a sixteenth, equivalent to that price. But mine
had been the risk, and I was determined mine should be
the triumph. So elated was I with my success, in spite of
all obstacles and false prophets, that I do not think half a
million of dollars would have tempted me to relinquish
the enterprise.

Upon settling the receipts of the first concert, they
were found to be somewhat less than I anticipated. The
sums bid at the auction sales, together with the tickets
purchased at private sale, amounted to more than $20,-
000. It proved, however, that several of the tickets bid
off at from $12 to $25 each, were not called for. In some
instances, probably the zeal of the bidders cooled down
when they came out from the scene of excitement, and
once more breathed the fresh sea-breeze which came
sweeping up from "the Narrows," while perhaps, in
other instances, bids were made by parties who never
intended to take the tickets. I can only say, once for all,
that I was never privy to a false bid, and was so particular
upon that point, that I would not permit one of my em-
ployees to bid on, or purchase a ticket at auction, though
requested to do so for especial friends.

The amount of money received for tickets to the first
concert was $17,864.05. As this made Miss Lind's por-

tion too small to realize the $10,000 which had been announced as devoted to charity, I proposed to divide equally with her the proceeds of the first two concerts, and not count them at all in our regular engagement. Accordingly, the second concert was given September 13th, and the receipts, amounting to $14,203.03, were, like those of the first concert, equally divided. Our third concert, but which, as between ourselves, we called the "first regular concert," was given Tuesday, September 17, 1850.

CHAPTER XIX.

Successful Management.

No one can imagine the amount of head-work and hand-work which I performed during the first four weeks after Jenny Lind's arrival. Anticipating much of this, I had spent some time in August at the White Mountains to recruit my energies. Of course I had not been idle during the summer. I had put innumerable means and appliances into operation for the furtherance of my object, and little did the public see of the hand that indirectly pulled at their heart-strings, preparatory to a relaxation of their purse-strings; and these means and appliances were continued and enlarged throughout the whole of that triumphal musical campaign.

The first great assembly at Castle Garden was not gathered by Jenny Lind's musical genius and powers alone. She was effectually introduced to the public before they had seen or heard her. She appeared in the presence of a jury already excited to enthusiasm in her behalf. She more than met their expectations, and all the means I had adopted to prepare the way were thus abundantly justified.

As a manager, I worked by setting others to work. Biographies of the Swedish Nightingale were largely circulated; "Foreign Correspondence" glorified her talents and triumphs by narratives of her benevolence; and "printer's ink" was invoked in every possible form, to put and keep Jenny Lind before the people. I am happy to say that the press generally echoed the voice of her praise

197

from first to last. I could fill many volumes with printed extracts which are nearly all of a similar tenor to the following unbought, unsolicited editorial article, which appeared in the *New York Herald* of Sept. 10, 1850 (the day before the first concert given by Miss Lind in the United States):

"JENNY LIND AND THE AMERICAN PEOPLE.—What ancient monarch was he, either in history or in fable, who offered half his kingdom (the price of box tickets and choice seats in those days) for the invention of an original sensation, or the discovery of a fresh pleasure? That sensation—that pleasure which royal power in the old world failed to discover—has been called into existence at a less price, by Mr. Barnum, a plain republican, and is now about to be enjoyed by the sovereigns of the new world.

"Jenny Lind, the most remarkable phenomenon in musical art which has for the last century flashed across the horizon of the old world, is now among us, and will make her *début* to-morrow night to a house of nearly ten thousand listeners, yielding in proceeds by auction, a sum of forty or fifty thousand dollars. For the last ten days our musical reporters have furnished our readers with every matter connected with her arrival in this metropolis, and the steps adopted by Mr. Barnum in preparation for her first appearance. The proceedings of yesterday, consisting of the sale of the remainder of the tickets, and the astonishing, the wonderful sensation produced at her first rehearsal on the few persons, critics in musical art, who were admitted on the occasion, will be found elsewhere in our columns.

"We concur in everything that has been said by our musical reporter, describing her extraordinary genius— her unrivalled combination of power and art. Nothing has been exaggerated, not an iota. Three years ago, more or less, we heard Jenny Lind on many occasions when she made the first great sensation in Europe, by her *début* at the London Opera House. Then she was great in power—in art—in genius; now she is greater in all. We speak from experience and conviction. Then she astonished, and pleased, and fascinated the thousands of the British aristocracy; now she will fascinate, and please, and delight, and almost make mad with musical excitement, the millions of the American democracy. To-morrow night, this new sensation—this fresh movement—this excitement excelling all former excitements—will be called into existence, when she pours out the notes of *Casta Diva*, and exhibits her astonishing powers—her wonderful peculiarities, that seem more of heaven than of earth—more of a voice from eternity, than from the lips of a human being.

"We speak soberly—seriously—calmly. The public expectation has run very high for the last week—higher than at any former period of our past musical annals. But high as it has risen, the reality—the fact—the concert—the voice and power of Jenny Lind—will far surpass all past expectation. Jenny Lind is a wonder, and a prodigy in song—and no mistake."

As usual, however, the *Herald* very soon "took it all back" and roundly abused Miss Lind and persistently attacked her manager. As usual, too, the public paid no attention to the *Herald* and doubled their patronage of the Jenny Lind concerts.

After the first month the business became thoroughly systematized, and by the help of such agents as my faithful treasurer, L. C. Stewart, and the indefatigable Le Grand Smith, my personal labors were materially relieved; but from the first concert on the 11th of September, 1850, until the ninety-third concert on the 9th of June, 1851, a space of nine months, I did not know a waking moment that was entirely free from anxiety.

I could not hope to be exempted from trouble and perplexity in managing an enterprise which depended altogether on popular favor, and which involved great consequences to myself; but I did not expect the numerous petty annoyances which beset me, especially in the early period of the concerts. Miss Lind did not dream, nor did any one else, of the unparalleled enthusiasm that would greet her; and the first immense assembly at Castle Garden somewhat prepared her, I suspect, to listen to evil advisers. It would seem that the terms of our revised contract were sufficiently liberal to her and sufficiently hazardous to myself, to justify the expectation of perfectly honorable treatment; but certain envious intermeddlers appeared to think differently. "Do you not see, Miss Lind, that Mr. Barnum is coining money out of your genius?" said they; of course she saw it, but the high-minded Swede despised and spurned the advisers who recommended her to repudiate her contract with me at all hazards, and take the enterprise into her own hands—possibly to put it into theirs. I, however, suffered much from the unreasonable interference of her lawyer, Mr. John Jay. Benedict and Belletti behaved like men, and Jenny afterwards expressed to me her regret that she had for a moment listened to the vexatious exactions of her legal counsellor.

To show the difficulties with which I had to contend thus early in my enterprise, I copy a letter which I wrote, a little more than one month after Miss Lind commenced her engagement with me, to my friend Mr. Joshua Bates, of Messrs. Baring, Brothers & Co., London:

NEW YORK, Oct. 23, 1850.

JOSHUA BATES ESQ:

DEAR SIR,—I take the liberty to write you a few lines, merely to say that we are getting along as well as could reasonably be expected. In this country you are aware that the rapid accumulation of wealth always creates much envy, and envy soon augments to malice. Such are the elements at work to a limited degree against myself, and although Miss Lind, Benedict and myself have never, as yet, had the slightest feelings between us, to my knowledge, except those of friendship, yet I cannot well see how this can long continue in face of the fact that, nearly every day, they allow persons (some moving in the first classes of society) to approach them, and spend hours in traducing me; even her attorney, Mr. John Jay, has been so blind to her interests, as to aid in poisoning her mind against me, by pouring into her ears the most silly twaddle, all of which amounts to nothing and less than nothing—such as the regret that I was a 'showman,' exhibitor of Tom Thumb, etc., etc.

Without the elements which I possess for business, as well as my knowledge of human nature, acquired in catering for the public, the result of her concerts here would not have been pecuniarily one half as much as at present—and such men as the Hon. Edward Everett, G. G. Howland, and others will tell you that there is no charlatanism or lack of dignity in my management of these concerts. I know as well as any person that the merits of Jenny Lind are the best capital to depend upon to secure public favor, and I have thus far acted on this knowledge. Everything which money and attention can procure for their comfort, they have, and I am glad to know that they are satisfied on this score. All I fear is, that these continual backbitings, if listened to by her, will, by and by, produce a feeling of distrust or regret, which will lead to unpleasant results.

The fact is, her mind ought to be as free as air, and she herself as free as a bird, and, being satisfied of my probity and ability, she should turn a deaf ear to all envious and malevolent attacks on me. I have hoped that by thus briefly stating to you the facts in the case, you might be induced for her interests as well as mine to drop a line of advice to Mr. Benedict and another to Mr. Jay on this subject. If I am asking or expecting too much, I pray you to not give it a thought, for I feel myself fully able to carry through my rights alone, although I should deplore nothing so much as to be obliged to do so in a feeling of unfriendliness. I have risked much money on the issue of this speculation—it has proved successful. I am full of perplexity and anxiety, and labor continually for success, and I cannot allow ignorance or envy to rob me of the fruits of my enterprise.

Sincerely and gratefully, yours,

P. T. BARNUM.

It is not my purpose to enter into full details of all of the Lind concerts, though I have given elsewhere a transcript from the account books of my treasurer, presenting a table of the place and exact receipts of each concert. This will gratify curiosity, and at the same time indicate our route of travel. Meanwhile, I devote a few pages to interesting incidents connected with Miss Lind's visit to America.

Jenny Lind's character for benevolence became so

generally known, that her door was beset by persons asking charity, and she was in the receipt, while in the principal cities, of numerous letters, all on the same subject. Her secretary examined and responded favorably to some of them. He undertook at first to answer them all, but finally abandoned that course in despair. I knew of many instances in which she gave sums of money to applicants, varying in amount from $20, $50, $500, to $1,000, and in one instance she gave $5,000 to a Swedish friend.

One night, while giving a concert in Boston, a girl approached the ticket-office, and laying down $3 for a ticket, remarked, "There goes half a month's earnings, but I am determined to hear Jenny Lind." Miss Lind's secretary heard the remark, and a few minutes afterwards coming into her room, he laughingly related the circumstance. "Would you know the girl again?" asked Jenny, with an earnest look. Upon receiving an affirmative reply, she instantly placed a $20 gold-piece in his hand, and said, "Poor girl! give her that with my best compliments." He at once found the girl, who cried with joy when she received the gold-piece, and heard the kind words with which the gift was accompanied.

The night after Jenny's arrival in Boston, a display of fireworks was given in her honor, in front of the Revere House, after which followed a beautiful torch-light procession by the Germans of that city.

On her return from Boston to New York, Jenny, her companion, and Messrs. Benedict and Belletti, stopped at Iranistan, my residence in Bridgeport, where they remained until the following day. The morning after her arrival, she took my arm and proposed a promenade through the grounds. She seemed much pleased, and said, "I am astonished that you should have left such a beautiful place for the sake of travelling through the country with me."

The same day she told me in a playful mood, that she

had heard a most extraordinary report. "I have heard that you and I are about to be married," said she; "now how could such an absurd report ever have originated?"

"Probably from the fact that we are 'engaged,' " I replied. She enjoyed a joke, and laughed heartily.

"Do you know, Mr. Barnum," said she, "that if you had not built Iranistan, I should never have come to America for you?"

I expressed my surprise, and asked her to explain.

"I had received several applications to visit the United States," she continued, "but I did not much like the appearance of the applicants, nor did I relish the idea of crossing 3,000 miles of ocean; so I declined them all. But the first letter which Mr. Wilton, your agent, addressed me, was written upon a sheet headed with a beautiful engraving of Iranistan. It attracted my attention. I said to myself, a gentleman who has been so successful in his business as to be able to build and reside in such a palace cannot be a mere 'adventurer.' So I wrote to your agent, and consented to an interview, which I should have declined, if I had not seen the picture of Iranistan!"

"That, then, fully pays me for building it, " I replied; "for I intend and expect to make more by this musical enterprise than Iranistan cost me."

"I really hope so," she replied; "but you must not be too sanguine, you know, 'man proposes but God disposes.' "

Jenny Lind always desired to reach a place in which she was to sing, without having the time of her arrival known, thus avoiding the excitement of promiscuous crowds. As a manager, however, I knew that the interests of the enterprise depended in a great degree upon these excitements. Although it frequently seemed inconceivable to her how so many thousands should have discovered her secret and consequently gathered together to receive her, I was not so much astonished, inasmuch as my agent always had early telegraphic intelligence of the time of her anticipated arrival, and was not slow in communicating the information to the public.

On reaching Philadelphia, a large concourse of persons awaited the approach of the steamer which conveyed her. With difficulty we pressed through the crowd, and were followed by many thousands to Jones's Hotel. The street in front of the building was densely packed by the populace, and poor Jenny, who was suffering from a severe headache, retired to her apartments. I tried to induce the crowd to disperse, but they declared they would not do so until Jenny Lind should appear on the balcony. I would not disturb her, and knowing that the tumult might prove an annoyance to her, I placed her bonnet and shawl upon her companion, Miss Ahmansen, and led her out on the balcony. She bowed gracefully to the multitude, who gave her three hearty cheers and quietly dispersed. Miss Lind was so utterly averse to any thing like deception, that we never ventured to tell her the part which her bonnet and shawl had played in the absence of their owner.

Jenny was in the habit of attending church whenever she could do so without attracting notice. She always preserved her nationality, also, by inquiring out and attending Swedish churches wherever they could be found. She gave $1,000 to a Swedish church in Chicago.

While in Boston, a poor Swedish girl, a domestic in a family at Roxbury, called on Jenny. She detained her visitor several hours, talking about home, and other matters, and in the evening took her in her carriage to the concert, gave her a seat, and sent her back to Roxbury in a carriage, at the close of the performances. I have no doubt the poor girl carried with her substantial evidences of her countrywoman's bounty.

My eldest daughter, Caroline, and her friend, Mrs. Lyman, of Bridgeport, accompanied me on the tour from New York to Havana, and thence home, *via* New Orleans and the Mississippi.

We were at Baltimore on the Sabbath, and my daughter, accompanying a friend, who resided in the city, to church, took a seat with her in the choir, and joined in the singing. A number of the congregation, who had seen Caroline with me the day previous, and supposed her to be Jenny Lind, were yet laboring under the same mistake, and it was soon whispered through the church that Jenny Lind was in the choir! The excitement was worked to its highest pitch when my daughter rose as one of the musical group. Every ear was on the alert to catch the first notes of her voice, and when she sang, glances of satisfaction passed through the assembly. Caroline, quite unconscious of the attention she attracted, continued to sing to the end of the hymn. Not a note was lost upon the ears of the attentive congregation. "What an exquisite singer!" "Heavenly sounds!" "I never heard the like!" and similar expressions were whispered through the church.

At the conclusion of the services, my daughter and her friend found the passage way to their carriage blocked by a crowd who were anxious to obtain a nearer view of the "Swedish Nightingale," and many persons that afternoon boasted, in good faith, that they had listened to the extraordinary singing of the great songstress. The pith of the joke is that we have never discovered that my daughter has any extraordinary claims as a vocalist.

Our orchestra in New York consisted of sixty. When we started on our southern tour, we took with us permanently as the orchestra, twelve of the best musicians we could select, and in New Orleans augmented the force to sixteen. We increased the number to thirty-five, forty or fifty, as the case might be, by choice of musicians residing where the concerts were given. On our return to New York from Havana, we enlarged the orchestra to one hundred performers.

The morning after our arrival in Washington, President Fillmore called, and left his card, Jenny being out.

When she returned and found the token of his attention, she was in something of a flurry. "Come," said she, "we must call on the President immediately."

"Why so?" I inquired.

"Because he has called on me, and of course that is equivalent to a command for me to go to his house."

I assured her that she might make her mind at ease, for whatever might be the custom with crowned heads, our Presidents were not wont to "command" the movements of strangers, and that she would be quite in time if she returned his call the next day. She did so, and was charmed with the unaffected bearing of the President, and the warm kindnesses expressed by his amiable wife and daughter, and consented to spend the evening with them in conformity with their request. She was accompanied to the "White House" by Messrs. Benedict, Belletti and myself, and several happy hours were spent in the private circle of the President's family.

Mr. Benedict, who engaged in a long quiet conversation with Mr. Fillmore, was highly pleased with the interview. A foreigner, accustomed to court etiquette, is generally surprised at the simplicity which characterizes the Chief Magistrate of this Union. In 1852 I called on the President with my friend the late Mr. Brettell, of London, who resided in St. James Palace, and was quite a worshipper of the Queen, and an ardent admirer of all the dignities and ceremonies of royalty. He expected something of the kind in visiting the President of the United States, and was highly pleased with his disappointment.

Both concerts in Washington were attended by the President and his family, and every member of the Cabinet. I noticed, also, among the audience, Henry Clay, Benton, Foote, Cass and General Scott, and nearly every member of Congress. On the following morning, Miss Lind was called upon by Mr. Webster, Mr. Clay, General Cass, and Colonel Benton, and all parties were evidently gratified. I had introduced Mr. Webster

to her in Boston. Upon hearing one of her wild mountain songs in New York, and also in Washington, Mr. Webster signified his approval by rising, drawing himself up to his full height, and making a profound bow. Jenny was delighted by this expression of praise from the great statesman. When I first introduced Miss Lind to Mr. Webster, at the Revere House, in Boston, she was greatly impressed with his manners and conversation, and after his departure, walked up and down the room in great excitement, exclaiming: "Ah! Mr. Barnum, that is a man; I have never before seen such a man!"

We visited the Capitol while both Houses were in session. Miss Lind took the arm of Hon. C. F. Cleveland, representative from Connecticut, and was by him escorted into various parts of the Capitol and the grounds, with all of which she was much pleased.

While I was in Washington an odd reminiscence of my old show-days in the South came back to me in a curious way. Some years before, in 1836, my travelling show company had stopped at a hotel in Jackson, Mississippi, and, as the house was crowded, soon after I went to bed five or six men came into the room with cards and a candle and asked permission, as there was no other place, to sit down and play a quiet game of "brag." I consented on condition that I might get up and participate, which was permitted and in a very little while, as I knew nothing whatever of the game, I lost fifty dollars. Good "hands" and good fortune soon enabled me to win back my money, at which point one of the players who had been introduced to me as "Lawyer Foote" said:

"Now the best thing you can do is to go back to bed; you don't know anything about the game, and these fellows do, and they'll skin you."

I acted upon his advice. And now, years afterwards, when Senator Foote called upon Miss Lind the story came back to me, and while I was talking with him I remarked:

"Fifteen years ago, when I was in the South, I became

acquainted with a lawyer named Foote, at Jackson, Mississippi."

"It must have been me," said the Senator, "I am the only 'lawyer Foote, of Jackson, Mississippi.'"

"Oh! no, it could not have been you," and I told him the story.

"It was me," he whispered in my ear, and added, "I used to gamble like h——l in those days."

During the week I was invited with Miss Lind and her immediate friends, to visit Mount Vernon, with Colonel Washington, the then proprietor, and Mr. Seaton, ex-Mayor of Washington, and Editor of the *Intelligencer*. Colonel Washington chartered a steamboat for the purpose. We were landed a short distance from the tomb, which we first visited. Proceeding to the house, we were introduced to Mrs. Washington, and several other ladies. Much interest was manifested by Miss Lind in examining the mementoes of the great man whose home it had been. A beautiful collation was spread out and arranged in fine taste. Before leaving, Mrs. Washington presented Jenny with a book from the library, with the name of Washington written by his own hand. She was much overcome at receiving this present, called me aside, and expressed her desire to give something in return. "I have nothing with me," she said, "excepting this watch and chain, and I will give that if you think it will be acceptable." I knew the watch was very valuable, and told her that so costly a present would not be expected, nor would it be proper. "The expense is nothing, compared to the value of that book," she replied, with deep emotion; "but as the watch was a present from a dear friend, perhaps I should not give it away." Jenny Lind, I am sure, never forgot the pleasurable emotions of that day.

At Richmond, half an hour previous to her departure, hundreds of young ladies and gentlemen had crowded into the halls of the house to secure a glimpse of her at parting. I informed her that she would find difficulty in

passing out. "How long is it before we must start?" she asked. "Half an hour," I replied. "Oh, I will clear the passages before that time," said she, with a smile; whereupon she went into the upper hall, and informed the people that she wished to take the hands of every one of them, upon one condition, viz: they should pass by her in rotation, and as fast as they had shaken hands, proceed down stairs, and not block up the passages. They joyfully consented to the arrangement, and in fifteen minutes the course was clear. Poor Jenny had shaken hands with every person in the crowd, and I presume she had a feeling remembrance of the incident for an hour or two at least. She was waited on by many members of the Legislature while in Richmond, that body being in session while we were there.

The voyage from Wilmington to Charleston was an exceedingly rough and perilous one. We were about thirty-six hours in making the passage, the usual time being seventeen. There was really great danger of our steamer being swamped, and we were all apprehensive that we should never reach the Port of Charleston alive. Some of the passengers were in great terror. Jenny Lind exhibited more calmness upon this occasion than any other person, the crew excepted. We arrived safely at last, and I was grieved to learn that for twelve hours the loss of the steamer had been considered certain, and had even been announced by telegraph in the Northern cities.

We remained at Charleston about ten days, to take the steamer "Isabella" on her regular trip to Havana. Jenny had been through so much excitement at the North, that she determined to have quiet here, and therefore declined receiving any calls. This disappointed many ladies and gentlemen. One young lady, the daughter of a wealthy planter near Augusta, was so determined upon seeing her in private, that she paid one of the servants to allow her to put on a cap and white apron, and carry in the tray for Jenny's tea. I afterwards told Miss Lind of the joke, and suggested that after such an evidence of admiration, she should receive a call from the young lady.

"It is not admiration—it is only curiosity," replied Jenny, "and I will not encourage such folly."

Christmas was at hand, and Jenny Lind determined to honor it in the way she had often done in Sweden. She had a beautiful Christmas tree privately prepared, and from its boughs depended a variety of presents for members of the company. These gifts were encased in paper, with the names of the recipients written on each.

After spending a pleasant evening in her drawing-room, she invited us into the parlor, where the "surprise" awaited us. Each person commenced opening the packages bearing his or her address, and although every individual had one or more pretty presents, she had prepared a joke for each. Mr. Benedict, for instance, took off wrapper after wrapper from one of his packages, which at first was as large as his head, but after having removed some forty coverings of paper, it was reduced to a size smaller than his hand, and the removal of the last envelope exposed to view a piece of cavendish tobacco. One of my presents, choicely wrapped in a dozen coverings, was a jolly young Bacchus in Parian marble, intended as a pleasant hit at my temperance principles!

The night before New Year's day was spent in her apartment with great hilarity. Enlivened by music, singing, dancing and story-telling, the hours glided swiftly away. Miss Lind asked me if I would dance with her. I told her my education had been neglected in that line, and that I had never danced in my life. "That is all the better," said she; "now dance with me in a cotillion. I am sure you can do it." She was a beautiful dancer, and I never saw her laugh more heartily than she did at my awkwardness. She said she would give me the credit of being the poorest dancer she ever saw!

About a quarter before twelve, Jenny suddenly checked Mr. Burke,—formerly celebrated as the musical prodigy, "Master Burke,"—who was playing on the piano, by saying, "Pray let us have quiet; do you see, in fifteen minutes more, this year will be gone forever!"

She immediately took a seat, and rested her head upon her hand in silence. We all sat down, and for a quarter of an hour the most profound quiet reigned in the apartment. The remainder of the scene I transcribe from a description written the next day by Mrs. Lyman, who was present on the occasion:

"The clock of a neighboring church struck the knell of the dying year. All were silent—each heart was left to its own communings, and the bowed head and tearful eye told that memory was busy with the Past. It was a brief moment, but thoughts and feelings were crowded into it, which render it one never to be forgotten. A moment more—the last stroke of the clock had fallen upon the ear—the last faint vibration ceased; another period of time had passed forever away—a new one had dawned, in which each felt that they were to live and act. This thought recalled them to a full consciousness of the present, and all arose and quietly, but cordially, presented to each other the kind wishes of the season. As the lovely hostess pressed the hands of her guests, it was evident that she, too, had wept,—she, the gifted, the admired, the almost idolized one. Had she, too, cause for tears? Whence were they?—from the overflowings of a grateful heart, from tender associations, or from sad remembrances? None knew, none could ask, though they awakened deep and peculiar sympathy. And from one heart, at least, arose the prayer, that when the dial of time should mark the last hour of her earthly existence, she should greet its approach with joy and not with grief—that to her soul spirit-voices might whisper, 'Come, sweet sister! come to the realms of unfading light and love—come, join your seraphic tones with ours, in singing the praises of Him who loved us, and gave himself for us'—while she, with meekly-folded hands and faith-uplifted eye, should answer, 'Yes, gladly and without fear I come, for I know that my Redeemer liveth.' "

I had arranged with a man in New York to transport furniture to Havana, provide a house, and board Jenny Lind and our immediate party during our stay. When we arrived, we found the building converted into a semi-hotel, and the apartments were any thing but comfortable. Jenny was vexed. Soon after dinner, she took a volante and an interpreter, and drove into the suburbs. She was absent four hours. Whither or why she had gone, none of us knew. At length she returned and informed us that she had hired a commodious furnished house in a delightful location outside the walls of the city, and invited us all to go and live with her during our stay in Havana, and we accepted the invitation. She was now freed from all annoyances; her time was her own, she received no calls, went and came when she pleased, had no meddlesome advisers about her, legal or otherwise, and was as merry as a cricket. We had a large court-yard in the rear of the house, and here she would come and romp and run, sing and laugh, like a young school-girl. "Now, Mr. Barnum, for another game of ball," she would say half a dozen times a day; whereupon, she would take an india-rubber ball, (of which she had two or three,) and commence a game of throwing and catching, which would be kept up until, being completely tired out, I would say, "I give it up." Then her rich, musical laugh would be heard ringing through the house, as she exclaimed, "Oh, Mr. Barnum, you are too fat and too lazy; you cannot stand it to play ball with me!"

Her celebrated countrywoman, Miss Frederika Bremer, spent a few days with us very pleasantly, and it is difficult to conceive of a more delightful month than was passed by the entire party at Jenny Lind's house in the outskirts of Havana.

CHAPTER XXIII.

Other Enterprises.

While I was managing the Lind concerts, in addition to the American Museum I had other business matters in operation which were more than enough to engross my entire attention and which, of course, I was compelled to commit to the hands of associates and agents.

In 1849 I had projected a great travelling museum and menagerie, and, as I had neither time nor inclination to manage such a concern, I induced Mr. Seth B. Howes, justly celebrated as a "showman," to join me, and take the sole charge. Mr. Sherwood E. Stratton, father of General Tom Thumb, was also admitted to partnership, the interest being in thirds.

In carrying out a portion of the plan, we chartered the ship "Regatta," Captain Pratt, and despatched her, together with our agents, Messrs. June and Nutter, to Ceylon. The ship left New York in May, 1850, and was absent one year. Their mission was to procure, either by capture or purchase, twelve or more living elephants, besides such other wild animals as they could secure. In order to provide sufficient drink and provender for a cargo of these huge animals, we purchased a large quantity of hay in New York. Five hundred tons were left at the Island of St. Helena, to be taken on the return trip of the ship, and staves and hoops of water-casks were also left at the same place.

As our agents were unable to purchase the required number of elephants, either in Columbo or Kandy, the principal towns of the island, (Ceylon,) they took one hundred and sixty native assistants, and plunged into the jungles, where, after many most exciting adventures, they succeeded in securing thirteen elephants of a suitable size for their purpose, with a female and her calf, or "baby" elephant, only six months old. In the course of the expedition, Messrs. Nutter and June killed large numbers of the huge beasts, and had numerous encounters of the most terrific description with the formidable animals, one of the most fearful of which took place near Anarajah Poora, while they were endeavoring, by the aid of the natives and trained elephants, to drive the wild herd of beasts into an Indian kraal.

They arrived in New York in 1851 with ten of the elephants, and these, harnessed in pairs to a chariot, paraded up Broadway past the Irving House, while Jenny Lind was staying at that hotel, on the occasion of her second visit to New York. Messrs. Nutter and June also brought with the elephants a native who was competent to manage and control them. We added a caravan of wild animals and many museum curiosities, the entire outfit, including horses, vans, carriages, tent, etc., costing $109,000, and commenced operations, with the presence and under the "patronage" of General Tom Thumb, who travelled nearly four years as one of the attractions of "Barnum's Great Asiatic Caravan, Museum and Menagerie," returning us immense profits.

At the end of that time, after exhibiting in all sections of the country, we sold out the entire establishment—animals, cages, chariots and paraphernalia, excepting one elephant, which I retained in my own possession two months for agricultural purposes. It occurred to me that if I could put an elephant to plowing for a while on my farm at Bridgeport, it would be a capital advertisement for the American Museum, which was then, and always during my proprietorship of that establishment, foremost in my thoughts.

So I sent him to Connecticut in charge of his keeper, whom I dressed in Oriental costume, and keeper and elephant were stationed on a six-acre lot which lay close beside the track of the New York and New Haven Railroad. The keeper was furnished with a time-table of the road, with special instructions to be busily engaged in his work whenever passenger trains from either way were passing through. Of course, the matter soon appeared in the papers and went the entire rounds of the press in this country and even in Europe, and it was everywhere announced that P. T. Barnum, "Proprietor of the celebrated American Museum in New York"—and here is where the advertisement came in—had introduced elephants upon his farm, to do his plowing and heavy draft work. Hundreds of people came many miles to witness the novel spectacle. Letters poured in upon me from the secretaries of hundreds of State and County agricultural societies throughout the Union, stating that the presidents and directors of such societies had requested them to propound to me a series of questions in regard to the new power I had put in operation on my farm. These questions were greatly diversified, but the "general run" of them were something like the following:

1. "Is the elephant a profitable agricultural animal?"
2. "How much can an elephant plow in a day?"
3. "How much can he draw?"
4. "How much does he eat?"—this question was invariably asked, and was a very important one.
5. "Will elephants make themselves generally useful on a farm?" I suppose some of my inquirers thought the elephant would pick up chips, or even pins as they have been taught to do, and would rock the baby and do all the chores, including the occasional carrying of a trunk, other than his own, to the depot.

6. "What is the price of an elephant?"

7. "Where can elephants be purchased?"

Then would follow a score of other inquiries, such as, whether elephants were easily managed; if they would quarrel with cattle; if it was possible to breed them; how old calf elephants must be before they would earn their own living; and so on indefinitely. I began to be alarmed lest some one should buy an elephant, and so share the fate of the man who drew one in a lottery, and did not know what to do with him. I accordingly had a general letter printed, which I mailed to all my anxious inquirers. It was headed "strictly confidential," and I then stated, begging my correspondents "not to mention it," that to me the elephant was a valuable agricultural animal, because he was an excellent advertisement to my Museum; but that to other farmers he would prove very unprofitable for many reasons. In the first place, such an animal would cost from $3,000 to $10,000; in cold weather he could not work at all; in any weather he could not earn even half his living; he would eat up the value of his own head, trunk, and body every year; and I begged my correspondents not to do so foolish a thing as to undertake elephant farming.

Newspaper reporters came from far and near, and wrote glowing accounts of the elephantine performances. One of them, taking a political view of the matter, stated that the elephant's sagacity showed that he knew more than did any laborer on the farm, and yet, shameful to say, he was not allowed to vote. Another said that Barnum's elephant built all the stone wall on the farm; made all the rail fences; planted corn with his trunk, and covered it with his foot; washed my windows and sprinkled the walks and lawns, by taking water from the fountain-basin with his trunk; carried all the children to school, and put them to bed at night, tucking them up with his trunk; fed the pigs; picked fruit from branches that could not otherwise be reached; turned the fanning mill and corn-

sheller; drew the mowing machine, and turned and
cocked the hay with his trunk; carried and brought my
letters to and from the post-office (it was a male elephant); and did all the chores about the house, including
milking the cows, and bringing in eggs. Pictures of Barnum's plowing elephant appeared in illustrated papers at
home and abroad, and as the cars passed the scene of the
performance, passengers' heads were out of every window, and among many and varied exclamations, I heard
of one man's saying:

"Well, I declare! That is certainly a real elephant and
any man who has so many elephants that he can afford to
work them on his farm, must have lots of wild animals
and curious 'critters' in his Museum, and I am bound to
go there the first thing after my arrival in New York."

The six acres were plowed over at least sixty times
before I thought the advertisement sufficiently circulated, and I then sold the elephant to Van Amburgh's
Menagerie.

A substantial farmer friend of mine, Mr. Gideon
Thompson, called at Iranistan during the elephant excitement and asked me to accompany him to the field to let
him see "how the big animal worked." I knew him to be
a shrewd, sharp man and a good farmer, and I tried to
excuse myself, as I did not wish to be too closely ques-
tioned. Indeed, for the same reason, I made it a point at
all times to avoid being present when the plowing was
going on. But the old farmer was a particular friend and
he refused to take "no" for an answer; so I went with him
"to see the elephant."

Arriving at the field, Mr. Thompson said nothing, but
stood with folded arms and sedately watched the elephant
for at least fifteen minutes. Then he walked out on to the
plowed ground, and found it so mellow that he sank
nearly up to his knees; for it had already been plowed
over and over many times. As usual, several spectators
were present. Mr. Thompson walked up to where I was

standing, and, looking me squarely in the eyes, he asked with much earnestness:

"What is your object, sir, in bringing that great Asiatic animal on to a New England farm?"

"To plow," I replied very demurely.

"To plow!" said Thompson; "don't talk to me about plowing! I have been out where he has plowed, and the ground is so soft I thought I should go through and come out in China. No, sir! You can't humbug me. You have got some other object in bringing that elephant up here; now what is it?"

"Don't you see for yourself that I am plowing with him?" I asked.

"Nonsense," said Thompson "that would never pay; I have no doubt he eats more than he earns every day; you have some other purpose in view, I am sure you have."

"Perhaps he does not eat so much as you think," I replied; "and you see he draws nobly—in fact, I expect he will be just the animal by and by, to draw saw logs to mill, and do other heavy work."

But Uncle Gid., was not to be put aside so easily so he asked very sharply:

"How much does he eat in a day?"

"Oh," I replied carelessly, "not more than a quarter of a ton of hay and three or four bushels of oats."

"Exactly," said Thompson, his eyes glistening with delight; "that is just about what I expected. He can't draw so much as two pair of my oxen can, and he costs more than a dozen pair."

"You are mistaken, friend Thompson," I replied with much gravity; "that elephant is a powerful animal; he can draw more than forty yoke of oxen, and he pays me well for bringing him here."

"Forty yoke of oxen!" contemptuously replied the old farmer; "I don't want to tell you I doubt your word, but I would just like to know what he can draw."

"He can draw the attention of twenty millions of American citizens to Barnum's Museum," I replied.

"Oh, you can make him pay in that way, of course," responded the old farmer.

"None but a greenhorn could ever have expected he would pay in any other way," I replied.

The old man gave a hearty laugh, and said, "Well, I give it up. I have been a farmer thirty-five years, and I have only just discovered that an elephant is a very useful and profitable animal on a farm—provided the farmer also owns a museum."

In 1851 I became a part owner of the steamship "North America." Our intention in buying it was to run it to Ireland as a passenger and freight ship. The project was, however, abandoned, and Commodore Cornelius Vanderbilt bought one half of the steamer, while the other half was owned by three persons, of whom I was one. The steamer was sent around Cape Horn to San Francisco, and was put into the Vanderbilt line.

After she had made several trips I called upon Mr. Vanderbilt, at his office, and introduced myself, as this was the first time we had met.

"Is it possible you are Barnum?" exclaimed the Commodore, in surprise, "why, I expected to see a monster, part lion, part elephant, and a mixture of rhinoceros and tiger! Is it possible," he continued, "that you are the showman who has made so much noise in the world?"

I laughingly replied that I was, and added that if I too had been governed in my anticipation of his personal appearance by the fame he had achieved in his line, I should have expected to have been saluted by a steam whistle, and to have seen him dressed in a pea jacket, blowing off steam, and crying out "all aboard that's going."

"Instead of which," replied Mr. Vanderbilt, "I suppose you have come to ask me, 'to walk up to the Captain's office and settle.'"

After this interchange of civilities, we talked about the success of the "North America" in having got safely around the Horn, and of the acceptable manner in which she was doing her duty on the Pacific side.

"We have received no statement of her earnings yet," said the Commodore, "but if you want money, give your receipt to our treasurer, and take some."

A few months subsequent to this, I sold out my share in the steamship to Mr. Daniel Drew. The day after closing with Mr. Drew, I discovered an error of several hundred dollars (a matter of interest on some portion of the purchase money, which had been overlooked). I called on Mr. Drew, and asked him to correct it, but could get no satisfaction. I then wrote him a threatening letter, but received no response. I was on the eve of suing him for the amount due me, when the news came that the steamship "North America" was lying at the bottom of the Pacific. It turned out that she was sunk several days before I sold out, and as the owners were mulcted in the sum of many thousands of dollars damages by their passengers, besides suffering a great loss in their steamship, I said no more to the millionnaire Drew about the few hundreds which he had withheld from the showman.

Some reference to the various enterprises and "side shows" connected with and disconnected from my Museum, is necessary to show how industriously I have catered for the public's amusement, not only in America but abroad. When I was in Paris in 1844, in addition to the purchase of Robert Houdin's ingenious automaton writer, and many other costly curiosities for the Museum, I ordered, at an expense of $3,000, a panoramic diorama of the obsequies of Napoleon. Every event of that grand pageant, from the embarkation of the body at St. Helena, to its entombment at the Hotel des Invalides, amid the most gorgeous parade ever witnessed in France, was wonderfully depicted. This exhibition, after having had its day at the American Museum, was sold, and extensively and profitably exhibited elsewhere. While I was in London, during the same year, I engaged a company of "Campanalogians, or Lancashire Bell Ringers," then performing in Ireland, to make an American tour. They were really admirable performers, and by means of their numerous bells, of various sizes, they produced the most delightful music. They attracted much attention in various parts of the United States, in Canada, and in Cuba.

As a compensation to England for the loss of the Bell Ringers, I despatched an agent to America for a party of Indians, including squaws. He proceeded to Iowa, and returned to London with a company of sixteen. They were exhibited by Mr. Catlin on our joint account, and were finally left in his sole charge.

On my first return visit to America from Europe, I engaged Mr. Faber, an elderly and ingenious German, who had constructed an automaton speaker. It was of life-size, and when worked with keys similar to those of a piano, it really articulated words and sentences with surprising distinctness. My agent exhibited it for several months in Egyptian Hall, London, and also in the provinces. This was a marvellous piece of mechanism, though for some unaccountable reason it did not prove a success. The Duke of Wellington visited it several times, and at first he thought that the "voice" proceeded from the exhibitor, whom he assumed to be a skillful ventriloquist. He was asked to touch the keys with his own fingers, and after some instruction in the method of operating, he was able to make the machine speak, not only in English but also in German, with which language the Duke seemed familiar. Thereafter, he entered his name on the exhibitor's autograph book, and certified that the "Automaton Speaker" was an extraordinary production of mechanical genius.

During my first vist to England I obtained, verbally, through a friend, the refusal of the house in which Shakespeare was born, designing to remove it in sections to my Museum in New York; but the project leaked out, British pride was touched, and several English gentlemen interfered and purchased the premises for a Shakespearian Association. Had they slept a few days longer, I should have made a rare speculation, for I was subsequently assured that the British people, rather than suffer that house to be removed to America, would have bought me off with twenty thousand pounds. I did not hesitate to engage, or attempt to secure anything, at any expense, to please my patrons in the United States, and I made an effort to transfer Madame Tussaud's world-wide celebrated wax-work collection entire to New York. The papers were actually drawn up for this engagement, but the enterprise finally fell through.

The models of machinery exhibited in the Royal Polytechnic Institution in London, pleased me so well that I procured a duplicate; also duplicates of the "Dissolving Views," the Chromatrope and Physioscope, including many American scenes painted expressly to my order, at an aggregate cost of $7,000. After they had been exhibited in my Museum, they were sold to itinerant showmen, and some of them were afterwards on exhibition in various parts of the United States.

In June 1850, I added the celebrated Chinese Collection to the attractions of the American Museum. I also engaged the Chinese Family, consisting of two men, two "small-footed" women and two children. My agent exhibited them in London during the World's Fair. It may be stated here, that I subsequently sent to London the celebrated artist De Lamano to paint a panorama of the Crystal Palace, in which the World's Fair was held, and Colonel John S. Dusolle, an able and accomplished editor, whom I sent with De Lamano, wrote an accompanying descriptive lecture. Like most panoramas, however, the exhibition proved a failure.

The giants whom I sent to America were not the greatest of my curiosities, though the dwarfs might have been the least. The "Scotch Boys" were interesting, not so much on account of their weight, as for the mysterious method by which one of them, though blind-folded, answered questions put by the other respecting objects presented by persons who attended the surprising exhibition. The mystery, which was merely the result of patient practice, consisted wholly in the manner in which the question was propounded; in fact, the question invariably carried its own answer; for instance:

"What is this?" meant gold; "Now what is this?" silver; "Say what is this?" copper; "Tell me what this is," iron; "What is the shape?" long; "Now what shape?" round; "Say what shape," square; "Please say what this is," a watch; "Can you tell what is in this lady's hand?" a purse; "Now please say what this is?" a key; "Come now, what is this?" money; "How much?" a penny; "Now how much?" sixpence; "Say how much," a quarter of a dollar; "What color is this?" black; "Now what color is this?" red; "Say what color," green; and so on, *ad infinitum*. To such perfection was this brought that it was almost impossible to present any object that could not be quite closely described by the blind-folded boy. This is the key to all exhibitions of what is called "second sight."

In 1850, the celebrated Bateman children acted for several weeks at the American Museum and in June of that year I sent them to London with their father and Mr. Le Grand Smith, where they played in the St. James Theatre, and afterwards in the principal provincial theatres. The elder of these children, Miss Kate Bateman, subsequently attained the highest histrionic distinction in America and abroad, and reached the very head of her profession.

In October, 1852, having stipulated with Mr. George A. Wells and Mr. Bushnell that they should share in the enterprise and take the entire charge, I engaged Miss Catherine Hayes and Herr Begnis to give a series of sixty concerts in California, and the engagement was fulfilled to our entire satisfaction. Mr. Bushnell afterwards went to Australia with Miss Hayes and they were subsequently married. Both of them are dead.

Before setting out for California, Miss Catherine Hayes, her mother and sister spent several days at Iranistan and were present at the marriage of my eldest daughter, Caroline, to Mr. David W. Thompson. The wedding was to take place in the evening, and in the afternoon I was getting shaved in a barber-shop in Bridge-port, when Mr. Thompson drove up to the door in great haste and exclaimed;

"Mr. Barnum, Iranistan is in flames!"

I ran out half-shaved, with the lather on my face, jumped into his wagon and bade him drive home with all speed. I was greatly alarmed, for the house was full of visitors who had come from a distance to attend the wedding, and all the costly presents, dresses, refreshments, and everything prepared for a marriage celebration to which nearly a thousand guests had been invited, were already in my house. Mr. Thompson told me that he had seen the flames bursting from the roof and it seemed to me that there was little hope of saving the building.

My mind was distressed, not so much at the great pecuniary loss which the destruction of Iranistan would involve as at the possibility that some of my family or visitors would be killed or seriously injured in attempting to save something from the fire. Then I thought of the sore disappointment this calamity would cause to the young couple, as well as to those who were invited to the wedding. I saw that Mr. Thompson looked pale and anxious.

"Never mind!" said I; "we can't help these things; the house will probably be burned; but if no one is killed or injured, you shall be married to-night, if we are obliged to perform the ceremony in the coach-house."

On our way, we overtook a fire-company and I implored them to "hurry up their machine." Arriving in sight of Iranistan we saw huge volumes of smoke rolling out from the roof and many men on the top of the house were passing buckets of water to pour upon the fire. Fortunately, several men had been engaged during the day in repairing the roof, and their ladders were against the house. By these means and with the assistance of the men employed upon my grounds, water was passed very rapidly and the flames were soon subdued without serious damage. The inmates of Iranistan were thoroughly frightened; Catherine Hayes and other visitors packed their trunks and had them carried out on the lawn; and the house came as near destruction as it well could, and escape.

While Miss Hayes was in Bridgeport I induced her to give a concert for the benefit of the "Mountain Grove Cemetery," and the large proceeds were devoted to the erection of the beautiful stone tower and gateway at the entrance of that charming ground. The land for this cemetery, about eighty acres, had been bought by me, years before, from several farmers. I had often shot over the ground while hunting a year or two before, and had then seen its admirable capabilities for the purpose to which it was eventually devoted. After deeds for the property were secured, it was offered for a cemetery, and at a meeting of citizens several lots were subscribed for, enough, indeed, to cover the amount of the purchase money. Thus was begun the "Mountain Grove Cemetery," which is now beautifully laid out and adorned with many tasteful and costly monuments. Among these are my own substantial granite monument, the family monuments of Harral, Bishop, Hubbell, Lyon, Wood, Loomis, Wordin, Hyde, and others, and General Tom Thumb has erected a tall marble shaft which is surmounted by a life-size statue of himself. There is no more charming burial ground in the whole country; yet when the project was suggested, many persons preferred an intermural cemetery to this rural resting-place for their departed friends; though now, all concur in considering it fortunate that this adjunct was secured to Bridgeport before the land could be permanently devoted to other purposes.

Some time afterwards, when Mr. Dion Boucicault visited me at Bridgeport, at my solicitation he gave a lecture for the benefit of this cemetery. I may add that on several occasions I have secured the services of General Tom Thumb and others for this and equally worthy objects in

Bridgeport. When the General first returned with me from England, he gave exhibitions for the benefit of the Bridgeport Charitable Society. September 28, 1867, I induced him and his wife, with Commodore Nutt and Minnie Warren to give their entertainment for the benefit of the Bridgeport Library, thus adding $475 to the funds of that institution; and on one occasion I lectured to a full house in the Methodist Church, and the entire receipts were given to the library, of which I was already a life member, on account of previous subscriptions and contributions.

CHAPTER XXIV.

Work and Play.

In the summer, I think, of 1853, I saw it announced in the newspapers that Mr. Alfred Bunn, the great ex-manager of Drury Lane Theatre, in London, had arrived in Boston. Of course, I knew Mr. Bunn by reputation, not only from his managerial career, but from the fact that he made the first engagement with Jenny Lind to appear in London. This engagement, however, Mr. Lumley, of Her Majesty's Theatre, induced her to break, he standing a lawsuit with Mr. Bunn, and paying heavy damages. I had never met Mr. Bunn, but he took it for granted that I had seen him, for one day after his arrival in this country, a burly Englishman abruptly stepped into my private office in the Museum, and assuming a theatrical attitude, addressed me:

"Barnum, do you remember me?"

I was confident I had never seen the man before, but it struck me at once that no Englishman I ever heard of would be likely to exhibit more presumption or assumption than the ex-manager of Drury Lane, and I jumped at the conclusion:

"Is not this Mr. Bunn?"

"Ah! Ah! my boy!" he exclaimed, slapping me familiarly on the back, "I thought you would remember me. Well, Barnum, how have you been since I last saw you?"

I replied in a manner that would humor his impression that we were old acquaintances, and during his two hours'

227

visit we had much gossip about men and things in London. He called upon me several times, and it probably never entered into his mind that I could possibly have been in London two or three years without having made the personal acquaintance of so great a lion as Alfred Bunn.

I met Mr. Bunn again in 1858, in London, at a dinner party of a mutual friend, Mr. Levy, proprietor of the London *Daily Telegraph*. Of course, Bunn and I were great chums and very old and intimate acquaintants. At the same dinner, I met several literary and dramatic gentlemen.

In 1851, 1852, and 1853, I spent much of my time at my beautiful home in Bridgeport, going very frequently to New York, to attend to matters in the Museum, but remaining in the city only a day or two at a time. I resigned the office of President of the Fairfield County Agricultural Society in 1853, but the members accepted my resignation, only on condition that it should not go into effect until after the fair of 1854. During my administration, the society held six fairs and cattle-shows,—four in Bridgeport and two in Stamford,—and the interest in these gatherings increased from year to year.

Pickpockets are always present at these country fairs, and every year there were loud complaints of the depredations of these operators. In 1853 a man was caught in the act of taking a pocket-book from a country farmer, nor was this farmer the only one who had suffered in the same way. The scamp was arrested, and proved to be a celebrated English pickpocket. As the Fair would close the next day, and as most persons had already visited it, we expected our receipts would be light.

Early in the morning the detected party was legally examined, plead guilty, and was bound over for trial. I obtained consent from the sheriff that the culprit should be put in the Fair room for the purpose of giving those who had been robbed an opportunity to identify him. For this purpose he was handcuffed, and placed in a conspicuous position, where of course he was "the observed of all observers." I then issued handbills, stating that as it was the last day of the Fair, the managers were happy to announce that they had secured extra attractions for the occasion, and would accordingly exhibit, safely handcuffed, and without extra charge, a live pickpocket, who had been caught in the act of robbing an honest farmer the day previous. Crowds of people rushed in "to see the show." Some good mothers brought their children ten miles for that purpose, and our treasury was materially benefited by the operation.

At the close of my presidency in 1854, I was requested to deliver the opening speech at our County Fair, which was held at Stamford. As I was not able to give agricultural advice, I delivered a portion of my lecture on the "Philosophy of Humbug." The next morning, as I was being shaved in the village barber's shop, which was at the time crowded with customers, the ticket-seller to the Fair came in.

"What kind of a house did you have last night?" asked one of the gentlemen in waiting.

"Oh, first-rate, of course. Barnum always draws a crowd," was the reply of the ticket-seller, to whom I was not known.

Most of the gentlemen present, however, knew me, and they found much difficulty in restraining their laughter.

"Did Barnum make a good speech?" I asked.

"I did not hear it. I was out in the ticket-office. I guess it was pretty good, for I never heard so much laughing as there was all through his speech. But it makes no difference whether it was good or not," continued the ticket-seller, "the people will go to see Barnum."

"Barnum must be a curious chap," I remarked.

"Well, I guess he is up to all the dodges."

"Do you know him?" I asked.

"Not personally," he replied; "but I always get into

the Museum for nothing. I know the doorkeeper, and he slips me in free."

"Barnum would not like that, probably, if he knew," I remarked.

"But it happens he don't know it," replied the ticket-seller, in great glee.

"Barnum was on the cars the other day, on his way to Bridgeport," said I, "and I heard one of the passengers blowing him up terribly as a humbug. He was addressing Barnum at the time, but did not know him. Barnum joined in lustily, and indorsed everything the man said. When the passenger learned whom he had been addressing, I should think he must have felt rather flat."

"I should think so, too," said the ticket-seller.

This was too much, and we all indulged in a burst of laughter; still the ticket-seller suspected nothing. After I had left the shop, the barber told him who I was. I called into the ticket-office on business several times during the day, but the poor ticket-seller kept his face turned from me, and appeared so chap-fallen that I did not pretend to recognize him as the hero of the joke in the barber's shop.

This incident reminds me of numerous similar ones which have occurred at various times. On one occasion—it was in 1847—I was on board the steamboat from New York to Bridgeport. As we approached the harbor of the latter city, a stranger desired me to point out "Barnum's house" from the upper deck. I did so, whereupon a bystander remarked, "I know all about that house, for I was engaged in painting there for several months while Barnum was in Europe." He then proceeded to say that it was the meanest and most ill-contrived house he ever saw. "It will cost old Barnum a mint of money, and not be worth two cents after it is finished," he added.

"I suppose old Barnum don't pay very punctually," I remarked.

"Oh, yes, he pays punctually every Saturday night—there's no trouble about that; he has made half a million by exhibiting a little boy whom he took from Bridgeport, and whom we never considered any great shakes till Barnum took him and trained him."

Soon afterwards one of the passengers told him who I was, whereupon he secreted himself, and was not seen again while I remained on the boat.

On another occasion, I went to Boston by the Fall River route. Arriving before sunrise, I found but one carriage at the depot. I immediately engaged it, and giving the driver the check for my baggage, told him to take me directly to the Revere House, as I was in great haste, and enjoined him to take in no other passengers, and I would pay his demands. He promised compliance with my wishes, but soon afterwards appeared with a gentleman, two ladies, and several children, whom he crowded into the carriage with me, and placing their trunks on the baggage rack, started off. I thought there was no use in grumbling, and consoled myself with the reflection that the Revere House was not far away. He drove up one street and down another, for what seemed to me a very long time, but I was wedged in so closely that I could not see what route he was taking.

After half an hour's drive he halted, and I found we were at the Lowell Railway depot. Here my fellow-passengers alighted, and after a long delay the driver delivered their baggage, received his fare, and was about closing the carriage door preparatory to starting again. I was so thoroughly vexed at the shameful manner in which he had treated me, that I remarked;

"Perhaps you had better wait till the Lowell train arrives; you may possibly get another load of passengers. Of course my convenience is of no consequence. I suppose if you land me at the Revere House any time this week, it will be as much as I have a right to expect."

"I beg your pardon," he replied, "but that was Barnum and his family. He was very anxious to get here in time for the first train, so I stuck him for $2, and now I'll carry you to the Revere House free."

"What Barnum is it?" I asked.

"The Museum and Jenny Lind man," he replied.

The compliment and the shave both having been intended for me, I was of course mollified, and replied, "You are mistaken, my friend, *I* am Barnum."

"Coachee" was thunderstruck, and offered all sorts of apologies.

"A friend at the other depot told me that I had Mr. Barnum on board," said he, "and I really supposed he meant the other man. When I come to notice you, I perceive my mistake, but I hope you will forgive me. I have carried you frequently before, and hope you will give me your custom while you are in Boston. I never will make such a mistake again." I had to be satisfied.

Late in August, 1851, I was visited at Bridgeport by a gentleman who was interested in an English invention patented in this country, and known as Phillips' Fire Annihilator. He showed me a number of certificates from men of eminence and trustworthiness in England, setting forth the merits of the invention in the highest terms. The principal value of the machine seemed to consist in its power to extinguish flame, and thus prevent the spread of fire when it once broke out. Besides, the steam or vapor generated in the Annihilator was not prejudicial to human life. Now, as water has no effect whatever upon flame, it was obvious that the Annihilator would at the least prove a great *assistant* in extinguishing conflagrations, and that, especially in the incipient stage of a fire, it would extinguish it altogether, without damage to goods or other property, as is usually the case with water.

Hon. Elisha Whittlesey, First Comptroller of the United States Treasury at Washington, was interested in the American patent, and the gentleman that called upon me desired that I should also take an interest in it. I had no disposition to engage in any speculation; but, believing this might prove a beneficent invention, and be the means of saving a vast amount of human life as well as property, I visited Washington City for the purpose of conferring with Mr. Whittlesey, Hon. J. W. Allen and other parties interested.

I was there shown numerous certificates of fires having been extinguished by the machine in Great Britain, and property to the amount of many thousands of pounds saved. I also saw that Lord Brougham had proposed in Parliament that every Government vessel should be compelled to have the Fire Annihilator on board. Mr. Whittlesey expressed his belief in writing, that "if there is any reliance to be placed on human testimony, it is one of the greatest discoveries of this most extraordinary age." I fully agreed with him, and have never yet seen occasion to change that opinion.

I agreed to join in the enterprise. Mr. Whittlesey was elected President, and I was appointed Secretary and General Agent of the Company. I opened the office of the Company in New York, and sold and engaged machines and territory in a few months to the amount of $180,000. I refused to receive more than a small portion of the purchase money until a public experiment had tested the powers of the machine, and I voluntarily delivered to every purchaser an agreement, signed by myself, in the following words:

"If the public test and demonstration are not perfectly successful, I will at any time when demanded, within ten days after the public trial, refund and pay back every shilling that has been paid into this office for machines or territory for the sale of the patent."

The public trial came off in Hamilton Square on the 18th December, 1851. It was an exceedingly cold and inclement day. Mr. Phillips, who conducted the experiment, was interfered with and knocked down by some rowdies who were opposed to the invention, and the building was ignited and consumed after he had extinguished the previous fire. Subsequently to this unexpected and unjust opposition, I refunded every cent which I had received, sometimes against the wishes of those who had purchased, for they were willing to wait the result of further experiments; but I was utterly disgusted with the course of a large portion of the public upon a subject in which they were much more deeply interested than I was.

The arrangements of the Annihilator Company with Mr. Phillips, the inventor, predicated all payments which he was to receive on *bona fide* sales which we should actually make; therefore he really received nothing, and the entire losses of the American Company, which were merely for advertising and the expense of trying the experiments, hire of an office, etc., amounted to nearly $30,000, of which my portion was less than $10,000.

In the spring of 1851 the Connecticut Legislature chartered the Pequonnock Bank of Bridgeport, with a capital of two hundred thousand dollars. I had no interest whatever in the charter, and did not even know that an application was to be made for it. More banking capital was needed in Bridgeport in consequence of the great increase of trade and manufactures in that growing and prosperous city, and this fact appearing in evidence, the charter was granted as a public benefit. The stockbooks were opened under the direction of State Commissioners, according to the laws of the Commonwealth, and nearly double the amount of capital was subscribed on the first day. The stock was distributed by the Commissioners among several hundred applicants. Circumstances unexpectedly occurred which induced me to accept the presidency of the bank, in compliance with the unanimous vote of its directors. Feeling that I could not, from my many avocations, devote the requisite personal attention to the duties of the office, C. B. Hubbell, Esq., then Mayor of Bridgeport, was at my request appointed Vice-President of the institution.

In the fall of 1852 a proposition was made by certain

parties to commence the publication of an illustrated weekly newspaper in the City of New York. The field seemed to be open for such an enterprise, and I invested twenty thousand dollars in the concern, as special partner, in connection with two other gentlemen, who each contributed twenty thousand dollars, as general partners. Within a month after the publication of the first number of the *Illustrated News,* which was issued on the first day of January, 1853, our weekly circulation had reached seventy thousand. Numerous and almost insurmountable difficulties, for novices in the business, continued however to arise, and my partners becoming weary and disheartened with constant over-exertion, were anxious to wind up the enterprise at the end of the first year. The good-will and the engravings were sold to *Gleason's Pictorial,* in Boston, and the concern was closed without loss.

In 1851, when the idea of opening a World's Fair in New York was first broached, I was waited upon by Mr. Riddell and the other originators of the scheme, and invited to join in getting it up. I declined, giving as a reason that such a project was, in my opinion, premature. I felt that it was following quite too closely upon its London prototype, and assured the projectors that I could see in it nothing but certain loss. The plan, however, was carried out, and a charter obtained from the New York Legislature. The building was erected on a plot of ground upon Reservoir Square, leased to the association, by the City of New York, for one dollar per annum. The location, being four miles distant from the City Hall, was enough of itself to kill the enterprise. The stock was readily taken up, however, and the Crystal Palace opened to the public in July, 1853. Many thousands of strangers were brought to New York, and however disastrous the enterprise may have proved to the stockholders, it is evident that the general prosperity of the city has been promoted far beyond the entire cost of the whole speculation.

In February, 1854, numerous stockholders applied to

me to accept the Presidency of the Crystal Palace, or, as it was termed, "The Association for the Exhibition of the Industry of all Nations." I utterly declined listening to such a project, as I felt confident that the novelty had passed away, and that it would be difficult to revive public interest in the affair.

Shortly afterwards, however, I was waited upon by numerous influential gentlemen, and strongly urged to allow my name to be used. I repeatedly objected to this, and at last consented, much against my own judgment. Having been elected one of the directors, I was by that body chosen President. I accepted the office conditionally, reserving the right to decline if I thought, upon investigation, that there was no vitality left in the institution. Upon examining the accounts said to exist against the Association, many were pronounced indefensible by those who I supposed knew the facts in the case, while various debts existing against the concern were not exhibited when called for, and I knew nothing of their existence until after I accepted the office of President. I finally accepted it, only because no suitable person could be found who was willing to devote his entire time and services to the enterprise, and because I was frequently urged by directors and stockholders to take hold of it for the benefit of the city at large, inasmuch as it was well settled that the Palace would be permanently closed early in April, 1854, if I did not take the helm.

These considerations moved me, and I entered upon my duties with all the vigor which I could command. To save it from bankruptcy, I advanced large sums of money for the payment of debts, and tried by every legitimate means to create an excitement and bring it into life. By extraneous efforts, such as the Re-inauguration, the Monster Concerts of Jullien, the Celebration of Independence, etc., it was temporarily galvanized, and gave several life-like kicks, generally without material results, except prostrating those who handled it too familiarly;

but it was a corpse long before I touched it, and I found, after a thorough trial, that my first impression was correct, and that so far as my ability was concerned, "the dead could not be raised." I therefore resigned the presidency and the concern soon went into liquidation. . . .

CHAPTER XXV.

The Jerome Clock Company Entanglement.

I now come to a series of events which, all things considered, constitute one of the most remarkable experiences of my life—an experience which brought me much
pain and many trials; which humbled my pride and
threatened me with hopeless financial ruin; and yet, nevertheless, put new blood in my veins, fresh vigor in my
action, warding off all temptation to rust in the repose
which affluence induces, and developed, I trust, new and
better elements of manliness in my character. This trial
carried me through a severe and costly discipline, and
now that I have passed through it and have triumphed
over it, I can thank God for sending it upon me, though I
feel no special obligations to the human instruments employed in the severe chastening.

When the blow fell upon me, I thought that I could
never recover; the event has shown, however, that I have
gained both in character and fortune, and what threatened, for years, to be my ruin, has proved one of the most
fortunate happenings of my career. The "Bull Run" of
my life's battle was a crushing defeat, which, unknown to
me at the time, only presaged the victories which were
to follow.

In my general plan of presenting the facts and incidents of my life in chronological order, I shall necessarily
introduce in the history of the next seven years, an account of my entanglement in the "Jerome Clock Com-

pany,"—how I was drawn into it, how I got out of it, and what it did to me and for me. The great notoriety given to my connection with this concern—the fact that the journals throughout the country made it the subject of news, gossip, sympathy, abuse, and advice to and about me, my friends, my persecutors, and the public generally—seems to demand that the story should be briefly but plainly told. The event itself has passed away and with it the passions and excitements that were born of it; and I certainly have no desire now to deal in personalities or to go into the question of the motives which influenced those who were interested, any farther than may be strictly essential to a fair and candid statement of the case.

It is vital to the narrative that I should give some account of the new city, East Bridgeport, and my interests therein, which led directly to my subsequent complications with the Jerome Clock Company.

In 1851, I purchased from Mr. William H. Noble, of Bridgeport, the undivided half of his late father's homestead, consisting of fifty acres of land, lying on the east side of the river, opposite the City of Bridgeport. We intended this as the nucleus of a new city, which we concluded could soon be built up, in consequence of many natural advantages that it possesses.

Before giving publicity to our plans, however, we purchased one hundred and seventy-four acres contiguous to that which we already owned, and laid out the entire property in regular streets, and lined them with trees, reserving a beautiful grove of six or eight acres, which we inclosed, and converted into a public park. We then commenced selling alternate lots, at the same price which the land cost us by the acre. Our sales were always made on the condition that a suitable dwelling-house, store, or manufactory should be erected upon the land, within one year from the date of purchase; that every building should be placed at a certain distance from the street, in a style of architecture approved by us; that the grounds should be enclosed with acceptable fences, and kept clean and neat, with other conditions which would render the locality a desirable one for respectable residents, and operate for the mutual benefit of all persons who should become settlers in the new city.

This entire property consists of a beautiful plateau of ground, lying within less than half a mile of the centre of Bridgeport city. Considering the superiority of the situation, it is a wonder that the City of Bridgeport was not originally founded upon that side of the river. The late Dr. Timothy Dwight, for a long time President of Yale College, in his "Travels in New England in 1815," says of the locality:

"There is not in the State a prettier village than the borough of Bridgeport. In the year 1783, there were scarcely half a dozen houses in this place. It now contains probably more than one hundred, built on both sides of Pughquonnuck (Pequonnock) river, a beautiful mill-stream, forming at its mouth the harbor of Bridgeport. The situation of this village is very handsome, particularly on the eastern side of the river. A more cheerful and elegant piece of ground can scarcely be imagined than the point which stretches between the Pughquonnuck and the old mill-brook; and the prospects presented by the harbors at the mouths of these streams, the Sound, and the surrounding country, are, in a fine season, gay and brilliant, perhaps without a parallel."

This "cheerful and elegant piece of ground," as Dr. Dwight so truly describes it, had only been kept from market by the want of means of access. A new foot-bridge was built, connecting this place with the City of Bridgeport, and a public toll-bridge which belonged to us was thrown open to the public free. We also obtained from the State Legislature a charter for erecting a toll-bridge between the two bridges already existing, and under that charter we put up a fine covered draw-bridge at a cost of $16,000 which also we made free to the public for several years. We built and leased to a union company of young coach makers a large and elegant coach manufactory, which was one of the first buildings erected there, and which went into operation on the first of January, 1852, and was the beginning of the extensive manufactories which were subsequently built in East Bridgeport.

Besides the inducement which we held out to purchasers to obtain their lots at a merely nominal price, we advanced one half, two-thirds, and frequently all the funds necessary to erect their buildings, permitting them to repay us in sums as small as five dollars, at their own convenience. This arrangement enabled many persons to secure and ultimately pay for homes which they could not otherwise have obtained. We looked for our profits solely to the rise in the value of the reserved lots, which we were confident must ensue. Of course, these extraordinary inducements led many persons to build in the new city, and it began to develop and increase with a rapidity rarely witnessed in this section of the country. Indeed, our speculation, which might be termed a profitable philanthropy, soon promised to be so remunerative, that I offered Mr. Noble for his interest in the estate, $60,000 more than the prime cost, which offer he declined.

It will thus be seen that, in 1851, my pet scheme was to build up a city in East Bridgeport. I had made a large fortune and was anxious to be released from the harassing cares of active business. But I could not be idle, and if I could be instrumental in giving value to land comparatively worthless; if I could by the judicious investment of a portion of my capital open the way for new industries and new homes, I should be of service to my fellow men and find grateful employment for my energies and time. I saw that in case of success there was profit in my project, and I was enough like mankind in general to look upon the enlargement of my means as a consummation devoutly and legitimately to be wished.

Yet, I can truly say that mere money-making was a secondary consideration in my scheme. I wanted to build a city on the beautiful plateau across the river; in the expressive phrase of the day, I "had East Bridgeport on the brain." Whoever approached me with a project which looked to the advancement of my new city, touched my weak side and found me an eager listener. The serpent that beguiled me was any plausible proposition that promised prosperity to East Bridgeport, and it was in this way that the coming city connected me with that source of so many annoyances and woes, the Jerome Clock Company.

There was a small clock manufactory in the town of Litchfield, Connecticut, in which I became a stock-holder to the amount of six or seven thousand dollars, and my duties as a director in the company called me occasionally to Litchfield and made me somewhat acquainted with the clock business. Thinking of plans to forward my pet East Bridgeport enterprise, it occurred to me that if the Litchfield clock concern could be transferred to my prospective new city, it would necessarily bring many families, thus increasing the growth of the place and the value of the property. Negotiations were at once commenced and the desired transfer of the business was the result. A new stock company was formed under the name of the "Terry & Barnum Manufacturing Company," and in 1852 a factory was built in East Bridgeport.

In 1855, I received a suggestion from a citizen of New Haven, that the Jerome Clock Company, then reputed to be a wealthy concern, should be removed to East Bridgeport, and shortly afterwards I was visited at Iranistan by Mr. Chauncey Jerome, the President of that company. The result of this visit was a proposition from the agent of the company, who also held power of attorney for the president, that I should lend my name as security for $110,000 in aid of the Jerome Clock Company, and the proffered compensation was the transfer of this great manufacturing concern, with its seven hundred to one thousand operatives, to my beloved East Bridgeport. It was just the bait for the fish; I was all attention; yet I must do my judgment the justice to say that I called for proofs, strong and ample, that the great company deserved its reputation as a substantial enterprise that might safely be trusted.

Accordingly, I was shown an official report of the directors of the company, exhibiting a capital of $400,-000, and a surplus of $187,000, in all, $587,000. The need for $110,000 more, was on account of a dull season, and the market glutted with the goods, and immediate money demands which must be met. I was also impressed with the pathetic tale that the company was exceedingly loth to dismiss any of the operatives, who would suffer greatly if their only dependence for their daily food was taken away.

The official statement seemed satisfactory, and I cordially sympathized with the philanthropic purpose of keeping the workmen employed, even in the dull season. The company was reputed to be rich; the President, Mr. Chauncey Jerome, had built a church in New Haven, at a cost of $40,000, and proposed to present it to a congregation; he had given a clock to a church in Bridgeport, and these things showed that he, at least, thought he was wealthy. The Jerome clocks were for sale all over the world, even in China, where the Celestials were said to take out the "movements," and use the cases for little temples for their idols, thus proving that faith was possible without "works." So wealthy and so widely-known a company would surely be a grand acquisition to my city.

Further testimony came in the form of a letter from the cashier of one of the New Haven banks, expressing the highest confidence in the financial strength of the concern, and much satisfaction that I contemplated giving temporary aid which would keep so many workmen and their families from suffering, and perhaps starvation. I had not, at the time, the slightest suspicion that my voluntary correspondent had any interest in the transfer of the Jerome Company from New Haven to East Bridgeport, though I was subsequently informed that the bank, of which my correspondent was the cashier, was almost the largest, if not the largest, creditor of the clock company.

Under all the circumstances, and influenced by the rose-colored representations made to me, not less than by my mania to push the growth of my new city, I finally accepted the proposition and consented to an agreement that I would lend the clock company my notes for a sum not to exceed $50,000, and accept drafts to an amount not to exceed $60,000. It was thoroughly understood that I was in no case to be responsible for one cent in excess of $110,000. I also received the written guaranty of Chauncey Jerome that in no event should I lose by the loan, as he would become personally responsible for the repayment. I was willing that my notes, when taken up, should be renewed, I cared not how often, provided the stipulated maximum of $110,000 should never be exceeded. I was weak enough, however, under the representation that it was impossible to say exactly when it would be necessary to use the notes, to put my name to several notes for $3,000, $5,000, and $10,000, leaving the date of payment blank; but it was agreed that the blanks should be filled to make the notes payable in five, ten, or even sixty days from the date, according to the exigencies of the case, and I was careful to keep a memorandum of the several amounts of the notes.

On the other side it was agreed that the Jerome Company should exchange its stock with the Terry & Barnum stockholders and thus absorb that company and unite the entire business in East Bridgeport. It was scarcely a month before the secretary wrote me that the company would soon be in condition to "snap its fingers at the banks."

Nevertheless, three months after the consolidation of the companies, a reference to my memoranda showed that I had already become responsible for the stipulated sum of $110,000. I was then called upon in New York by the agent who wanted five notes of $5,000 each and I declined to furnish them, unless I should receive in return an equal amount in my own cancelled notes, since he assured me they were cancelling these "every week." The cancelled notes were brought to me next day and I renewed them. This I did frequently, always receiving cancelled notes, till finally my confidence in the company became so established that I did not ask to see the notes that had been taken up, but furnished new accommodation paper as it was called for.

By and by I heard that the banks began to hesitate about discounting my paper, and knowing that I was good for $110,000 several times over, I wondered what was the matter, till the discovery came at last that my notes had not been taken up as was represented, and that some of the blank date notes had been made payable in twelve, eighteen, and twenty-four months. Further investigation revealed the frightful fact that I had endorsed for the clock company to the extent of more than half a million dollars, and most of the notes had been exchanged for old Jerome Company notes due to the banks and other creditors. My agent who made these startling discoveries came back to me with the refreshing intelligence that I was a ruined man!

Not quite; I had the mountain of Jerome debts on my back, but I found means to pay every claim against me at my bank, all my store and shop debts, notes to the amount of $40,000, which banks in my neighborhood, relying upon my personal integrity, had discounted for the Clock Company, and then I—failed!

What a dupe had I been! Here was a great company pretending to be worth $587,000, asking temporary assistance to the amount of $110,000, coming down with a crash, so soon as my helping hand was removed, and sweeping me down with it. It failed; and even after absorbing my fortune, it paid but from twelve to fifteen per cent of its obligations, while, to cap the climax, it never removed to East Bridgeport at all, notwithstanding this was the only condition which ever prompted me to advance one dollar to the rotten concern!

If at any time my vanity had been chilled by the fear that after my retirement from the Jenny Lind enterprise the world would forget me, this affair speedily reassured me; I had notice enough to satisfy the most inordinate craving for notoriety. All over the country, and even across the ocean, "Barnum and the Jerome Clock Bubble" was the great newspaper theme. I was taken to pieces, analyzed, put together again, kicked, "pitched into," tumbled about, preached to, preached about, and made to serve every purpose to which a sensation-loving world could put me. Well! I was now in training, in a new school, and was learning new and strange lessons.

Yet, these new lessons conveyed the old, old story. There were those who had fawned upon me in my prosperity, who now jeered at my adversity; people whom I had specially favored, made special efforts to show their ingratitude; papers which, when I had the means to make it an object for them to be on good terms with me, overloaded me with adulation, now attempted to overwhelm me with abuse; and then the immense amount of moralizing over the "instability of human fortunes," and especially the retributive justice that is sure to follow "ill-gotten gains," which my censors assumed to be the sum and substance of my honorably acquired and industriously worked for property. I have no doubt that much of this kind of twaddle was believed by the twaddlers to be sincere; and thus my case was actual capital to certain preachers and religious editors who were in want of fresh illustrations wherewith to point their morals.

As for myself, I was in the depths, but I did not despond. I was confident that with energetic purpose and divine assistance I should, if my health and life were spared, get on my feet again; and events have since fully justified and verified the expectation and the effort.

CHAPTER XXVII.

Rest, But Not Rust.

In the summer of 1855, previous to my financial troubles, feeling that I was independent and could retire from active business, I sold the American Museum collection and good will to Messrs. John Greenwood, Junior, and Henry D. Butler. They paid me double the amount the collection had originally cost, giving me notes for nearly the entire amount secured by a chattel mortgage, and hired the premises from my wife, who owned the Museum property lease, and on which, by the agreement of Messrs. Greenwood and Butler, she realized a profit of $19,000 a year. The chattel mortgage of Messrs. Greenwood and Butler, was, of course, turned over to the New York assignee with the other property.

And now there came to me a new sensation which was at times terribly depressing and annoying. My widespread reputation for shrewdness as a showman had induced the general belief that my means were still ample, and certain outside creditors who had bought my clock notes at a tremendous discount and entirely on speculation, made up their minds that they must be paid at once without waiting for the slow process of the sale of my property by the assignees.

They therefore took what are termed "supplementary proceedings," which enabled them to haul me any day before a judge for the purpose, as they phrased it, of "putting Barnum through a course of sprouts," and which meant an examination of the debtor under oath, compelling him to disclose everything with regard to his property, his present means of living, and so on.

I repeatedly answered all questions on these points; and reports of the daily examinations were published. Still another and another, and yet another creditor would haul me up; and his attorney would ask me the same questions which had already been answered and published half a dozen times. This persistent and unnecessary annoyance created considerable sympathy for me, which was not only expressed by letters I received daily from various parts of the country, but the public press, with now and then an exception, took my part, and even the Judges, before whom I appeared, said to me on more than one occasion, that as men they sincerely pitied me, but as judges of course they must administer the law. After a while, however, the judges ruled that I need not answer any question propounded to me by an attorney if I had already answered the same question to some other attorney in a previous examination in behalf of other creditors. In fact, one of the judges, on one occasion, said pretty sharply to an examining attorney:

"This, sir, has become simply a case of persecution. Mr. Barnum has many times answered every question that can properly be put to him to elicit the desired information; and I think it is time to stop these examinations. I advise him to not answer one interrogatory which he has replied to under any previous inquiries."

These things gave me some heart, so that at last, I went up to the "sprouts" with less reluctance, and began to pay off my persecutors in their own coin.

On one occasion, a dwarfish little lawyer, who reminded me of "Quilp," commenced his examination in behalf of a note-shaver who held a thousand dollar note, which it seemed he had bought for seven hundred dollars. After the oath had been administered the little "limb of the law" arranged his pen, ink and paper, and in a loud voice, and with a most peremptory and supercilious air, asked:

"What is your name, sir?"

I answered him, and his next question, given in a louder and more peremptory tone, was:

"What is your business?"

"Attending bar," I meekly replied.

"Attending bar!" he echoed, with an appearance of much surprise; "Attending bar! Why, don't you profess to be a temperance man—a teetotaler?"

"I do," I replied.

"And yet, sir, do you have the audacity to assert that you peddle rum all day, and drink none yourself?"

"I doubt whether that is a relevant question," I said in a low tone of voice.

"I will appeal to his honor the judge, if you don't answer it instantly," said Quilp in great glee.

"I attend bar, and yet never drink intoxicating liquors," I replied.

"Where do you attend bar, and for whom?" was the next question.

"I attend the bar of this court, nearly every day, for the benefit of two-penny, would-be lawyers and their greedy clients," I answered.

A loud tittering in the vicinity only added to the vexation which was already visible on the countenance of my interrogator, and he soon brought his examination to a close.

On another occasion, a young lawyer was pushing his inquiries to a great length, when, in a half laughing, apologetic tone, he said:

"You see, Mr. Barnum, I am searching after the small things; I am willing to take even the crumbs which fall from the rich man's table!"

"Which are you, Lazarus, or one of the dogs?" I asked.

"I guess a blood-hound would not smell out much on

this trail," he said good-naturedly, adding that he had no more questions to ask.

I still continued to receive many offers of pecuniary assistance, which, whenever proposed in the form of a gift, I invariably refused. In a number of instances, personal friends tendered me their checks for $500, $1,000, and other sums, but I always responded in substance: "Oh, no, I thank you; I do not need it; my wife has considerable property, besides a large income from her Museum lease. I want for nothing; I do not owe a dollar for personal obligations that is not already secured, and when the clock creditors have fully investigated and thought over the matter, I think they will be content to divide my property among themselves and let me up."

Just after my failure, and on account of the ill-health of my wife, I spent a portion of the summer with my family in the farmhouse of Mr. Charles Howell, at Westhampton, on Long Island. The place is a mile west of Quogue, and was then called "Ketchebonneck." The thrifty and intelligent farmers of the neighborhood were in the habit of taking summer boarders, and the place had become a favorite resort. Mr. Howell's farm lay close upon the ocean and I found the residence a cool and delightful one. Surf bathing, fishing, shooting and fine roads for driving made the season pass pleasantly and the respite from active life and immediate annoyance from my financial troubles was a very great benefit to me.

Our landlord was an eccentric character, who took great pleasure in showing me to his friends and neighbors as "the Museum man," and consequently, as a great curiosity for in his estimation, the American Museum was chief among the institutions of New York. He was in a habit of gathering shells and such rarities as came within his reach, which he took to the city and disposed of at the Museum. He often spoke of certain phenomena in his neighborhood, which he thought would take well with the public, if they were properly brought out. One day he said:

"Mr. Barnum, I am going to Moriches this
and I want you to go along with me and see a great curiosity there is there."

"What is it?" I asked.

"It is a man who has got a natural 'honk,' " replied
Howell, "and it is worth fifty dollars a year to him."

"A what?" I inquired.

"A honk! a honk! a perfectly natural honk! he makes
fifty dollars a year out of it," Howell reiterated.

I could not comprehend what a "honk" was, but concluded that if it was worth fifty dollars a year among the
Long Island fishermen and farmers who could hardly be
expected to pay much for mere sight-seeing, it would be
much more valuable to exhibit in the Museum. So I remarked that as I was authorized by Messrs. Greenwood
and Butler to purchase curiosities for them, I would go
with him and buy the honk from its possessor if I could
get it at a reasonable price.

"Buy it!" exclaimed Howell; "I guess you can't buy it!
You don't seem to understand me; the man has got a natural honk, I tell you; that is, he honks exactly like a wild
goose; when flocks are flying over he goes out and honks
and the geese, supposing that some goose has settled and
is honking for the rest of the flock to come down and
feed, all fly towards the ground and he 'lets into 'em' with
his gun, thus killing a great many, and in this way his
honk is worth fifty dollars a year to him, and perhaps
more."

I decided not to attempt to buy the "honk," but my
eagerness to do so and my entire ignorance of the character of the curiosity furnished food for laughter to Howell
and his neighbors for a long time.

One morning we discovered that the waves had
thrown upon the beach a young black whale some twelve
feet long. It was dead, but the fish was hard and fresh and
I bought it for a few dollars from the men who had taken
possession of it. I sent it at once to the Museum, where it
was exhibited in a huge refrigerator for a few days,

creating considerable excitement, the general public considering it "a big thing on ice," and the managers gave
me a share of the profits, which amounted to a sufficient
sum to pay the entire board bill of my family for the
season.

This incident both amused and amazed my Long Island landlord. "Well, I declare," said he, "that beats all;
you are the luckiest man I ever heard of. Here you come
and board for four months with your family, and when
your time is nearly up, and you are getting ready to leave,
out rolls a black whale on our beach, a thing never heard
of before in this vicinity, and you take that whale and pay
your whole bill with it! I wonder if that ain't 'providential'? Why, that beats the 'natural honk' all to pieces!"
This was followed by such a laugh as only Charles Howell
could give, and like one of his peculiar sneezes, it re-
sounded, echoed, and re-echoed through the whole
neighborhood.

Soon after my return to New York, something occurred which I foresaw, I thought, at the time, was likely
indirectly to lead me out of the wilderness into a clear
field again, and, indeed, it eventually did so. Strange to
say, my new city which had been my ruin was to be my
redemption, and dear East Bridgeport which plunged me
into the slough was to bring me out again. "Dear" as the
place had literally proved to me, it was to be yet dearer, in
another and better sense, hereafter.

The now gigantic Wheeler & Wilson Sewing Machine Company was then doing a comparatively small,
yet rapidly growing business at Watertown, Connecticut.
The Terry & Barnum clock factory was standing idle,
almost worthless, in East Bridgeport, and Wheeler &
Wilson saw in the empty building, the situation, the ease
of communication with New York, and other advantages, precisely what they wanted, provided they could
procure the premises at a rate which would compensate them for the expense and trouble of removing their
establishment from Watertown. It is enough to say here,

that the clock factory was sold for a trifle and the Wheeler & Wilson Company moved into it and speedily enlarged it. I felt then that this was providential; the fact that the empty building could be cheaply purchased was the main motive for the removal of this Watertown enterprise to East Bridgeport, and was one of the first indications that my failure might prove a "blessing in disguise." It was a fresh impulse towards the building up of the new city and the consequent increase of the value of the land belonging to my estate. Many persons did not see these things in the same light in which they were presented to me, but I had so long pondered upon the various means which were to make the new city prosperous, that I was quick to catch any indication which promised benefit to East Bridgeport.

This important movement of the Wheeler and Wilson Company gave me the greatest hope, and moreover, Mr. Wheeler kindly offered me a loan of $5,000, without security, and as I was anxious to have it used in purchasing the East Bridgeport property, when sold at public auction by my assignees, and also in taking up such clock notes as could be bought at a reasonable percentage, I accepted the offer and borrowed the $5,000. This sum, with many thousand dollars more belonging to my wife, was devoted to these purposes.

It seemed as if I had now got hold of the thread which would eventually lead me out of the labyrinth of financial difficulty in which the Jerome entanglement had involved me. Though the new plan promised relief, and actually did succeed, even beyond my most sanguine expectations, eventually putting more money into my pocket than the Jerome complication had taken out—yet I also foresaw that the process would necessarily be very slow. In fact, two years afterwards I had made very little progress. But I concluded to let the new venture work out itself and it would go on as well without my personal presence and attention, perhaps even better. Growing trees, money at interest, and rapidly rising real estate, work for their owners all night as well as all day, Sundays included, and when the proprietors are asleep or away, and with the design of cooperating in the new accumulation and of saving something to add to the amount, I made up my mind to go to Europe again. I was anxious for a change of scene and for active employment, and equally desirous of getting away from the immediate pressure of troubles which no effort on my part could then remove. While my affairs were working out themselves in their own way and in the speediest manner possible, I might be doing something for myself and for my family.

Accordingly, leaving all my business affairs at home in the hands of my friends, early in 1857 I set sail once more for England, taking with me General Tom Thumb, and also little Cordelia Howard and her parents. This young girl had attained an extended reputation for her artistic personation of "Little Eva," in the play of "Uncle Tom," and she displayed a precocious talent in her rendering of other juvenile characters. With these attractions, and with what else I might be able to do myself, I determined to make as much money as I could, intending to remit the same to my wife's friends, for the purpose of repurchasing a portion of my estate, when it was offered at auction, and of redeeming such of the clock notes as could be obtained at reasonable rates.

CHAPTER XXVIII.

Abroad Again.

On arriving at Liverpool, I found that my old friends, Mr. and Mrs. Lynn, of the Waterloo Hotel, had changed very little during my ten years' absence from England. Even the servants in the hotel were mainly those whom I left there when I last went away from Liverpool—which illustrates, in a small way, how much less changeable, and more "conservative" the English people are than we are. The old head-waiter, Thomas, was still head-waiter, as he had been for full twenty years. His hair was more silvered, his gait was slower, his shoulders had rounded, but he was as ready to receive, as I was to repeat, the first order I ever gave him, to wit: "Fried soles and shrimp sauce."

And among my many friends in Liverpool and London, but one death had occurred, and with only two exceptions they all lived in the same buildings, and pursued the same vocations as when I left them in 1847. When I reached London, I found one of these exceptions to be Mr. Albert Smith, who, when I first knew him, was a dentist, a literary hack, a contributor to *Punch,* and a writer for the magazines,—and who was now transformed to a first-class showman in the full tide of success, in my own old exhibition quarters in Egyptian Hall, Piccadilly.

A year or two before, he had succeeded in reaching the top of Mont Blanc, and after publishing a most interesting account, which was re-published and translated into several languages, the whole world over, he concluded to make further use of his expedition by adapting it to a popular entertainment. He therefore illustrated his ascent by means of a finely painted and accurate panorama, and he accompanied the exhibition with a descriptive lecture full of amusing and interesting incidents, illustrative of his remarkable experiences in accomplishing the difficult ascent. He also gave a highly-colored and exciting narrative of his entire journey from London to Switzerland, and back again, including his trip up and down the Rhine, and introducing the many peculiar characters of both sexes, he claimed to have met at different points during his tour. These he imitated and presented in so life-like a manner, as to fairly captivate and convulse his audiences.

It was one of the most pleasing and popular entertainments ever presented in London, and was immensely remunerative to the projector,—resulting, indeed, in a very handsome fortune. The entertainments were patronized by the most cultivated classes, for information was blended with amusement, and in no exhibition then in London was there so much genuine fun. Two or three times Albert Smith was commanded to appear before the Queen at Buckingham Palace, and at Windsor, and as he gave his entertainment with great success on these occasions, spite of the fact that he could not take his panorama with him, it can readily be imagined that the frame was quite as good as the picture, and that the lecture as compared with the panorama, admirable as both were, was by no means the least part of the "show."

Calling upon Albert Smith, I found him the same kind, cordial friend as ever, and he at once put me on the free list at his entertainment, and insisted upon my dining frequently with him at his favorite club, the Garrick.

The first time I witnessed his exhibition he gave me a sly wink from the stage at the moment of his describing a scene in the golden chamber of St. Ursula's church in

Cologne, where the old sexton was narrating the story of the ashes and bones of the eleven thousand innocent virgins who, according to tradition, were sacrificed on a certain occasion. One of the characters whom he pretended to have met several times on his trip to Mont Blanc, was a Yankee, whom he named "Phineas Cutecraft." The wink came at the time he introduced Phineas in the Cologne Church, and made him say at the end of the sexton's story about the Virgins' bones:

"Old fellow, what will you take for that hull lot of bones? I want them for my Museum in America!"

When the question had been interpreted to the old German, he exclaimed in horror, according to Albert Smith:

"Mine Gott! it is impossible! We will never sell the Virgins' bones!"

"Never mind," replied Phineas Cutecraft, "I'll send another lot of bones to my Museum, swear mine are the real bones of the Virgins of Cologne, and burst up your show!"

This always excited the heartiest laughter; but Mr. Smith knew very well that I would at once recognize it as a paraphrase of the scene wherein he had figured with me in 1844 at the porter's lodge of Warwick Castle. In the course of the entertainment, I found he had woven in numerous anecdotes I had told him at that time, and many incidents of our excursion were also travestied and made to contribute to the interest of his description of the ascent of Mont Blanc.

When we went to the Garrick club that day, Albert Smith introduced me to several of his acquaintances as his "teacher in the show business." As we were quietly dining together, he remarked that I must have recognized several old acquaintances in the anecdotes at his entertainment. Upon my answering that I did, "indeed," he remarked, "you are too old a showman not to know that in order to be popular, we must snap up and localize all the good things which we come across." By thus engrafting his various experiences upon his Mont Blanc entertainment, Albert Smith succeeded in serving up a salmagundi feast, which was relished alike by royal and less distinguished palates.

At one of the Egyptian Hall matinees, Albert Smith, espying me in the audience, sent an usher to me with a note of invitation to dine with him and a number of friends immediately after the close of the entertainment. To this invitation he added the request that as soon as he concluded his lecture I should at once come to him through the small door under the stage at the end of the orchestra, and by thus getting ahead of the large crowd of ladies and gentlemen composing the audience we should save time and reach the club at an hour for an early dinner.

As soon as he uttered the last word of his lecture, I pushed for the little door, the highly distinguished audience, which on this occasion was mainly made up of ladies, meanwhile slowly progressing towards the exits, while the orchestra was "playing them out" with selections of popular music. Closing the stage door behind me, I instantly found myself enveloped in that Egyptian darkness which was peculiar, I suppose, if not appropriate, to that part of Egyptian Hall. I could hear Smith and his assistants walking on the stage over my head, but I dare not call out lest some nervous Duchess or Countess should faint under the apprehension that the hall was on fire, or that some other severe disaster threatened.

Groping my way blindly and hitting my head several times against sundry beams, at last, to my joy, I reached the knob of the door which led me into this hole, but to my dismay it had been locked from the outside! In feeling about, however, I discovered a couple of bell pulls, both of which I desperately jerked and heard a faint tinkling in two opposite directions. Next, I heard the heavy canvas drop-curtain roll down rapidly till it struck the stage with a thud. Then the music in the orchestra suddenly ceased, and I could readily understand by the shrieks of the

women and the loud protestations of masculine voices
that the gas had been turned off and the whole house left
in darkness. This was followed by hurried and heavy
footsteps on the stage, the imprecations of stage car-
penters and gasmen, jargon of foreign musicians in the
orchestra, and the earnest voice of my friend Smith excitedly exclaiming: "Who rung those bells? why are we all
left in the dark? Light up here at once; bless my soul!
what does all this mean?"

I was amazed, yet amused and half alarmed. What to
do, I did not know, so I sat still on a box which I had
stumbled over, as well as upon, afraid to move or put out
my hand lest I might touch some machinery which would
give the signal for thunder and lightning, or an earth-
quake, or more likely, a Mont Blanc avalanche. Restored
tranquility overhead assured me that the gas had been
relighted. I knew Smith must be anxiously awaiting me,
for he was not a man to be behind time when so important a matter as dinner was the motive of the appointment. Something desperate must be done; so I carefully
groped my way to the stage door again and with a strong
effort managed to wrench it open. Covered with dust and
perspiration I followed behind the rear of the out-going
audience and found Smith, to whom I narrated my
under-ground experiences.

Brushes, water and towels soon put me once more in
presentable condition and we went to the Garrick Club
where we dined with several gentlemen of note. Smith
could not refrain from relating my mishaps and their
consequences in my search for him under difficulties, and
worse yet, under his stage, and great was the merriment
over the idea that an old manager like myself should so
lose his reckoning in a place with which he might well be
supposed to be perfectly familiar.

When the late William M. Thackeray made his first
visit to the United States, I think in 1852, he called on me
at the Museum with a letter of introduction from our mutual friend Albert Smith. He spent an hour with me,

mainly for the purpose of asking my advice in regard to the management of the course of lectures on "The English Humorists of the Eighteenth Century," whic! he proposed to deliver, as he did afterwards, with very great success, in the principal cities of the Union. I gave him the best advice I could as to management, and the cities he ought to visit, for which he was very grateful and he called on me whenever he was in New York. I also saw him repeatedly when he came to America the second time with his admirable lectures on "The Four Georges," which, it will be remembered he delivered in the United States in the season of 1855–56, before he read these lectures to audiences in Great Britain. My relations with this great novelist, I am proud to say, were cordial and intimate; and now, when I called upon him, in 1857, at his own house he grasped me heartily by the hand and said:

"Mr. Barnum, I admire you more than ever. I have read the accounts in the papers of the examinations you underwent in the New York courts, and the positive pluck you exhibit under your pecuniary embarrassments is worthy of all praise. You would never have received credit for the philosophy you manifest, if these financial misfortunes had not overtaken you."

I thanked him for his compliment, and he continued:

"But tell me, Barnum, are you really in need of present assistance? for if you are you must be helped."

"Not in the least," I replied, laughing; "I need more money in order to get out of bankruptcy and I intend to earn it; but so far as daily bread is concerned, I am quite at ease, for my wife is worth £30,000 or £40,000."

"Is it possible?" he exclaimed, with evident delight; "well now, you have lost all my sympathy; why, that is more than I ever expect to be worth; I shall be sorry for you no more."

During my stay in London, I met Thackeray several times, and on one occasion I dined with him. He was a most genial, noble-hearted gentleman. In our conversations he spoke with the warmest appreciation of America, and of his numerous friends in this country, and he repeatedly expressed his obligations to me for the advice and assistance I had given him on the occasion of his first lecturing visit to the United States.

The late Charles Kean, then manager of the Princess's Theatre, in London, was also exceedingly polite and friendly to me. He placed a box at my disposal at all times, and took me through his theatre to show me the stage, dressing rooms, and particularly the valuable "properties" he had collected. Among other things, he had twenty or more complete suits of real armor and other costumes and appointments essential to the production of historical plays, in the most complete and authentic manner. In the mere matter of stage-setting, Charles Kean has never been surpassed.

Otto Goldschmidt, the husband of Jenny Lind, also called on me in London. He and his wife were then living in Dresden, and he said the first thing his wife desired him to ask me was, whether I was in want. I assured him that I was not, although I was managing to live in an economical way and my family would soon come over to reside in London. He then advised me to take them to Dresden, saying that living was very cheap there; and, he added, "my wife will gladly look up a proper house for you to live in." I thankfully declined his proffered kindness, as Dresden was too far away from my business. A year subsequent to this, a letter was generally published in the American papers, purporting to have been written to me by Jenny Lind, and proffering me a large sum of money. I immediately pronounced the letter a forgery, and I soon afterwards received a communication from a young reporter in Philadelphia acknowledging himself as the author, and saying that he wrote it from a good motive, hoping it would benefit me. On the contrary it annoyed me exceedingly.

My old friends Julius Benedict and Giovanni Belletti, called on me and we had some very pleasant dinners together, when we talked over incidents of their travels in America. Among the gentlemen whom I met in London, some of them quite frequently at dinners, were Mr. George Augustus Sala, Mr. Edmund Yates, Mr. Horace Mayhew, Mr. Alfred Bunn, Mr. Lumley, of Her Majesty's Theatre, Mr. Buckstone, of the Haymarket, Mr. Charles Kean, our princely countrymen Mr. George Peabody, Mr. J. M. Morris, the manager, Mr. Bates, of Baring, Brothers & Co., Mr. Oxenford, dramatic critic of the London *Times,* Dr. Ballard, the American dentist, and many other eminent persons.

I had numerous offers from professional friends on both sides of the Atlantic who supposed me to be in need of employment. Mr. Barney Williams, who had not then acted in England, proposed in the kindest manner to make me his agent for a tour through Great Britain, and to give me one-third of the profits which he and Mrs. Williams might make by their acting. Mr. S. M. Pettengill, of New York, the newspaper advertising agent, offered me the fine salary of $10,000 a year to transact business for him in Great Britain. He wrote to me: "when you failed in consequence of the Jerome clock notes, I felt that your creditors were dealing hard with you; that they should have let you up and give you a chance, and they would have fared better and I wish I was a creditor so as to show what I would do." These offers, both from Mr. Williams and Mr. Pettengill, I was obliged to decline.

Mr. Lumley, manager of Her Majesty's Theatre, used to send me an order for a private box for every opera night, and I frequently availed myself of his courtesy. I had an idea that much money might be made by transferring his entire opera company, which then included Piccolomini and Titjiens to New York for a short season. The plan included the charter of a special steamer for the company and the conveyance of the entire troup, including the orchestra, with their instruments, and the chorus, costumes, scores, and properties of the company. It was a gigantic scheme, which would no doubt have been pecuniarily successful, and Mr. Lumley and I went so far as to draw up the preliminaries of an arrangement, in which I was to share a due proportion of the profits for my assistance in the management; but after a while, and to the evident regret of Mr. Lumley, the scheme was given up.

Meanwhile, I was by no means idle. Cordelia Howard as "Little Eva," with her mother as the inimitable "Topsy," were highly successful in London and other large cities, while General Tom Thumb, returning after so long an absence, drew crowded houses wherever he went. These were strong spokes in the wheel that was moving slowly but surely in the effort to get me out of debt, and, if possible, to save some portion of my real estate. Of course, it was not generally known that I had any interest whatever in either of these exhibitions; if it had been, possibly some of the clock creditors would have annoyed me; but I busied myself in these and in other ways, working industriously and making much money, which I constantly remitted to my trusty agent at home. . . .

CHAPTER XXXI.

The Art of
Money Getting.

S eeing the necessity of making more money to assist in
extricating me from my financial difficulties, and
leaving my affairs in the hands of Mr. James D. Johnson—my wife and youngest daughter, Pauline, boarding
with my eldest daughter, Mrs. Thompson, in Bridgeport—early in 1858, I went back to England, and took
Tom Thumb to all the principal places in Scotland and
Wales, giving many exhibitions and making much money
which was remitted, as heretofore, to my agents and assignees in America.

Finding, after a while, that my personal attention was
not needed in the Tom Thumb exhibitions and confiding
him almost wholly to agents who continued the tour
through Great Britain, under my general advice and instruction, I turned my individual attention to a new field.
At the suggestion of several American gentlemen, resident in London, I prepared a lecture on "The Art of
Money Getting." I told my friends that, considering my
clock complications, I thought I was more competent to
speak on "The Art of Money Losing"; but they encouraged me by reminding me that I could not have lost
money, if I had not previously possessed the faculty of
making it. They further assured me that my name having
been intimately associated with the Jenny Lind concerts
and other great money-making enterprises, the lecture
would be sure to prove attractive and profitable.

The old clocks ticked in my ear the reminder that I should improve every opportunity to "turn an honest penny," and my lecture was duly announced for delivery in the great St. James' Hall, Regent Street, Piccadilly. It was thoroughly advertised—a feature I never neglected—and, at the appointed time, the hall, which would hold three thousand people, was completely filled, at prices of three and two shillings, (seventy-five and fifty cents,) per seat, according to location. It was the evening of December 29, 1858. Since my arrival in Great Britain the previous spring, I had spent months in travelling with General Tom Thumb, and now I was to present myself in a new capacity to the English public as a lecturer. I could see in my audience all my American friends who had suggested this effort; all my theatrical and literary friends; and as I saw several gentlemen whom I knew to be connected with the leading London papers, I felt sure that my success or failure would be duly chronicled next morning. There was, moreover, a general audience that seemed eager to see the "showman" of whom they had heard so much, and to catch from his lips the "art" which, in times past, had contributed so largely to his success in life. Stimulated by these things, I tried to do my best and I think I did it. . . .

After delivering my lecture many times in different places, a prominent publishing house in London, offered me £1,200 ($6,000,) for the copyright. This offer I declined, not that I thought the lecture worth more money, but because I had engaged to deliver it in several towns and cities, and I thought the publication would be detrimental to the public delivery of my lecture. It was a source of very considerable emolument to me, bringing in much money, which went towards the redemption of my pecuniary obligations, so that the lecture itself was an admirable illustration of "The Art of Money Getting."

CHAPTER XXXIII.

Richard's Himself Again.

In 1859 I returned to the United States. During my last visit abroad I had secured many novelties for the Museum, including the Albino Family, which I engaged at Amsterdam, and Thiodon's mechanical theatre, which I found at Southampton, beside purchasing many curiosities. These things all afforded me a liberal commission, and thus, by constant and earnest effort, I made much money, besides what I derived from the Tom Thumb exhibitions, my lectures, and other enterprises. All of this money, as well as my wife's income and a considerable sum raised by selling a portion of her property, was faithfully devoted to the one great object of my life at that period—my extrication from those crushing clock debts. I worked and I saved. When my wife and youngest daughter were not boarding in Bridgeport, they lived frugally in the suburbs, in a small one-story house which was hired at the rate of $150 a year. I had now been struggling about four years with the difficulties of my one great financial mistake, and the end still seemed to be far off. I felt that the land, purchased by my wife in East Bridgeport at the assignees' sale, would, after a while, increase rapidly in value; and on the strength of this expectation more money was borrowed for the sake of taking up the clock notes, and some of the East Bridgeport property was sold in single lots, the proceeds going to the same object.

them. I had once retired from the establishment a man of independent fortune; I was now ready to return, to make, if possible, another fortune.

On the 17th of March, 1860, Messrs. Butler & Greenwood signed an agreement to sell and deliver to me on the following Saturday, March 24th, their good will and entire interest in the Museum collection. This fact was thoroughly circulated and it was everywhere announced in blazing posters, placards and advertisements which were headed, "Barnum on his feet again." It was furthermore stated that the Museum would be closed, March 24th, for one week for repairs and general renovation, to be re-opened, March 31st, under the management and proprietorship of its original owner. It was also announced that on the night of closing I would address the audience from the stage.

The American Museum, decorated on that occasion, as on holidays, with a brilliant display of flags and banners, was filled to its utmost capacity, and I experienced profound delight at seeing hundreds of old friends of both sexes in the audience. I lacked but four months of being fifty years of age; but I felt all the vigor and ambition that fired me when I first took possession of the premises twenty years before; and I was confident that the various experiences of that score of years would be valuable to me in my second effort to secure an independence. . . .

At last, in March 1860, all the clock indebtedness was satisfactorily extinguished, excepting some $20,000 which I had bound myself to take up within a certain number of months, my friend, James D. Johnson, guaranteeing my bond to that effect. Mr. Johnson was by far my most effective agent in working me through these clock troubles, and in aiding to bring them to a successful conclusion. Another man, however, who pretended to be my friend, and whom I liberally paid to assist in bringing me out of my difficulties, gained my confidence, possessed himself of a complete knowledge of the situation of my affairs, and then coolly proposed to Mr. Johnson to counteract all my efforts to get out of debt, and to divide between them what could be got out of my estate. Failing in this, the scoundrel, taking advantage of the confidence reposed in him, slyly arranged with the owners of clock notes to hold on to them, and share with him whatever they might gain by adopting his advice, he assuming that he knew all my secrets and that I would soon come out all right again. Thus I had to contend with foes from within as well as without; but the "spotting" of this traitor was worth something, for it opened my eyes in relation to former transactions in which I had intrusted large sums of money to his hands, and it put me on guard for the future. But I bear no malice towards him; I only pity him, as I do any man who knows so little of the true road to contentment and happiness as to think that it lies in the direction of dishonesty.

I need not dwell upon the details of what I suffered from the doings of those heartless, unscrupulous men who fatten upon the misfortunes of others. It is enough to say that I triumphed over them and all my troubles. I was once more a free man. At last I was able to make proclamation that "Richard's himself again"; that Barnum was once more on his feet. The Museum had not flourished greatly in the hands of Messrs. Greenwood & Butler, and so, when I was free, I was quite willing to take back the property upon terms that were entirely satisfactory to

CHAPTER XXXV.

East Bridgeport.

For nearly five years my family had been knocked about, the sport of adverse fortune, without a settled home. Sometimes we boarded, and at other times we lived in a small hired house. Two of my daughters were married, and my youngest daughter, Pauline, was away at boarding school. The health of my wife was much impaired, and she especially needed a fixed residence which she could call "home." Accordingly, in 1860, I built a pleasant house adjoining that of my daughter Caroline, in Bridgeport, and one hundred rods west of the grounds of Iranistan. I had originally a tract of twelve acres, but half of it had been devoted to my daughter, and on the other half I now proposed to establish my own residence. To prepare the site it was necessary to cart in several thousands of loads of dirt to fill up the hollow and to make the broad, beautiful lawn, in the centre of which I erected the new house, and after supplying the place with fountains, shrubbery, statuary and all that could adorn it, I named my new home "Lindencroft." It was, in truth, a very delightful place, complete and convenient in all respects, and there is scarcely a more beautiful residence in Bridgeport now.

Meanwhile, my pet city, East Bridgeport, was progressing with giant strides. The Wheeler and Wilson Sewing Machine manufactory had been quadrupled in size, and employed about a thousand workmen. Numerous other large factories had been built, and scores of first-class houses were erected, besides many neat, but smaller and cheaper houses for laborers and mechanics. That piece of property, which, but eight years before, had been farm land, with scarcely six houses upon the whole tract, was now a beautiful new city, teeming with busy life, and looking as neat as a new pin. The greatest pleasure which I then took, or even now take, was in driving through those busy streets, admiring the beautiful houses and substantial factories, with their thousands of prosperous workmen, and reflecting that I had, in so great a measure, been the means of adding all this life, bustle and wealth to the City of Bridgeport. And reflection on this subject only confirmed in my mind the great doctrine of compensations. How plain was it in my case, that an "apparent evil" was a "blessing in disguise!" How palpable was it now, that, had it not been for the clock failure, this prosperity could not have existed here. An old citizen of Bridgeport used to say to me, when, a few years before, he had noticed my zeal in trying to build up the east side:

"Mr. Barnum, your contemplated new city is like a fire made with chestnut wood; it burns so long as you keep blowing it, and when you stop, it goes out!"

I like, now-a-days to laugh at him about his "chestnut wood fire." Of course, I did blow the fire in all possible ways, but the result proved that the wood which fed the fire was not chestnut, but the best and soundest old hickory. The situation was everything that could be desired, and I knew that in order to induce manufacturers to establish their business in the new city, a prime requisite was the advantage I could offer to employers, agents and workmen, to secure good and cheap homes in the vicinity of their place of labor. . . .

The land in East Bridgeport was originally purchased by me at from $50 to $75, and from those sums to $300 per acre; and the average cost of all I bought on that side of the river was $200 per acre. Some portions of this land are now assessed in the Bridgeport tax-list at from $3,-000 to $4,000 per acre. At the time I joined Mr. Noble in this enterprise, the site we purchased was not a part of the City of Bridgeport. It is now, however, a most important section of the city, and the three bridges connecting the two banks of the river, and originally chartered as toll-bridges, have been bought by the city and thrown open as free highways to the public. A horse railroad, in which I took one-tenth part of the stock, connects the two portions of the city, extending westerly beyond Iranistan and Lindencroft, while a branch road runs to the beautiful "Sea-side Park" on the Sound shore.

The eastern line of East Bridgeport, when I first purchased so large a portion of the property, was bounded by a long, narrow swale or valley of salt meadow, through which a small stream passed, and which was flooded with salt water at every tide. At considerable expense, I erected a dam at the foot of this meadow, and thus converted this heretofore filthy, repulsive, mosquito-inhabited and malaria-breeding marsh into a charming sheet of water, which is now known as Pembroke Lake. If this improvement had not been made, in all probability the eastern portion of my property would never have been devoted to dwelling houses; as it is, Barnum Street has been extended by means of a bridge across the lake, and the eastern shore is already studded with houses. The land on that side of the lake lies in the town of Stratford, and the growth of the new settlement promises to be as rapid as that of East Bridgeport. . . .

CHAPTER XXXVI.

More About the Museum.

On the 13th of October, 1860, the American Museum was the scene of another re-opening, which was, in fact, the commencement of the fall dramatic season, the summer months having been devoted to pantomime. A grand flourish of trumpets in the way of newspaper advertisements and flaming posters drew a crowded house. Among other attractions, it was announced that Mr. Barnum would introduce a mysterious novelty never before seen in that establishment. I appeared upon the stage behind a small table, in front of which was nailed a white sack, on which was inscribed, in large letters, "The cat let out of the bag." I then stated that, having spent two of the summer months in the country, leaving the Museum in charge of Mr. Greenwood, he had purchased a curiosity with which he was not satisfied; but, for my part, I thought he had received his money's worth, and I proposed to exhibit it to the audience, for the purpose of getting their opinion on the subject. I stated that a farmer came in from the country, and said he had got a "cherry-colored cat" at home which he would like to sell; that Mr. Greenwood gave him a writing promising to pay him twenty-five dollars for such a cat delivered in good health, provided it was not artificially colored; and that the cat was then in the bag in front of the table, ready for exhibition. Whereupon, my assistant drew from the bag a common black cat, and I informed the audience that when the farmer brought his "cherry-colored cat," he quietly remarked to Mr. Greenwood, that, of course, he meant "a cat of the color of black cherries." The laughter that followed this narration was uproarious, and the audience unanimously voted that the "cherry-colored cat," all things considered, was well worth twenty-five dollars. The cat, adorned with a collar bearing the inscription, "The Cherry-colored Cat," was then placed in the cage of the "Happy Family," and the story getting into the newspapers, it became another advertisement of the Museum.

In 1861, I learned that some fishermen at the mouth of the St. Lawrence had succeeded in capturing a living white whale, and I was also informed that a whale of this kind, if placed in a box lined with sea-weed and partially filled with salt water, could be transported by land to a considerable distance, and be kept alive. It was simply necessary that an attendant, supplied with a barrel of salt water and a sponge, should keep the mouth and blow-hole of the whale constantly moist. It seemed incredible that a living whale could be "expressed" by railroad on a five days' journey, and although I knew nothing of the white whale or its habits, since I had never seen one, I determined to experiment in that direction. Landsman as I was, I believed that I was quite as competent as a St. Lawrence fisherman to superintend the capture and transportation of a live white whale.

When I had fully made up my mind to attempt the task, I made every provision for the expedition, and took precaution against every conceivable contingency. I determined upon the capture and transport to my Museum of at least two living whales, and prepared in the basement of the building a brick and cement tank, forty feet long, and eighteen feet wide, for the reception of the marine monsters. When this was done, taking two trusty assistants, I started upon my whaling expedition. Going by rail to Quebec, and thence by the Grand Trunk Railroad, ninety miles, to Wells River, where I chartered a sloop to Elbow Island (Isle au Coudres), in the St.

Lawrence River, and found the place populated by Canadian French people of the most ignorant and dirty description. They were hospitable, but frightfully filthy, and they gained their livelihood by farming and fishing. Immense quantities of maple-sugar are made there, and in exploring about the island, we saw hundreds of birch-bark buckets suspended to the trees to catch the sap. After numerous consultations, extending over three whole days, with a party of twenty-four fishermen, whose gibberish was almost as untranslatable as it was unbearable, I succeeded in contracting for their services to capture for me, alive and unharmed, a couple of white whales, scores of which could at all times be discovered by their "spouting" within sight of the island. I was to pay these men a stipulated price per day for their labor, and if they secured the whales, they were to have a liberal bonus.

The plan decided upon was to plant in the river a "kraal," composed of stakes driven down in the form of a V, leaving the broad end open for the whales to enter. This was done in a shallow place, with the point of the kraal towards shore; and if by chance one or more whales should enter the trap at high water, my fishermen were to occupy the entrance with their boats, and keep up a tremendous splashing and noise till the tide receded, when the frightened whales would find themselves nearly "high and dry," or with too little water to enable them to swim, and their capture would be the next thing in order. This was to be effected by securing a slip-noose of stout rope over their tails, and towing them to the sea-weed lined boxes in which they were to be transported to New York.

All this was simple enough "on paper"; but several days elapsed before a single spout was seen inside the kraal, though scores of whales were constantly around and near it. In time, it became exceedingly aggravating to see the whales glide so near the trap without going into it, and our patience was sorely tried. One day a whale actually went into the kraal, and the fishermen proposed to capture it; but I wanted another, and while we waited for number two to go in, number one, knowing the proverb, probably, and having an eye to his own interests, went out. Two days afterwards, I was awakened at daylight by a great noise, and amid the clamor of many voices, I caught the cheering news that two whales were even then within the kraal, and hastily dressing myself, I took a boat for the exciting scene. The real difficulty, which was to get the whales into the trap, was now over, and the details of capture and transportation could safely be left to my trusty assistants and the fishermen. What they were to do until the tide went out and thereafter was once more fully explained; and after depositing money enough to pay the bill, if the capture was successful, I started at once for Quebec. There I learned by telegraph that both whales had been caught, boxed, and put on board sloop for the nearest point where they could be transshipped in the cars. I had made every arrangement with the railway officials, and had engaged a special car for the precious and curious freight.

Elated as I was at the result of this novel enterprise, I had no idea of hiding my light under a bushel, and I immediately wrote a full account of the expedition, its intention, and its success, for publication in the Quebec and Montreal newspapers. I also prepared a large number of brief notices which I left at every station on the line, instructing telegraph operators to "take off" all "whaling messages" that passed over the wires to New York, and to inform their fellow townsmen at what hour the whales would pass through each place. The result of these arrangements may be imagined; at every station crowds of people came to the cars to see the whales which were travelling by land to Barnum's Museum, and those who did not see the monsters with their own eyes, at least saw some one who had seen them, and I thus secured a tremendous advertisement, seven hundred miles long, for the American Museum.

When I arrived in New York, a dozen despatches had

come from the "whaling expedition," and they continued
to come every few hours. These I bulletined in front of
the Museum and sent copies to the papers. The excitement was intense, and, when at last, these marine monsters arrived and were swimming in the tank that had
been prepared for them, anxious thousands literally
rushed to see the strangest curiosities ever exhibited in
New York.

Thus was my first whaling expedition a great success;
but I did not know how to feed or to take care of the
monsters, and, moreover, they were in fresh water, and
this, with the bad air in the basement, may have hastened
their death, which occurred a few days after their arrival,
but not before thousands of people had seen them. Not at
all discouraged, I resolved to try again. My plan now was
to connect the water of New York bay with the basement
of the Museum by means of iron pipes under the street,
and a steam engine on the dock to pump the water. This
I actually did at a cost of several thousand dollars, with an
extra thousand to the aldermanic "ring" for the privilege,
and I constructed another tank in the second floor of the
building. This tank was built of slate and French glass
plates six feet long, five feet broad, and one inch thick,
imported expressly for the purpose, and the tank,
when completed, was twenty-four feet square, and cost
$4,000. It was kept constantly supplied with what would
be called Hibernically, "fresh" salt water, and inside of it
I soon had two white whales, caught, as the first had
been, hundreds of miles below Quebec, to which city
they were carried by a sailing vessel, and from thence
were brought by railway to New York.

Of this whole enterprise, I confess I was very proud
that I had originated it and brought it to such successful
conclusion. It was a very great sensation, and it added
thousands of dollars to my treasury. The whales, however, soon died—their sudden and immense popularity
was too much for them—and I then despatched agents to
the coast of Labrador, and not many weeks thereafter I

had two more live whales disporting themselves in my monster aquarium. Certain envious people started the report that my whales were only porpoises, but this petty malice was turned to good account, for Professor Agassiz, of Harvard University, came to see them, and gave me a certificate that they were genuine white whales, and this indorsement I published far and wide.

The tank which I had built in the basement served for a yet more interesting exhibition. On the 12th of August, 1861, I began to exhibit the first and only genuine hippopotamus that had ever been seen in America, and for several weeks the Museum was thronged by the curious who came to see the monster. I advertised him extensively and ingeniously, as "the great behemoth of the Scriptures," giving a full description of the animal and his habits, and thousands of cultivated people, biblical students, and others, were attracted to this novel exhibition. There was quite as much excitement in the city over this wonder in the animal creation as there was in London when the first hippopotamus was placed in the zoölogical collection in Regent's Park.

Having a stream of salt water at my command at every high tide, I was enabled to make splendid additions to the beautiful aquarium, which I was the first to introduce into this country. I not only procured living sharks, porpoises, sea horses, and many rare fish from the sea in the vicinity of New York, but in the summer of 1861, I despatched a fishing smack and crew to the Island of Bermuda and its neighborhood, whence they brought scores of specimens of the beautiful "angel fish," and numerous other tropical fish of brilliant colors and unique forms. These fish were a great attraction to all classes, and especially to naturalists and others, who commended me for serving the ends of science as well as amusement. But as cold weather approached, these tropical fish began to die, and before the following spring, they were all gone. I, therefore, replenished this portion of my aquaria during the summer, and for several summers in succession, by sending a special vessel to the Gulf for specimens. These operations were very expensive, but I really did not care for the cost, if I could only secure valuable attractions.

In the same year, I bought out the Aquarial Gardens in Boston, and soon after removed the collection to the Museum. I had now the finest assemblage of fresh as well as salt water fish ever exhibited, and with a standing offer of one hundred dollars for every living brook-trout, weighing four pounds or more, which might be brought to me, I soon had three or four of these beauties, which trout-fishermen from all parts of the country came to New York to see. But the trout department of my Museum required so much care, and was attended with such constant risks, that I finally gave it up.

In December, 1861, I made one of my most "palpable hits." I was visited at the Museum by a most remarkable dwarf, who was a sharp, intelligent little fellow, with a deal of drollery and wit. He had a splendid head, was perfectly formed, was very attractive, and, in short, for a "showman," he was a perfect treasure. His name, he told me, was George Washington Morrison Nutt, and his father was Major Rodnia Nutt, a substantial farmer, of Manchester, New Hampshire. I was not long in despatching an efficient agent to Manchester, and in overcoming the competition with other showmen who were equally eager to secure this extraordinary pigmy. The terms upon which I engaged him for three years were so large that he was christened the $30,000 Nutt; I, in the mean time, conferring upon him the title of Commodore. As soon as I engaged him, placards, posters and the columns of the newspapers proclaimed the presence of "Commodore Nutt," at the Museum. I also procured for the Commodore a pair of Shetland ponies, miniature coachman and footman, in livery, gold-mounted harness and an elegant little carriage, which, when closed, represented a gigantic English walnut. The little Commodore attracted great attention and grew rapidly in public favor. General Tom Thumb was then travelling in the South and West. For some years he had not been exhibited in New York, and during these years he had increased considerably in rotundity and had changed much in his general appearance. It was a singular fact, however, that Commodore Nutt was almost a *fac-simile* of General Tom Thumb, as he looked half-a-dozen years before. Consequently, very many of my patrons, not making allowance for the time which had elapsed since they had last seen the General, declared that I was trying to play "Mrs. Gamp" with my "Mrs. Harris"; that there was, in fact, no such person as "Commodore Nutt"; and that I was exhibiting my old friend Tom Thumb under a new name. The mistake was very natural, and to me it was very laughable, for the more I tried to convince people of their error, the more they winked and looked wise, and said, "It's pretty well done, but you can't take me in."

Commodore Nutt enjoyed the joke very much. He would sometimes half admit the deception, simply to add to the bewilderment of the doubting portion of my visitors. After he had been in the Museum a few weeks, I took the Commodore to Bridgeport to spend a couple of days by way of relaxation. Many of the citizens of Bridgeport, who had known Tom Thumb from his birth, would salute the Commodore as the General Tom Thumb. The little fellow would return these salutes, for he delighted in keeping up the illusion.

Going into a crowded barber-shop one morning with the little Commodore, we met my friend Mr. Gideon Thompson, who was sitting there, and who called out:

"Good morning, Charley; how are you? When did you get home?"

"I'm quite well, thank you, and I arrived last night," responded the Commodore, with due gravity.

"I've got a horse now that will beat yours," said Mr. Thompson.

"He must be pretty fast, then."

"Well, Charley, I'll drive out by your mother's the first fine day, and give you a trial."

"All right," said little Nutt, "but you had better not wager too much on your fast horse, for you know mine is some pumpkins."

"Well, Uncle Gid.," I exclaimed, "you are 'had' this time; this little gentleman is not General Tom Thumb, but Commodore Nutt."

"What!" roared friend Gid.; "do you think I am an infernal fool? Why, I knew Charley Stratton years before you ever saw him, didn't I, General?"

No one in the room suspected that my little friend was any other than General Tom Thumb, till Mr. William Bassett, the General's brother-in-law, came in and remarked the "wonderful resemblance to our little Charley, as he looked years ago."

"Is not this the General?" inquired half a dozen astonished men, who were speedily assured he was not, but was quite another person. This gave rise to a proposition to exhibit the Commodore to the General's mother, and a coach was procured, and Mr. Bassett, the Commodore, and I went to Mrs. Stratton's house. When we arrived, the Commodore shouted out:

"How are you, mother?"

But the mother, of all persons in Bridgeport, was not to be deceived, though she expressed her astonishment at the very striking likeness the Commodore bore to her son as he once looked. Mrs. Bassett concurred in the testimony and said the Commodore looked so much like her brother that she was loth to let him go. It is no wonder that other people were deceived by the resemblance.

It was evident that here was an opportunity to turn all doubts into hard cash by simply bringing the two dwarf Dromios together, and showing them on the same platform. I therefore induced Tom Thumb to bring his Western engagements to a close, and to appear for four weeks, beginning with August 11, 1862, in my Museum. Announcements headed "The Two Dromios," and "Two Smallest Men, and Greatest Curiosities Living," as I expected, drew large crowds to see them, and many came especially to solve their doubts with regard to the genuineness of the "Nutt." But here I was considerably nonplussed, for astonishing as it may seem, the doubts of many of the visitors were confirmed! The sharp people who were determined "not to be humbugged, anyhow," still declared that Commodore Nutt was General Tom Thumb, and that the little fellow whom I was trying to pass off as Tom Thumb, was no more like the General than he was like the man in the Moon. It is very amusing to see how people will sometimes deceive themselves by being too incredulous.

As an illustration—the "Australian Golden Pigeons" which deceived Old Adams were the occasion of another ludicrous incident. A shrewd lady, one of my neighbors in Connecticut, was visiting the Museum, and after inspecting the "Golden Angel Fish" swimming in one of the aquaria, she abruptly addressed me:

"You can't humbug me, Mr. Barnum; that fish is painted!"

"Nonsense!" said I, with a laugh; "the thing is impossible."

"I don't care, I know it is painted; it is as plain as can be."

"But, my dear Mrs. H., paint would not adhere to a fish in the water; and if it would, it would kill him."

She left the Museum not more than half convinced, and in the afternoon of the same day I met her in the California Menagerie. She knew I was part proprietor in the establishment, and seeing me in conversation with Old Adams, she came to me, her eyes glistening with excitement, and exclaimed—

"Oh, Mr. Barnum, I never saw anything so beautiful as those elegant "Golden Pigeons"; you must give me some of their eggs for my own pigeons to hatch; I should prize them beyond measure."

"Oh, you don't want 'Golden Pigeons,' " I said; "they are painted."

"No, they are not painted," said she, with a laugh, "but I half think the 'Angel Fish' is."

I could scarcely control my laughter as I explained: "Now, Mrs. H., I never spoil a good joke, even when the exposure betrays a Museum secret. I assure you, upon honor, that the "Australian Golden Pigeons," as they are labelled, are really painted; I bought them for the sole purpose of giving Old Adams a lesson; in their natural state they are nothing more than common white ruff-neck pigeons." She was convinced, and to this day she blushes whenever any allusion is made to the "Angel Fish" or the "Golden Pigeons."

In 1862, I sent the Commodore to Washington, and joining him there, I received an invitation from President Lincoln to call at the White House with my little friend. Arriving at the appointed hour I was informed that the President was in a special cabinet meeting, but that he had left word if I called to be shown in to him with the Commodore. These were dark days in the rebellion and I felt that my visit, if not ill-timed, must at all events be brief. When we were admitted Mr. Lincoln received us cordially, and introduced us to the members of the cabinet. When Mr. Chase was introduced as the Secretary of the Treasury, the little Commodore remarked:

"I suppose you are the gentleman who is spending so much of Uncle Sam's money?"

"No, indeed," said Secretary of War Stanton, very promptly: "I am spending the money."

"Well," said Commodore Nutt, "it is in a good cause, anyhow, and I guess it will come out all right."

His apt remark created much amusement. Mr. Lincoln then bent down his long, lank body, and taking Nutt by the hand, he said:

"Commodore, permit me to give you a parting word of advice. When you are in command of your fleet, if you find yourself in danger of being taken prisoner, I advise you to wade ashore."

The Commodore found the laugh was against him, but

placing himself at the side of the President, and gradually raising his eyes up the whole length of Mr. Lincoln's very long legs, he replied:

"I guess Mr. President, you could do that better than I could."

Commodore Nutt and the Nova Scotia giantess, Anna Swan, illustrate the old proverb sufficiently to show how extremes occasionally met in my Museum. He was the shortest of men and she was the tallest of women. I first heard of her through a quaker who came into my office one day and told me of a wonderful girl, seventeen years of age, who resided near him at Pictou, Nova Scotia, and who was probably the tallest girl in the world. I asked him to obtain her exact height, on his return home, which he did and sent it to me, and I at once sent an agent who in due time came back with Anna Swan. She was an intelligent and by no means ill-looking girl, and during the long period while she was in my employ she was visited by thousands of persons. After the burning of my second Museum, she went to England where she attracted great attention.

For many years I had been in the habit of engaging parties of American Indians from the far West to exhibit at the Museum, and had sent two or more Indian companies to Europe, where they were regarded as very great "curiosities." In 1864, ten or twelve chiefs of as many different tribes, visited the President of the United States at Washington. By a pretty liberal outlay of money, I succeeded in inducing the interpreter to bring them to New York, and to pass some days at my Museum. Of course, getting these Indians to dance, or to give any illustration of their games or pastimes, was out of the question. They were real chiefs of powerful tribes, and would no more have consented to give an exhibition of themselves than the Chief Magistrate of our own nation would have done. Their interpreter could not therefore promise that they would remain at the Museum for any definite time; "for," said he, "you can only keep them just so long as they suppose all your patrons come to pay them visits of honor. If they suspected that your Museum was a place where people paid for entering," he continued, "you could not keep them a moment after the discovery."

On their arrival at the Museum, therefore, I took them upon the stage and personally introduced them to the public. The Indians liked this attention from me, as they had been informed that I was the proprietor of the great establishment in which they were invited and honored guests. My patrons were of course pleased to see these old chiefs, as they knew they were the *"real* thing," and several of them were known to the public, either as being friendly or cruel to the whites. After one or two appearances upon the stage, I took them in carriages and visited the Mayor of New York in the Governor's room at the City Hall. Here the Mayor made them a speech of welcome, which being interpreted to the savages was responded to by a speech from one of the chiefs, in which he thanked the great "Father" of the city for his pleasant words, and for his kindness in pointing out the portraits of his predecessors hanging on the walls of the Governor's room.

On another occasion, I took them by special invitation to visit one of the large public schools up town. The teachers were pleased to see them, and arranged an exhibition of special exercises by the scholars, which they thought would be most likely to gratify their barbaric visitors. At the close of these exercises, one old chief arose, and simply said, "This is all new to us. We are mere unlearned sons of the forest, and cannot understand what we have seen and heard."

On other occasions, I took them to ride in Central Park, and through different portions of the city. At every street corner which we passed, they would express their astonishment to each other, at seeing the long rows of houses which extended both ways on either side of each cross-street. Of course, between each of these outside visits I would return with them to the Museum, and secure two or three appearances upon the stage to receive the people who had there congregated "to do them honor."

As they regarded me as their host, they did not hesitate to trespass upon my hospitality. Whenever their eyes rested upon a glittering shell among my specimens of conchology, especially if it had several brilliant colors, one would take off his coat, another his shirt, and insist that I should exchange my shell for their garment. When I declined the exchange, but on the contrary presented them with the coveted article, I soon found I had established a dangerous precedent. Immediately, they all commenced to beg for everything in my vast collection, which they happened to take a liking to. This cost me many valuable specimens, and often "put me to my trumps" for an excuse to avoid giving them things which I could not part with.

The chief of one of the tribes one day discovered an ancient shirt of chain-mail which hung in one of my cases of antique armor. He was delighted with it, and declared he must have it. I tried all sorts of excuses to prevent his getting it, for it had cost me a hundred dollars and was a great curiosity. But the old man's eyes glistened, and he would not take "no" for an answer. "The Utes have killed my little child," he told me through the interpreter; and now he must have this steel shirt to protect himself; and when he returned to the Rocky Mountains he would have his revenge. I remained inexorable until he finally brought me a new buckskin Indian suit, which he insisted upon exchanging. I felt compelled to accept his proposal; and never did I see a man more delighted than he seemed to be when he took the mailed shirt into his hands. He fairly jumped up and down with joy. He ran to his lodging room, and soon appeared again with the coveted armor upon his body, and marched down one of the main halls of the Museum, with folded arms, and head erect, occasionally patting his breast with his right hand, as much as to say, "now, Mr. Ute, look sharp, for I will soon be on the war path!"

Among these Indians were War Bonnet, Lean Bear, and Hand-in-the-water, chiefs of the Cheyennes; Yellow Buffalo, of the Kiowas; Yellow Bear, of the same tribe; Jacob, of the Caddos; and White Bull, of the Apaches. The little wiry chief known as Yellow Bear had killed many whites as they had travelled through the "far West." He was a sly, treacherous, blood-thirsty savage, who would think no more of scalping a family of women and children, than a butcher would of wringing the neck of a chicken. But now he was on a mission to the "Great Father" at Washington, seeking for presents and favors for his tribe, and he pretended to be exceedingly meek and humble, and continually urged the interpreter to announce him as a "great friend to the white man." He would fawn about me, and although not speaking or understanding a word of our language, would try to convince me that he loved me dearly.

In exhibiting these Indian warriors on the stage, I explained to the large audiences the names and characteristics of each. When I came to Yellow Bear I would pat him familiarly upon the shoulder, which always caused him to look up to me with a pleasant smile, while he softly stroked down my arm with his right hand in the most loving manner. Knowing that he could not understand a word I said, I pretended to be complimenting him to the audience, while I was really saying something like the following:

"This little Indian, ladies and gentlemen, is Yellow Bear, chief of the Kiowas. He has killed, no doubt, scores of white persons, and he is probably the meanest, black-hearted rascal that lives in the far West." Here I patted him on the head, and he, supposing I was sounding his praises, would smile, fawn upon me, and stroke my arm, while I continued: "If the blood-thirsty little villain understood what I was saying, he would kill me in a moment; but as he thinks I am complimenting him, I can safely state the truth to you, that he is a lying, thieving, treacherous, murderous monster. He has tortured to death poor, unprotected women, murdered their husbands, brained their helpless little ones; and he would gladly do the same to you or to me, if he thought he could escape punishment. This is but a faint description of the character of Yellow Bear." Here I gave him another patronizing pat on the head, and he, with a pleasant smile, bowed to the audience, as much as to say that my words were quite true, and that he thanked me very much for the high encomiums I had so generously heaped upon him.

After they had been about a week at the Museum, one of the chiefs discovered that visitors paid money for entering. This information he soon communicated to the other chiefs, and I heard an immediate murmur of discontent. Their eyes were opened, and no power could induce them to appear again upon the stage. Their dignity had been offended, and their wild, flashing eyes were anything but agreeable. Indeed, I hardly felt safe in their presence, and it was with a feeling of relief that I witnessed their departure for Washington the next morning.

In the spring of 1864, the United States Consul at Larnica, Island of Cyprus, Turkish Dominions, wrote me a letter, declaring that he and the English Consul, an American physician, resident in the island, and a large company of Europeans as well as natives, had seen the most remarkable object, no doubt, in the world,—a *lusus naturæ*, a feminine phenomenon. This woman was represented to have "four cornicles on her head, and one large horn, equal in size to an ordinary ram's horn, growing out of the side of her head"; and the consistency of the horns was represented to be similar to that of cows' or goats' horns. This singular story continued: "These horns have been growing for ten or twelve years, and were carefully concealed by the woman until a few weeks since, when a vision appeared in the person of an old man, and warned her to remove the veil she wore, or God would punish her. She sent to the Greek priest (she being of that persuasion), and confessed to him, and was ordered to uncover her head, which she at once did." She was subsequently seen by the entire population, and the French consul, in company with others, offered her fifty thousand piastres to go to Paris for exhibition. The English consul, I was further informed, had pronounced this woman to be "worth her weight in gold"; and I was assured that if I wished to add her to my "wonderful Museum, and present to the American public the most remarkable object yet exhibited," I had only to "send an agent immediately to secure the prize."

Informing myself of the trustworthiness of my correspondent (who also wrote a similar account to the New York *Observer*), I was not long in making up my mind to secure this freak of nature; and I despatched Mr. John Greenwood, Jr., in the steamer "City of Baltimore," for Liverpool, April 30, 1864. He went to London and Paris, and thence to Marseilles, where he took a Syrian and Egyptian steamer to Palermo, and from thence proceeded to Cyprus. On arriving, if he could have seen the woman at once, he could have re-embarked on the steamer, which sailed again in a few hours for other islands; but unfortunately, the woman was a few miles in the interior, and poor Greenwood was detained a month on the island before he could take another steamer to get away. Worse yet, the woman, spite of the impression she had made upon so many and such respectable witnesses, was really no curiosity after all, as it proved upon examination, that her "horns" were not horns at all, but fleshy excrescences, which may have been singularly shaped tumors, or wens. It is needless to add that my agent did not engage her; and after a month of discomfort and hard living, he succeeded in getting away, and sailed for Constantinople, mainly to see what could be done in the way of securing one or more Circassian women for exhibition in my Museum.

On his way through the Mediterranean, he had the fol-

lowing adventure: On board the steamer, the harem of a
Turkish Pasha occupied one side of the quarter-deck,
which was divided off from the rest by a hurdle fence run
longitudinally through the middle of the deck. Greenwood was one day sitting in an easy chair with his back to
these women and their attendants, when feeling his chair
move, he turned and saw one of the Pasha's wives getting
over the hurdle, and as there was scarcely room for her to
squeeze herself between the chairs in which passengers
were sitting, he moved his own chair out of the way and
rising, offered his hand to assist the woman over the
fence. She indignantly jumped back, and Greenwood was
immediately seized by two of the Pasha's attendants,
violently shaken, and taken to task in Turkish for daring
to offer to touch the hand of one of his Excellency's
women. Greenwood had that day formed the acquaintance of a fellow-passenger, a young Greek from Scio,
who was going to Beyrout to act as clerk for a merchant
in that place. He spoke good English, and seeing
Greenwood in trouble among the Turks, and knowing
that he could speak neither Greek or Arabic, he went to
the rescue, and demanded an explanation of the difficulty.

Upon hearing what was the trouble, he informed the
turbulent fellows that Greenwood had no motive in his
act beyond simple common courtesy. The prisoner, however, was still detained in the grasp of the Turks, till the
will of the insulted Pasha could be known. On deck soon
came the irate Pasha, in company with an old gentleman
who was said to have been tutor, formerly, to the present
Sultan of Turkey. When the two heard the charge and
the explanation, and had consulted together a little while,
Greenwood was released. But for the friendly interposi-
tion of the Greek, he might have been bastinadoed, or
even bowstrung.

During the remainder of the voyage he was closely
watched, but he was very careful to be guilty of no act of
"politeness," and he went on shore at Constantinople

without so much as saying good-by to the Pasha. In Constantinople he had some very singular adventures. To carry out his purpose of getting access to the very interior of the slave-marts, he dressed himself in full Turkish costume, learned a few words and phrases which would be necessary in his assumed character as a slave-buyer, and, as the Turks are a notably reticent people, he succeeded very well in passing himself off for what he appeared, though he ran a risk of detection many times every day. In this manner, he saw a large number of Circassian girls and women, some of them the most beautiful beings he had ever seen, and after a month in Constantinople and in other Turkish cities, he sailed for Marseilles, then went to Paris, picking up many treasures for my Museum, and returned to New York, after a journey of 13,112 miles.

CHAPTER XXXVII.

Mr. and Mrs. General Tom Thumb.

In 1862 I heard of an extraordinary dwarf girl, named Lavinia Warren, who was residing with her parents at Middleboro', Massachusetts, and I sent an invitation to her and her parents to come and visit me at Bridgeport. They came, and I found her to be a most intelligent and refined young lady, well educated, and an accomplished, beautiful and perfectly-developed woman in miniature. I succeeded in making an engagement with her for several years, during which she contracted—as dwarfs are said to have the power to do—to visit Great Britain, France, and other foreign lands.

Having arranged the terms of her engagement, I took her to the house of one of my daughters in New York, where she remained quietly, while I was procuring her wardrobe and jewelry, and making arrangements for her debut. As yet, nothing had been said in the papers about this interesting young lady, and one day as I was taking her home with me to Bridgeport, I met in the cars the wife of a wealthy menagerie proprietor, who introduced me to her two daughters, young ladies of sixteen and eighteen years of age, and then said:

"You have disguised the little Commodore very nicely."

"That is not Commodore Nutt," I replied, "it is a young lady whom I have recently discovered."

"Very well done, Mr. Barnum," replied Mrs. B., with a look of self satisfaction.

"Really," I repeated, "this *is* a young lady."

"Thank you, Mr. Barnum, but I know Commodore Nutt in whatever costume you put him; and I recognized him the moment you brought him into the car."

"But, Mrs. B.," I replied, "Commodore Nutt is now exhibiting in the Museum, and this is a little lady whom I hope to bring before the public soon."

"Mr. Barnum," she replied, "you forget that I am a showman's wife, conversant with all the showman's tricks, and that I cannot be deceived."

Seeing there was no prospect of convincing her, I replied in a confidential whisper, for such chance for a joke was not to be lost:

"Well, I see you are too sharp for me, but I beg you not to mention it, for you are the only person on board this train who suspects it is the Commodore."

"I will say nothing," she replied, "but do please bring the little fellow over here, for my daughters have never seen him."

I stepped and told Lavinia the joke and asked her to help carry it out. I then took her over where she got a seat in the midst of the three ladies.

"Ah, Commodore," whispered Mrs. B., "you have done it pretty well, but bless you, I knew those eyes and that nose the moment I saw you."

"Your eyes must be pretty sharp, then," replied Lavinia.

"Oh, you see people in our line understand these things, and are never deceived by appearances; but let me introduce you to these two young ladies, my daughters."

"We are happy to see you, sir," said one of the young ladies. They then enjoyed a very animated conversation, in the course of which they asked the "Commodore" all about his family, and Lavinia managed to answer the questions in such a way as to avoid suspicion. The ladies then informed the "Commodore" that there was a sweet little lady living in their town only sixteen years old, and if he would visit them, they would introduce him; that her family was highly respectable, and she would make him a capital wife! Lavinia thanked them and promised to visit them if it should be convenient. As the ladies left the car, they shook hands with Lavinia, kissed her, and in a whisper said "good morning, sir." Meeting the husband of the lady, some weeks afterwards, I told him the joke, and he enjoyed it so highly that he will probably never let his wife and daughters hear the last of it.

I purchased a very splendid wardrobe for Miss Warren, including scores of the richest dresses that could be procured, costly jewels, and in fact everything that could add to the charms of her naturally charming little person. She was then placed on exhibition at the Museum and from the day of her *début* she was an extraordinary success. Commodore Nutt was on exhibition with her, and although he was several years her junior he evidently took a great fancy to her. One day I presented to Lavinia a diamond and emerald ring, and as it did not exactly fit her finger, I told her I would give her another one and that she might present this one to the Commodore in her own name. She did so, and an unlooked-for effect was speedily apparent; the little Commodore felt sure that this was a love-token, and poor Lavinia was in the greatest trouble, for she considered herself quite a woman, and regarded the Commodore only as a nice little boy. But she did not like to offend him, and while she did not encourage, she did not openly repel his attentions. Miss Lavinia Warren, however, was never destined to be Mrs. Commodore Nutt.

It was by no means an unnatural circumstance that I should be suspected of having instigated and brought about the marriage of Tom Thumb with Lavinia Warren. Had I done this, I should at this day have felt no regrets, for it has proved, in an eminent degree, one of the "happy marriages." I only say, what is known to all of their immediate friends, that from first to last their engagement was an affair of the heart—a case of "love at first sight"—that the attachment was mutual, and that it only grows with the lapse of time. But I had neither part nor lot in instigating or in occasioning the marriage. And as I am anxious to be put right before the public, and so to correct whatever of false impression may have gained ground, I have procured the consent of all the parties to a sketch of the wooing, winning and nuptials. Of course I should not lay these details before the public, except with the sanction of those most interested. In this they consent to pay the penalty of distinction. And if the wooings of kings and queens must be told, why not the courtship and marriage of General and Mrs. Tom Thumb? The story is an interesting one, and shall be told alike to exonerate me from the suspicion named, and to amuse those—and they count by scores of thousands—who are interested in the welfare of the distinguished couple.

In the autumn of 1862, when Lavinia Warren was on exhibition at the Museum, Tom Thumb had no business engagement with me; in fact, he was not on exhibition at the time at all; he was taking a "vacation" at his house in Bridgeport. Whenever he came to New York he naturally called me, his old friend, at the Museum. He happened to be in the city at the time referred to, and one day he called, quite unexpectedly to me, while Lavinia was holding one of her levees. Here he now saw her for the first time, and very naturally made her acquaintance. He had a short interview with her, after which he came directly to my private office and desired to see me alone. Of course I complied with his request, but without the remotest suspicion as to his object. I closed the door, and the General took a seat. His first question let in the light. He inquired about the family of Lavinia Warren. I gave him the facts, which I clearly perceived gave him satisfaction of a peculiar sort. He then said, with great frankness, and with no less earnestness:

"Mr. Barnum, that is the most charming little lady I ever saw, and I believe she was created on purpose to be my wife! Now," he continued, "you have always been a friend of mine, and I want you to say a good word for me to her. I have got plenty of money, and I want to marry and settle down in life, and I really feel as if I must marry that young lady."

The little General was highly excited, and his general manner betrayed the usual anxiety, which, I doubt not, most of my readers will understand without a description. I could not repress a smile, nor forget my joke; and I said:

"Lavinia is engaged already."

"To whom—Commodore Nutt?" asked Tom Thumb, with much earnestness, and some exhibition of the "green-eyed monster."

"No, General, to me," I replied.

"Never mind," said the General, laughing, "you can exhibit her for a while, and then give up the engagement; but I do hope you will favor my suit with her."

I told the General that this was too sudden an affair; that he must take time to think of it; but he insisted that years of thought would make no difference, for his mind was fully made up.

"Well, General," I replied, "I will not oppose you in your suit, but you must do your own courting. I tell you, however, the Commodore will be jealous of you, and more than that, Miss Warren is nobody's fool, and you will have to proceed very cautiously if you can succeed in winning her affections."

The General thanked me, and promised to be very discreet. A change now came suddenly over him in several particulars. He had been (much to his credit) very fond of his country home in Bridgeport, where he spent his intervals of rest with his horses, and especially with his yacht, for his fondness for the water was his great passion. But now he was constantly having occasion to visit the city, and horses and yachts were strangely neglected. He had a married sister in New York, and his visits to her multiplied, for, of course, he came to New York "to see his sister!" His mother, who resided in Bridgeport, remarked that Charles had never before shown so much brotherly affection, nor so much fondness for city life.

His visits to the Museum were very frequent, and it was noticeable that new relations were being established between him and Commodore Nutt. The Commodore was not exactly jealous, yet he strutted around like a bantam rooster whenever the General approached Lavinia. One day he and the General got into a friendly scuffle in the dressing-room, and the Commodore threw the General upon his back in "double quick" time. The Commodore is lithe, wiry, and quick in his movements, but the General is naturally slow, and although he was considerably heavier than the Commodore, he soon found that he could not stand before him in a personal encounter. Moreover, the Commodore is naturally quick-tempered, and when excited, he brags about his knowledge of "the manly art of self-defence," and sometimes talks about pistols and bowie knives, etc. Tom Thumb, on the contrary, is by natural disposition decidedly a man of peace; hence, in this, agreeing with Falstaff as to what constituted the "better part of valor," he was strongly inclined to keep his distance, if the little Commodore showed any belligerent symptoms.

In the course of several weeks the General found numerous opportunities to talk with Lavinia, while the Commodore was performing on the stage, or was otherwise engaged; and, to a watchful discerner, it was evident he was making encouraging progress in the affair of the heart. He also managed to meet Lavinia on Sunday afternoons and evenings, without the knowledge of the Commodore; but he assured me he had not yet dared to suggest matrimony.

He finally returned to Bridgeport, and privately begged that on the following Saturday I would take Lavinia up to my house, and also invite him.

His immediate object in this was, that his mother might get acquainted with Lavinia, for he feared opposi-

tion from that source whenever the idea of his marriage
should be suggested. I could do no less than accede to his
proposal, and on the following Friday, while Lavinia and
the Commodore were sitting in the green-room, I said:

"Lavinia, you may go up to Bridgeport with me to-
morrow morning, and remain until Monday."

"Thank you," she replied; "it will be quite a relief to
get into the country for a couple of days."

The Commodore immediately pricked up his ears, and
said:

"Mr. Barnum, *I* should like to go to Bridgeport to-
morrow."

"What for?" I asked.

"I want to see my little ponies; I have not seen them
for several months," he replied.

I whispered in his ear, "you little rogue, *that* is the
pony you want to see," pointing to Lavinia.

He insisted I was mistaken. When I remarked that he
could not well be spared from the Museum, he said:

"Oh! I can perform at half past seven o'clock, and then
jump on to the eight o'clock evening train, and go up by
myself, reaching Bridgeport before eleven, and return
early Monday morning."

I feared there would be a clashing of interests between
the rival pigmies; but wishing to please him, I consented
to his request, especially as Lavinia also favored it. I
wished I could then fathom that little woman's heart, and
see whether she (who must have discovered the secret of
the General's frequent visits to the Museum) desired the
Commodore's visit in order to stir up the General's ardor,
or whether, as seemed to me the more likely, she was
seeking in this way to prevent a *denouement* which she
was not inclined to favor. Certain it is, that though I was
the General's confidant, and knew all his desires upon the
subject, no person had discovered the slightest evidence
that Lavinia Warren had ever entertained the remotest
suspicion of his thoughts regarding marriage. If she had

made the discovery, as I assume, she kept the secret well. In fact, I assured Tom Thumb that every indication, so far as any of us could observe, was to the effect that his suit would be rejected. The little General was fidgety, but determined; hence he was anxious to have Lavinia meet his mother, and also see his possessions in Bridgeport, for he owned considerable land and numerous houses there.

The General met us at the depot in Bridgeport, on Saturday morning, and drove us to my house in his own carriage—his coachman being tidily dressed, with a broad velvet ribbon and silver buckle placed upon his hat expressly for the occasion. Lavinia was duly informed that this was the General's "turn out"; and after resting half an hour at Lindencroft, he took her out to ride. He stopped a few moments at his mother's house, where she saw the apartments which his father had built expressly for him, and filled with the most gorgeous furniture—all corresponding to his own diminutive size. Then he took her to East Bridgeport, and undoubtedly took occasion to point out in great detail all of the houses which he owned, for he depended much upon having his wealth make some impression upon her. They returned, and the General stayed to lunch. I asked Lavinia how she liked her ride; she replied:

"It was very pleasant, but," she added, "it seems as if you and Tom Thumb owned about all of Bridgeport!"

The General took his leave and returned at five o'clock to dinner, with his mother. Mrs. Stratton remained until seven o'clock. She expressed herself charmed with Lavinia Warren; but not a suspicion passed her mind that little Charlie was endeavoring to give her this accomplished young lady as a daughter-in-law. The General had privately asked me to invite him to stay over night, for, said he, "If I get a chance, I intend to 'pop the question' before the Commodore arrives." So I told his mother I thought the General had better stop with us over night, as the Commodore would be up in the late train, adding that it would be more pleasant for the little

folks to be together. She assented, and the General was happy.

After tea Lavinia and the General sat down to play backgammon. As nine o'clock approached, I remarked that it was about time to retire, but somebody would have to sit up until nearly eleven o'clock, in order to let in the Commodore. The General replied:

"I will sit up with pleasure, if Miss Warren will remain also."

Lavinia carelessly replied, that she was accustomed to late hours, and she would wait and see the Commodore. A little supper was placed upon the table for the Commodore, and the family retired.

Now it happened that a couple of mischievous young ladies were visiting at my house, one of whom was to sleep with Lavinia. They were suspicious that the General was going to propose to Lavinia that evening, and, in a spirit of ungovernable curiosity, they determined, notwithstanding its manifest impropriety, to witness the operation, if they could possibly manage to do so on the sly. Of course this was inexcusable, the more so as so few of my readers, had they been placed under the same temptation, would have been guilty of such an impropriety! Perhaps I should hesitate to use the testimony of such witnesses, or even to trust it. But a few weeks after, they told the little couple the whole story, were forgiven, and all had a hearty laugh over it.

It so happened that the door of the sitting room, in which the General and Lavinia were left at the backgammon board, opened into the hall just at the side of the stairs, and these young misses, turning out the lights in the hall, seated themselves upon the stairs in the dark, where they had a full view of the cosy little couple, and were within easy ear-shot of all that was said.

The house was still. The General soon acknowledged himself vanquished at backgammon, and gave it up. After sitting a few moments, he evidently thought it was best to put a clincher on the financial part of his abilities;

so he drew from his pocket a policy of insurance, and handing it to Lavinia, he asked her if she knew what it was.

Examining it, she replied, "It is an insurance policy. I see you keep your property insured."

"But the beauty of it is, it is not my property," replied the General, "and yet I get the benefit of the insurance in case of fire. You will see," he continued, unfolding the policy, "this is the property of Mr. Williams, but here, you will observe, it reads 'loss, if any, payable to Charles S. Stratton, as his interest may appear.' The fact is, I loaned Mr. Williams three thousand dollars, took a mortgage on his house, and made him insure it for my benefit. In this way, you perceive, I get my interest, and he has to pay the taxes."

"That is a very wise way, I should think," remarked Lavinia.

"That is the way I do all my business," replied the General, complacently, as he returned the huge insurance policy to his pocket. "You see," he continued, "I never lend any of my money without taking bond and mortgage security, then I have no trouble with taxes; my principal is secure, and I receive my interest regularly."

The explanation seemed satisfactory to Lavinia, and the General's courage began to rise. Drawing his chair a little nearer to hers, he said:

"So you are going to Europe, soon?"

"Yes," replied Lavinia, "Mr. Barnum intends to take me over in a couple of months."

"You will find it very pleasant," remarked the General; "I have been there twice, in fact I have spent six years abroad, and I like the old countries very much."

"I hope I shall like the trip, and I expect I shall," responded Lavinia; "for Mr. Barnum says I shall visit all the principal cities, and he has no doubt I will be invited to appear before the Queen of England, the Emperor and Empress of France, the King of Prussia, the Emperor of Austria, and at the courts of any other countries which

we may visit. Oh! I shall like that, it will be so new to me."

"Yes, it will be very interesting indeed. I have visited most of the crowned heads," remarked the General, with an evident feeling of self-congratulation. "But are you not afraid you will be lonesome in a strange country?" asked the General.

"No, I think there is no danger of that, for friends will accompany me," was the reply.

"I wish I was going over, for I know all about the different countries, and could explain them all to you," remarked Tom Thumb.

"That would be very nice," said Lavinia.

"Do you think so?" said the General, moving his chair still closer to Lavinia's.

"Of course," replied Lavinia, coolly, "for I, being a stranger to all the habits and customs of the people, as well as to the country, it would be pleasant to have some person along who could answer all my foolish questions."

"I should like it first rate, if Mr. Barnum would engage me," said the General.

"I thought you remarked the other day that you had money enough, and was tired of travelling," said Lavinia, with a slightly mischievous look from one corner of her eye.

"That depends upon my company while travelling," replied the General.

"You might not find my company very agreeable."

"I would be glad to risk it."

"Well, perhaps Mr. Barnum would engage you, if you asked him," said Lavinia.

"Would you really like to have me go?" asked the General, quietly insinuating his arm around her waist, but hardly close enough to touch her.

"Of course I would," was the reply.

The little General's arm clasped the waist closer as he turned his face nearer to hers, and said:

"Don't you think it would be pleasanter if we went as man and wife?"

The little fairy quickly disengaged his arm, and remarked that the General was a funny fellow to joke in that way.

"I am not joking at all," said the General, earnestly, "it is quite too serious a matter for that."

"I wonder why the Commodore don't come?" said Lavinia.

"I hope you are not anxious for his arrival, for I am sure *I* am not," responded the General, "and what is more, I do hope you will say 'yes,' before he comes at all!"

"Really, Mr. Stratton," said Lavinia, with dignity, "if you are in earnest in your strange proposal, I must say I am surprised."

"Well, I hope you are not *offended,*" replied the General, "for I was never more in earnest in my life, and I hope you will consent. The first moment I saw you I felt that you were created to be my wife."

"But this is so sudden."

"Not so very sudden; it is several months since we first met, and you know all about me, and my family, and I hope you find nothing to object to in me."

"Not at all; on the contrary, I have found you very agreeable, in fact I like you very much as a friend, but I have not thought of marrying, and——"

"And what? my dear," said the General, giving her a kiss. "Now, I beg of you, don't have any 'buts' or 'ands' about it. You say you like me as a friend, why will you not like me as a husband? You ought to get married; I love you dearly, and I want you for a wife. Now, deary, the Commodore will be here in a few minutes, I may not have a chance to see you again alone; do say that we will be married, and I will get Mr. Barnum to give up your engagement."

Lavinia hesitated, and finally said:

"I think I love you well enough to consent, but I have

always said I would never marry without my mother's consent."

"Oh! I'll ask your mother. May I ask your mother? Come, say yes to that, and I will go and see her next week. May I do that, pet?"

Then there was a sound of something very much like the popping of several corks from as many beer bottles. The young eaves-droppers had no doubt as to the character of these reports, nor did they doubt that they sealed the betrothal, for immediately after they heard Lavinia say:

"Yes, Charles, you may ask my mother." Another volley of reports followed, and then Lavinia said, "Now, Charles, don't whisper this to a living soul; let us keep our own secrets for the present."

"All right," said the General, "I will say nothing; but next Tuesday I shall start to see your mother."

"Perhaps you may find it difficult to obtain her consent," said Lavinia.

At that moment a carriage drove up to the door, and immediately the bell was rung, and the little Commodore entered.

"*You* here, General?" said the Commodore, as he espied his rival.

"Yes," said Lavinia, "Mr. Barnum asked him to stay, and we were waiting for you; come, warm yourself."

"I am not cold," said the Commodore; "where is Mr. Barnum?"

"He has gone to bed," remarked the General, "but a nice supper has been prepared for you."

"I am not hungry, I thank you; I am going to bed. Which room does Mr. Barnum sleep in?" said the little bantam, in a petulant tone of voice.

His question was answered; the young eaves-droppers scampered to their sleeping apartments, and the Commodore soon came to my room, where he found me indulging in the foolish habit of reading in bed.

"Mr. Barnum, does Tom Thumb board here?" asked the Commodore, sarcastically.

"No," said I, "Tom Thumb does not *board* here. I invited him to stop over night, so don't be foolish, but go to bed."

"Oh, it's no affair of mine. I don't care anything about it; but I thought he had taken up his board here," replied the Commodore, and off he went to bed, evidently in a bad humor.

Ten minutes afterwards Tom Thumb came rushing into my room, and closing the door, he caught hold of my hand in a high state of excitement and whispered:

"We are engaged, Mr. Barnum! we are engaged! we are engaged!" and he jumped up and down in the greatest glee.

"Is that possible?" I asked.

"Yes, sir, indeed it is; but you must not mention it," he responded; "we agreed to tell nobody, so please don't say a word. I must tell *you,* of course, but 'mum is the word.' I am going, Tuesday, to get her mother's consent."

I promised secrecy, and the General retired in as happy a mood as I ever saw him. Lavinia also retired, but not a hint did she give to the young lady with whom she slept regarding the engagement. Indeed, our family plied her upon the subject the next day, but not a breath passed her lips that would give the slightest indication of what had transpired. She was quite sociable with the Commodore, and as the General concluded to go home the next morning, the Commodore's equanimity and good feelings were fully restored. The General made a call of half an hour Sunday evening, and managed to have an interview with Lavinia. The next morning she and the Commodore returned to New York in good spirits, I remaining in Bridgeport.

The General called on me Monday, however, bringing a very nice letter which he had written to Lavinia's mother. He had concluded to send this letter by his trusty friend, Mr. George A. Wells, instead of going himself, and he had just seen Mr. Wells, who had consented to go to Middleborough with the letter the following day, and to urge the General's suit, if it should be necessary.

The General went to New York on Wednesday, and was there to await Mr. Wells' arrival. On Wednesday morning the General and Lavinia walked into my office, and after closing the door, the little General said:

"Mr. Barnum, I want somebody to tell the Commodore that Lavinia and I are engaged, for I am afraid there will be a 'row' when he hears of it."

"Do it yourself, General," I replied.

"Oh," said the General, almost shuddering, "I would not dare to do it, he might knock me down."

"I will do it," said Lavinia; and it was at once arranged that I should call the Commodore and Lavinia into my office, and either she or myself would tell him. The General, of course, "vamosed."

When the Commodore joined us and the door was closed, I said:

"Commodore, do you know what this little witch has been doing?"

"No, I don't," he answered.

"Well, she has been cutting up one of the greatest pranks you ever heard of," I replied. "She almost deserves to be shut up, for daring to do it. Can't you guess what she has done?"

He mused a moment, and then looking at me, said in a low voice, and with a serious looking face, "Engaged?"

"Yes," said I, "absolutely engaged to be married to General Tom Thumb. Did you ever hear of such a thing?"

"Is that so, Lavinia?" asked the Commodore, looking her earnestly in the face.

"That is so," said Lavinia; "and Mr. Wells has gone to obtain my mother's consent."

The Commodore turned pale, and choked a little, as if he was trying to swallow something. Then, turning on his heel, he said, in a broken voice:

"I hope you may be happy."

As he passed out of the door, a tear rolled down his cheek.

"That is pretty hard," I said to Lavinia.

"I am very sorry," she replied, "but I could not help it. That diamond and emerald ring which you bade me present in my name, has caused all this trouble."

Half an hour after this incident, the Commodore came to my office, and said:

"Mr. Barnum, do you think it would be right for Miss Warren to marry Charley Stratton if her mother should object?"

I saw that the little fellow had still a slight hope to hang on, and I said:

"No, indeed, it would not be right."

"Well, she says she shall marry him any way; that she gives her mother the chance to consent, but if she objects, she will have her own way and marry him," said the Commodore.

"On the contrary," I replied, "I will not permit it. She is engaged to go to Europe for me, and I will not release her, if her mother does not fully consent to her marrying Tom Thumb."

The Commodore's eyes glistened with pleasure, as he replied:

"Between you and me, Mr. Barnum, I don't believe she will give her consent."

But the next day dissipated his hopes. Mr. Wells returned, saying that Lavinia's mother at first objected, for she feared it was a contrivance to get them married for the promotion of some pecuniary advantage; but, upon reading the letter from the General, and one still more urgent from Lavinia, and also upon hearing from Mr. Wells that, in case of their marriage, I should cancel all claims I had upon Lavinia's services, she consented.

After the Commodore had heard the news, I said to him:

"Never mind, Commodore, Minnie Warren is a better match for you; she is a charming little creature, and two years younger than you, while Lavinia is several years your senior."

"I thank you, sir," replied the Commodore, pompously, "I would not marry the best woman living; I don't believe in women, any way."

I then suggested that he should stand with little Minnie, as groom and bridesmaid, at the approaching wedding.

"No, sir!" replied the Commodore, emphatically; "I won't do it!"

That idea was therefore abandoned. A few weeks subsequently, when time had reconciled the Commodore, he told me that Tom Thumb had asked him to stand as groom with Minnie, at the wedding, and he was going to do so.

"When I asked you, a few weeks ago, you refused," I said.

"It was not your business to ask me," replied the Commodore, pompously. "When the proper person invited me I accepted."

Of course the approaching wedding was announced. It created an immense excitement. Lavinia's levees at the Museum were crowded to suffocation, and her photographic pictures were in great demand. For several weeks she sold more than three hundred dollars' worth of her *cartes de visite* each day. And the daily receipts at the Museum were frequently over three thousand dollars. I engaged the General to exhibit, and to assist her in the sale of pictures, to which his own photograph, of course, was added. I could afford to give them a fine wedding, and I did so.

The little couple made a personal application to Bishop Potter to perform the nuptial ceremony, and obtained his consent; but the matter became public, and outside pressure from some of the most squeamish of his clergy was brought to bear upon the bishop, and he rescinded his engagement.

This fact of itself, as well as the opposition that caused it, onlv added to the notoriety of the approaching wedding, and increased the crowds at the Museum. The financial result to me was a piece of good fortune, which I was, of course, quite willing to accept, though in this instance the "advertisement," so far as the fact of the betrothal of the parties with its preliminaries were concerned, was not of my seeking, as the recital now given shows. But seeing the turn it was taking in crowding the Museum, and pouring money into the treasury, I did not hesitate to seek continued advantage from the notoriety of the prospective marriage. Accordingly, I offered the General and Lavinia fifteen thousand dollars if they would postpone the wedding for a month, and continue their exhibitions at the Museum.

"Not for fifty thousand dollars," said the General, excitedly.

"Good for you, Charley," said Lavinia, "only you ought to have said not for a *hundred thousand,* for I would not!"

They both laughed heartily at what they considered my discomfiture, and such, looked at from a business point of view, it certainly was. The wedding day approached and the public excitement grew. For several days, I might say weeks, the approaching marriage of Tom Thumb was the New York "sensation." For proof of this I did not need what, however, was ample, the newspaper paragraphs. A surer index was in the crowds that passed into the Museum, and the dollars that found their way into the ticket office.

It was suggested to me that a small fortune in itself could be easily made out of the excitement. "Let the ceremony take place in the Academy of Music, charge a big price for admission, and the citizens will come in crowds." I have no manner of doubt that in this way twenty-five thousand dollars could easily have been obtained. But I had no such thought. I had promised to give the couple a genteel and graceful wedding, and I kept my word.

The day arrived, Tuesday, February 10, 1863. The ceremony was to take place in Grace Church, New York. The Rev. Junius Willey, Rector of St. John's Church in Bridgeport, assisted by the late Rev. Dr. Taylor, of Grace Church, was to officiate. The organ was played by Morgan. I know not what better I could have done, had the wedding of a prince been in contemplation. The church was comfortably filled by a highly select audience of ladies and gentlemen, none being admitted except those having cards of invitation. Among them were governors of several of the States, to whom I had sent cards, and such of those as could not be present in person were represented by friends, to whom they had given their cards. Members of Congress were present, also generals of the army, and many other prominent public men. Numerous applications were made from wealthy and distinguished persons for tickets to witness the ceremony, and as high as sixty dollars was offered for a single admission. But not a ticket was sold; and Tom Thumb and Lavinia Warren were pronounced "man and wife" before witnesses.

The following entirely authentic correspondence, the only suppression being the name of the person who wrote to Dr. Taylor and to whom Dr. Taylor's reply is addressed, shows how a certain would-be "witness" was not a witness of the famous wedding. In other particulars, the correspondence speaks for itself.

To THE REV. DR. TAYLOR.—*Sir:* The object of my unwillingly addressing you this note is to inquire what right you had to exclude myself and other owners of pews in Grace Church from entering it yesterday, enforced, too, by a cordon of police for that purpose. If my pew is not my property, I wish to know it; and if it is, I deny your right to prevent me from occupying it whenever the church is open, even at a marriage of mountebanks, which I would not take the trouble to cross the street to witness.

Respectfully, your obedient servant,

W * * * S * * *

804 BROADWAY, NEW YORK, Feb. 16, 1863.

MR. W * * * S * * *—*Dear Sir:* I am sorry, my valued friend, that you should have written me the peppery letter that is now before me. If the matter of which you complain be so utterly insignificant and contemptible as "a marriage of mountebanks, which you would not take the trouble to cross the street to witness," it surprises me that you should have made such strenuous, but ill-directed efforts to secure a ticket of admission. And why—permit me to ask in the name of reason and philosophy—do you still suffer it to disturb you so sadly? It would perhaps be a sufficient answer to your letter, to say that your cause of complaint exists only in your imagination. You have never been excluded from your pew. As rector, I am the only custodian of the church, and you will hardly venture to say that you have ever applied to me for permission to enter, and been refused.

Here I might safely rest, and leave you to the comfort of your own reflections in the case. But as you, in common with many other worthy persons, would seem to have very crude notions as to your rights of "property" in pews you will pardon me for saying that a pew in a church is property only in a peculiar and restricted sense. It is not property, as your house or your horse is property. It vests you with no fee in the soil; you cannot use it in any way, and in every way, and at all times, as your pleasure or caprice may dictate; you cannot put it to any common or unhallowed uses; you cannot remove it, nor injure it, nor destroy it. In short, you hold by purchase, and may sell the right to the undisturbed possession of that little space within the church edifice which you call your pew during the hours of divine service. But even that right must be exercised decorously, and with a decent regard for time and place, or else you may at any moment be ignominiously ejected from it.

I regret to be obliged to add that by the law of custom, you may, during those said hours of divine service (but at no other time) sleep in your pew; you must, however, do so noiselessly and never to the disturbance of your sleeping neighbors; your

property in your pew has this extent and nothing more. Now, if
Mr. W * * * S * * * were at any time to come to me and say,
"Sir, I would that you should grant me the use of Grace Church
for a solemn service (a marriage, a baptism, or a funeral, as the
case may be), and as it is desirable that the feelings of the parties
should be protected as far as possible from the impertinent in-
trusion and disturbance of a crowd from the streets and lanes of
the city, I beg that no one may be admitted within the doors of
the church during the very few moments that we expect to be
there, but our invited friends only,"—it would certainly, in
such a case, be my pleasure to comply with your request, and to
meet your wishes in every particular; and I think that even Mr.
W * * * S * * * will agree that all this would be entirely reasonable and proper. Then, tell me, how would such a case differ
from the instance of which you complain? Two young persons,
whose only crimes would seem to be that they are neither so
big, nor so stupid, nor so ill-mannered, nor so inordinately selfish as some other people, come to me and say, sir, we are about
to be married, and we wish to throw around our marriage all the
solemnities of religion. We are strangers in your city, and as
there is no clergymen here standing in a pastoral relation to us,
we have ventured to ask the favor of the bishop of New York to
marry us, and he has kindly consented to do so; may we then
venture a little further, and request the use of your church in
which the bishop may perform the marriage service? We assure
you, sir, that we are no shams, no cheats, no mountebanks; we
are neither monsters nor abortions; it is true we are little, but
we are as God made us, perfect in our littleness. Sir, we are
simply man and woman of like passions and infirmities with you
and other mortals. The arrangements for our marriage are
controlled by no "showman," and we are sincerely desirous
that everything should be ordered with a most scrupulous regard to decorum. We hope to invite our relations and intimate
friends, together with such persons as may in other years have
extended civilities to either of us; but we pledge ourselves to
you most sacredly that no invitation can be bought with money.
Permit us to say further, that as we would most gladly escape
from the insulting jeers, and ribald sneers and coarse ridicule of
the unthinking multitude without, we pray you to allow us, at
our own proper charges, so to guard the avenues of access from
the street, as to prevent all unseemly tumult and disorder.

I tell you sir, that whenever, and from whomsoever, such an appeal is made to my Christian courtesy, although it should come from the very humblest of the earth, I would go calmly and cheerfully forward to meet their wishes, although as many W * * * S * * *'s as would reach from here to Kamtschatka, clothed in furs and frowns, should rise up to oppose me.

In conclusion, I will say that if the marriage of Charles S. Stratton and Lavinia Warren is to be regarded as a pageant, then it was the most beautiful pageant it has ever been my privilege to witness. If on the contrary, it is rather to be thought of as a solemn ceremony, then it was as touchingly solemn as a wedding can possibly be rendered. It is true the bishop was not present, but Mr. Stratton's own pastor, the Rev. Mr. Willey, of Bridgeport, Connecticut, read the service with admirable taste and impressiveness, and the bride was given away by her mother's pastor and her own "next friend," a venerable congregational clergyman from Massachusetts. Surely, there never was a gathering of so many hundreds of our best people, when everybody appeared so delighted with everything; surely it is no light thing to call forth so much innocent joy in so few moments of passing time; surely it is no light thing, thus to smooth the roughness and sweeten the acerbities which mar our happiness as we advance upon the wearing journey of life. Sir, it was most emphatically a high triumph of "Christian civilization"!

Respectfully submitted, by your obedient servant,

THOMAS HOUSE TAYLOR.

Several thousand persons attended the reception of Mr. and Mrs. Tom Thumb the same day at the Metropolitan Hotel. After this they started on a wedding tour, taking Washington in their way. They visited President Lincoln at the White House. After a couple of weeks they returned, and, as they then supposed, retired to private life.

Habit, however, is indeed second nature. The General and his wife had been accustomed to excitement, and after a few months' retirement, they again longed for the peculiar pleasures of a public life, and the public were eager to welcome them once more. They resumed their

public career, and have since travelled several years in
Europe, and considerably in this country, holding public
exhibitions more than half the time, and spending the res-
idue in leisurely viewing such cities and portions of the
country as they may happen to be in. Commodore Nutt
and Minnie Warren, I should add, usually travel with
them.

I met the little Commodore last summer, after his absence in Europe of three years, and said:

"Are you not married yet, Commodore?"

"No, sir; my fruit is plucked," he replied.

"You don't mean to say you will never marry," I remarked.

"No, not exactly," replied the Commodore, complacently, "but I have concluded not to marry until I am
thirty."

"I suppose you intend to marry one of your size?" I
said.

"I am not particular in that respect," but seeing my
jocose mood, he continued, with a comical leer, "I think I
should prefer marrying a good, green country girl, to
anybody else."

This was said with a degree of nonchalance, which
none can appreciate who do not know him.

To make sure that a lack of memory has not misled me
as to any of the facts in regard to the courtship and
wedding of Tom Thumb and Lavinia Warren, I will here
say that, after writing out the story, I read it to the parties
personally interested, and they give me leave to say that,
in all particulars, it is a correct statement of the affair,
except that Lavinia remarked:

"Well, Mr. Barnum, your story don't lose any by
the telling"; and the Commodore denies the "rolling
tear," when informed of the engagement of the little
pair.

In June 1869, the report was started, for the third or
fourth time in the newspapers, that Commodore Nutt
and Miss Minnie Warren were married—this time at

West Haven, in Connecticut. The story was wholly untrue, nor do I think that such a wedding is likely to take place, for, on the principle that people like their opposites, Minnie and the Commodore are likely to marry persons whom they can literally "look up to"—that is, if either of them marries at all it will be a tall partner.

Soon after the wedding of General Tom Thumb and Lavinia Warren, a lady came to my office and called my attention to a little six-paged pamphlet which she said she had written, entitled "Priests and Pigmies," and requested me to read it. I glanced at the title, and at once estimating the character of the publication, I promptly declined to devote any portion of my valuable time to its perusal.

"But you had better look at it, Mr. Barnum; it deeply interests you, and you may think it worth your while to buy it."

"Certainly, I will buy it, if you desire," said I, tendering her a sixpence, which I supposed to be the price of the little pamphlet.

"Oh! you quite misunderstand me: I mean buy the copyright and the entire edition, with the view of suppressing the work. Is says some frightful things, I assure you," urged the author.

I lay back in my chair and fairly roared at this exceedingly feeble attempt at black-mail.

"But," persisted the lady, "suppose it says that your Museum and Grace Church are all one, what then?"

"My dear madam," I replied, "you may say what you please about me or about my Museum; you may print a hundred thousand copies of a pamphlet stating that I stole the communion service, after the wedding from Grace Church altar, or anything else you choose to write; only have the kindness to say something about me, and then come to me and I will properly estimate the money value of your services to me as an advertising agent. Good morning, madam,"—and she departed.

CHAPTER XXXVIII.

Political and Personal.

I began my political life as a Democrat, and my newspaper, the *Herald of Freedom,* was a Jackson-Democratic journal. While always taking an active interest in political matters, I had no desire for personal preferment, and, up to a late period, steadily declined to run for office. Nevertheless, in 1852 or 1853, prominent members of the party with which I voted, urged the submission of my name to the State Convention, as a candidate for the office of Governor, and although the party was then in the ascendancy, and a nomination would have been equivalent to an election, I peremptorily refused; in spite of this refusal, which was generally known, several votes were cast for me in the Convention. The Kansas strifes, in 1854, shook my faith in my party, though I continued to call myself a Democrat, often declaring that if I thought there was a drop of blood in me that was not democratic, I would let it out if I had to cut the jugular vein. When, however, secession threatened in 1860, I thought it was time for a "new departure," and I identified myself with the Republican party.

During the active and exciting political campaign of 1860, which resulted in Mr. Lincoln's first election to the presidency, it will be remembered that "Wide-Awake" associations, with their uniforms, torches and processions, were organized in nearly every city, town and village throughout the North. Arriving at Bridgeport from New York at five o'clock one afternoon, I was informed

315

that the Wide-Awakes were to parade that evening and intended to march out to Lindencroft. So I ordered two boxes of sperm candles, and prepared for a general illumination of every window in the front of my house. Many of my neighbors, including several Democrats, came to Lindencroft in the evening to witness the illumination and see the Wide-Awake procession. My nearest neighbor, Mr. T., was a strong Democrat, and before he came to my house, he ordered his servants to stay in the basement, and not to show a light above ground, thus intending to prove his Democratic convictions and conclusions by the darkness of his "premises"; and so, while Lindencroft was all ablaze with a flood of light, the next house was as black as a coal-hole.

My neighbor, Mr. James D. Johnson, was also a Democrat, but I knew he would not spoil a good joke for the sake of politics, and I asked him to engage the attention of Mr. and Mrs. T., and to keep their faces turned towards Bridgeport and the approaching procession, the light of whose torches could already be seen in the distance, while another Democratic friend, Mr. George A. Wells, and I, ran over and illuminated Mr. T.'s house. This we did with great success, completing our work five minutes before the procession arrived. As the Wide-Awakes turned into my grounds and saw that the house of Mr. T. was brilliantly illuminated, they concluded that he had become a sudden convert to Republicanism, and gave three rousing cheers for him. Hearing his name thus cheered and wondering at the cause, he happened to turn and see that his house was lighted up from basement to attic, and uttering a single profane ejaculation, he rushed for home. He was not able, however, to put out the lights till the Wide-Awakes had gone on their way rejoicing under the impression that one more Republican had been added to their ranks.

When the rebellion broke out in 1861, I was too old to go to the field, but I supplied four substitutes, and contributed liberally from my means for the cause of the

Union. After the defeat at Bull Run, July 21, 1861, "peace meetings" began to be held in different parts of the Northern States, and especially in Fairfield and Litchfield Counties, in Connecticut. It was usual in these assemblages to display a white flag, bearing the word "Peace" above the National flag, and to make and listen to harangues denunciatory of the war. One of these meetings was advertised to be held, August 24th, at Stepney, ten miles north of Bridgeport. On the morning of that day, I met Elias Howe, Jr., who proposed to me that we should drive up to Stepney, attend the Peace meeting and hear for ourselves whether the addresses were disloyal or not. We agreed to meet at the post-office, at twelve o'clock at noon, and I went home for my carriage. On the way I met several gentlemen to whom I communicated my intention, asking them to go also; and as Mr. Howe invited several of his friends to accompany us, when we met at noon, at least twenty gentlemen were at the place of rendezvous with their carriages, ready to start for Stepney. I am quite confident that not one of us had any other intention in going to this meeting, than to quietly listen to the harangues, and if they were found to be in opposition to the government, and calculated to create disturbance or disaffection in the community, and deter enlistments, it would be best to represent the matter to the government at Washington, and ask that measures might be taken to suppress such gatherings.

As we turned into Main Street, we discovered two large omnibuses filled with soldiers, who were at home on furlough, and who were going to Stepney. Our lighter carriages outran them, and so arrived at Stepney in time to see the white peace flag run up over the stars and stripes, when we quietly stood in the crowd while the meeting was organized. It was a very large gathering, and some fifty ladies were on the seats in front of the platform, on which were the officers and speakers of the meeting. A "preacher,"—Mr. Charles Smith,— was invited to open the proceedings with prayer, and

"The Military and Civil History of Connecticut, during the War of 1861–65," by W. A. Croffut and John M. Morris, thus continues the record of this extraordinary gathering:

"He (Smith) had not, however, progressed far in his supplication, when he slightly opened his eyes, and beheld, to his horror, the Bridgeport omnibuses coming over the hill, garnished with Union banners, and vocal with loyal cheers. This was the signal for a panic; Bull Run, on a small scale was re-enacted. The devout Smith, and the undelivered orators, it is alleged, took refuge in a field of corn. The procession drove straight to the pole unresisted, the hostile crowd parting to let them pass; and a tall man,—John Platt,—amid some mutterings, climbed the pole, reached the halliards, and the mongrel banners were on the ground. Some of the peace-men, rallying, drew weapons on 'the invaders,' and a musket and a revolver were taken from them by soldiers at the very instant of firing. Another of the defenders fired a revolver, and was chased into the fields. Still others, waxing belligerent, were disarmed, and a number of loaded muskets found stored in an adjacent shed were seized. The stars and stripes were hoisted upon the pole, and wildly cheered. P. T. Barnum was then taken on the shoulders of the boys in blue, and put on the platform, where he made a speech full of patriotism, spiced with the humor of the occasion. Captain James E. Dunham also said a few words to the point. . . . 'The Star Spangled Banner' was then sung in chorus, and a series of resolutions passed, declaring that 'loyal men are the rightful custodians of the peace of Connecticut.' Elias Howe, Jr., chairman, made his speech, when the crowd threatened to shoot the speakers: 'If they fire a gun, boys, burn the whole town, and I'll pay for it!' After giving the citizens wholesome advice concerning the substituted flag, and their duty to the government, the procession returned to Bridgeport, with the white flag trailing in the mud behind an omnibus. . . . They were received at Bridgeport by approving crowds, and were greeted with continuous cheers as they passed along."

On our way back to Bridgeport, the soldiers threatened a descent upon the *Farmer* office, but I strongly appealed to them to refrain from such a riotous proceeding, telling them that as law-abiding citizens they should refrain from acts of violence and especially should make no appeal to the passions of a mob. So confident was I that the day's proceedings had ended with the reception of the soldiers on their return from Stepney, that in telegraphing a full account of the facts to the New York papers, I added that there was no danger of an attack upon the *Farmer* office, since leading loyal citizens were opposed to such action as unnecessary and unwise. But the enthusiasm with which the soldiers had been received, and the excitement of the day, prompted them to break through their resolutions, and, half an hour after my telegram had been sent to New York, they rushed into the *Farmer* office, tumbled the type into the street, and broke the presses. I did not approve of this summary suppression of the paper, and offered the proprietors a handsome subscription to assist in enabling them to renew the publication of the *Farmer*. One of the editors of this paper went South, and connected himself with a journal in Augusta, Georgia; the remaining proprietor shortly afterwards re-issued the *Farmer,* but the peace meetings which had been advertised for different towns were never held; the gathering at Stepney was the last of the kind.

Elias Howe, Jr., although he was a man of wealth and well advanced in years, enlisted as a private in the Seventeenth regiment of Connecticut volunteers and served in the Army of the Potomac. Once when his fellow-soldiers, not having been paid off, were in need of money, he advanced $13,000 due them, and when his regiment was disbanded and discharged from service, he chartered, at his own expense, a special train to bring them from New Haven to Bridgeport, where they had a public reception.

Mr. Howe, like all men of his reputed wealth and liberality, was constantly besieged by solicitors for all sorts of charities, nor was he free from such applications when he was serving as a common soldier in Virginia. On one occasion a worthy priest came to him and asked for a subscription to a church which was then building. "Who is it," exclaimed Howe, "that talks of building churches in this time of war?" The priest ventured to say that he was trying to build in his parish a church which was to be known as St. Peter's.

"St. Peter's is it?" asked Howe; "well, St. Peter was, in his way, a fighting man; he drew a sword once and cut off a man's ear; on the whole, I think," he added, as he gave a handsome sum of money to the priest, "I must do something for St. Peter, though about these days I am devoting my attention and money mainly to saltpetre."

After the draft riots in New York and in other cities, in July, 1863, myself and other members of the "Prudential Committee" which had been formed in Bridgeport were frequently threatened with personal violence, and rumors were especially rife that Lindencroft would some night be mobbed and destroyed. On several occasions, soldiers volunteered as a guard and came and stayed at my house, sometimes for several nights in succession, and I was also provided with rockets, so that in case of an attempted attack I could signal to my friends in the city and especially to the night watchman at the arsenal, who would see my rockets at Lindencroft and give the alarm. Happily these signals were never needed, but the rockets came in play, long afterwards, in another way.

My house was provided with a magnetic burglar-alarm and one night the faithful bell sounded. I was instantly on my feet and summoning my servants, one ran and rung the large bell on the lawn which served in the day time to call my coachman from the stable, another turned on the gas, while I fired a gun out of the window and I then went to the top of the house and set off several rockets. The whole region round about was instantly aroused; dogs barked, neighbors half-dressed, but armed, flocked over to my grounds, every time a rocket went up, and I was by no means sparing of my supply; the whole place was as light as day, and in the general glare and confusion we caught sight of two retreating burglars, one running one way, the other another way, and both as fast as their legs could carry them; nor do I believe that the panic-stricken would-be plunderers stopped running till they reached New York.

It always seemed to me that a man who "takes no interest in politics" is unfit to live in a land where the government rests in the hands of the people. Consequently, whether I expressed them or not, I always had pronounced opinions upon all the leading political questions of the day, and no frivolous reason ever kept me from the polls. Indeed, on one occasion, I even hastened my return from Europe, so that I could take part in a presidential election. I was a party man, but not a partisan, nor a wire-puller, and I had never sought or desired office, though it had often been tendered to me. This was notoriously true, among all who knew me, up to the year 1865, when I accepted from the Republican party a nomination to the Connecticut legislature from the town of Fairfield, and I did this because I felt that it would be an honor to be permitted to vote for the then proposed amendment to the Constitution of the United States to abolish slavery forever from the land.

I was elected, and on arriving at Hartford the night before the session began, I found the wire-pullers at work laying their plans for the election of a Speaker of the House. Watching the movements closely, I saw that the railroad interests had combined in support of one of the candidates, and this naturally excited my suspicion. I never believed in making State legislation a mere power to support monopolies. I do not need to declare my full appreciation of the great blessings which railroad interests and enterprises have brought upon this country and the world. But the vaster the enterprise and its power for good, the greater its opportunity for mischief if its power is perverted. The time was when a whole community was tied to the track of one or two railway companies, and it was too truthful to be looked upon as satire to call New Jersey the "State of Camden and Amboy." A great railroad company, like fire, is a good servant, but a bad master; and when it is considered that such a company, with its vast number of men dependent upon it for their daily bread, can sometimes elect State officers and legislatures, the danger to our free institutions from such a force may well be feared.

Thinking of these things, and seeing in the combination of railroad interests to elect a speaker, no promise of good to the community at large, I at once consulted with a few friends in the legislature, and we resolved to defeat the railroad "ring," if possible, in caucus. I had not even seen either of the candidates for the speakership, nor had I a single selfish end in view to gratify by the election of one candidate or the other; but I felt that if the railroad favorite could be defeated, the public interest would be subserved. We succeeded; their candidate was not nominated, and the railroad men were taken by surprise. They had had their own way in every legislature since the first railroad was laid down in Connecticut, and to be beaten now fairly startled them.

Immediately after the caucus, I sought the successful nominee, Hon. E. K. Foster, of New Haven, and begged him not to appoint as chairman of the railroad committee the man who had held that office for several successive years, and who was, in fact, the great railroad factotum in the State. He complied with my request, and he soon found how important it was to check the strong and growing monopoly; for, as he said, the "outside pressure" from personal friends in both political parties, to secure the appointment of the person to whom I had objected, was terrible.

Though I had not foreseen nor thought of such a thing until I reached Hartford, I soon found that a battle with the railroad commissioners would be necessary, and my course was shaped accordingly. It was soon discovered that a majority of the railroad commissioners were mere tools in the hands of the railroad companies, and that one of them was actually a hired clerk in the office of the New York and New Haven Railroad Company. It was also shown that the chairman of the railroad commissioners permitted most of the accidents which occurred on that road to be taken charge of and reported upon by the paid lobby agent of that railroad. This was so manifestly destructive to the interests of all parties who might suffer from accidents on the road, or have any controversy therefor with the company, that I succeeded in enlisting the farmers and other true men on the side of right; and we defeated the chairman of the railroad commissioners, who was a candidate for re-election, and elected our own candidate in his place. I also carried through a law that no person who was in the employ of any railroad in the State should serve as railroad commissioner.

But the great struggle which lasted nearly through the entire session was upon the subject of railroad passenger commutations. Commodore Vanderbilt had secured control of the Hudson River and Harlem railroads, and had increased the price of commuters' tickets from two hundred to four hundred per cent. Many men living on the line of these roads at distances of from ten to fifty miles from New York, had built fine residences in the country, on the strength of cheap transit to and from the city, and were compelled to submit to the extortion. Commodore Vanderbilt was a large shareholder in the New York and New Haven road; indeed, subsequent elections showed that he had a controlling interest, and it seemed evident to me that the same practice would be put in operation on the New Haven Railroad, that commuters were groaning under on the two other roads. I enlisted as many as I could in an effort to strangle this outrage before it became too strong to grapple with. Several lawyers in the Assembly had promised me their aid, but long before the final struggle came, every lawyer except one in that body was enlisted in favor of the railroads! What potent influence had been at work with these legal gentlemen could only be surmised. Certain it is that all the railroad interests in the State were combined; and while they had plenty of money with which to carry out their designs and desires, the chances looked slim in favor of those members of the legislature who had no pecuniary interest in the matter, but were struggling simply for justice and the protection of the people. But "Yankee stick-to-it-iveness" was always a noted feature in my character. Every inch of the ground was fought over, day after day, before the legislative railroad committee. Examinations and cross-examinations of railroad commissioners and lobbyists were kept up. Scarcely more than one man, Senator Ballard, of Darien, aided me personally in the investigations which took place. But he was a host in himself, and we left not a stone unturned; we succeeded by our persistence, in letting in considerable light upon a dark subject. The man whom I had prevented from being made chairman, succeeded in becoming a member of the railroad committee; but, from the mouths of unwilling witnesses, I exhibited his connection with railroad reports, railroad laws, and railroad lobbyings, in such a light that he took to his bed some ten days before the end of the session, and actually remained there, "sick," as he said, till the legislature adjourned. . . .

CHAPTER XLI.

Bennett and
The Herald.

When the old American Museum burned down, and while the ruins were still smoking, I had numerous applications for the purchase of the lease of the two lots, fifty-six by one hundred feet, which had still nearly eleven years to run. It will be remembered that in 1847 I came back from England, while my second lease of five years had yet three years more to run, and renewed that lease for twenty-five years from 1851 at an annual rental of $10,000. It was also stipulated that in case the building was destroyed by fire the proprietor of the property should expend twenty-four thousand dollars towards the erection of a new edifice, and at the end of the term of lease he was to pay me the appraised value of the building, not to exceed $100,000. Rents and real estate values had trebled since I took this twenty-five years' lease, and hence the remaining term was very valuable. I engaged an experienced and competent real estate broker in Pine Street to examine the terms of my lease, and in view of his knowledge of the cost of erecting buildings and the rentals they were commanding in Broadway, I enjoined him to take his time, and make a careful estimate of what the lease was worth to me, and what price I ought to receive if I sold it to another party. At the end of several days, he showed me his figures, which proved that the lease was fully worth $275,000. As I was inclined to have a museum higher up town, I did not wish to engage in erecting two buildings at once, so I concluded to offer my museum lease for sale. Accordingly, I put it into the hands of Mr. Homer Morgan, with directions to offer it for $225,000, which was $50,000 less than the value at which it had been estimated.

The next day I met Mr. James Gordon Bennett, who told me that he desired to buy my lease, and at the same time to purchase the fee of the museum property, for the erection thereon of a publication building for the New York *Herald*. I said I thought it was very fitting the *Herald* should be the successor of the Museum; and Mr. Bennett asked my price.

"Please to go or send immediately to Homer Morgan's office," I replied, "and you will learn that Mr. Morgan has the lease for sale at $225,000. This is $50,-000 less than its estimated value; but to you I will deduct $25,000 from my already reduced price, so you may have the lease for $200,000."

Bennett replied that he would look into the affair closely; and the next day his attorney sent for my lease. He kept it several days, and then appointed an hour for me to come to his office. I called according to appointment. Mr. Bennett and his attorney had thoroughly examined the lease. It was the property of my wife. Bennett concluded to accept my offer. My wife assigned the lease to him, and his attorney handed me Mr. Bennett's check on the Chemical Bank for $200,000. That same day I invested $50,000 in United States bonds; and the remaining $150,000 was similarly invested on the following day. I learned at that time that Bennett had agreed to purchase the fee of the property for $500,000. He had been informed that the property was worth some $350,-000 to $400,000, and he did not mind paying $100,000 extra for the purpose of carrying out his plans. But the parties who estimated for him the value of the land knew nothing of the fact that there was a lease upon the property, else of course they would in their estimate have deducted the $200,000 which the lease would cost.

When, therefore, Mr. Bennett saw it stated in the newspapers that the sum which he had paid for a piece of land measuring only fifty-six by one hundred feet was more than was ever before paid in any city in the world for a tract of that size, he discovered the serious oversight which he had made; and the owner of the property was immediately informed that Bennett would not take it. But Bennett had already signed a bond to the owner, agreeing to pay $100,000 cash, and to mortgage the premises for the remaining $400,000.

Supposing that by this step he had shaken off the owner of the fee, Bennett was not long in seeing that, as he was not to own the land, he would have no possible use for the lease, for which he had paid the $200,000; and accordingly his next step was to shake me off also, and get back the money he had paid me.

At this time Bennett was ruling the managers of the theatres and other amusements with a rod of iron. He had established a large job printing office in connection with the *Herald* office; and woe to the manager who presumed to have his bills printed elsewhere. Any manager who dared to decline employing Bennett's job office to print his small bills and posters, at Bennett's exorbitant prices, was ignored in the *Herald;* his advertisements were refused, and generally, he and his establishment were black-balled and blackguarded in the columns of the *Herald.* Of course most of the managers were somewhat sensitive to such attacks, and therefore submitted to his impositions in the job office, his double price for newspaper advertisements, and any other overbearing conditions the *Herald* might choose to dictate. The advertisements of the Academy of Music, then under the direction of Mr. Max Maretzek, had been refused on account of some dissatisfaction in the *Herald* office in regard to free boxes, and also because the prima donna, Miss Clara Louise Kellogg, had certain ideas of her own with regard to social intercourse with certain people, as Miss Jenny Lind had with regard to the same people, when she was under my management, and to some degree under my advice, and these ideas were not particularly relished by the power behind the *Herald* throne.

For my own part, I thoroughly understood Bennett and his concern, and I never cared one farthing for him or his paper. I had seen for years, especially as Bennett's enormously overestimated "influence" applied to public amusements, that whatever the *Herald* praised, sickened, drooped, and if the *Herald* persisted in praising it, finally died; while whatever the *Herald* attacked prospered, and all the more, the more it was abused. It was utterly impossible for Bennett to injure me, unless he had some more potent weapon than his *Herald.* And that this was the general opinion was quite evident from the fact that several years had elapsed since gentlemen were in the almost daily habit of cuffing, kicking and cowhiding Bennett in the streets and other public places for his scurrilous attacks upon them, or upon members of their families. It had come to be seen that what the *Herald* said, good or bad, was, like the editor himself, literally of "no account."

My business for many years, as manager of the Museum and other public entertainments, compelled me to court notoriety; and I always found Bennett's abuse far more remunerative than his praise, even if I could have had the praise at the same price, that is, for nothing. Especially was it profitable to me when I could be the subject of scores of lines of his scolding editorials free of charge, instead of paying him forty cents a line for advertisements, which would not attract a tenth part so much attention. Bennett had tried abusing me, off and on, for twenty years, on one occasion refusing my advertisement altogether for the space of about a year; but I always managed to be the gainer by his course. Now, however, when new difficulties threatened, all the leading managers in New York were members of the "Managers' Association," and as we all submitted to the arbitrary and extortionate demands of the *Herald,* Bennett thought he had but to crack his whip, in order to keep any and all of us within the traces. The great Ogre of the *Herald* supposed he could at all times frighten the little managerial boys into any holes which might be left open for them to hide in. Accordingly, one day Bennett's attorney wrote me a letter, saying that he would like to have me call on him at his office the following morning. Not dreaming of the object I called as desired, and after a few pleasant commonplace remarks about the weather, and other trifles, the attorney said:

"Mr. Barnum, I have sent for you to say that Mr. Bennett has concluded not to purchase the museum lots, and therefore that you had better take back the lease, and return the $200,000 paid for it."

"Are you in earnest?" I asked with surprise.

"Certainly, quite so," he answered.

"Really," I said, smiling, "I am sorry I can't accommodate Mr. Bennett; I have not got the little sum about me; in fact, I have spent the money."

"It will be better for you to take back the lease," said the attorney seriously.

"Nonsense," I replied, "I shall do nothing of the sort, I don't make child's bargains. The lease was cheap enough, but I have other business to attend to, and shall have nothing to do with it."

The attorney said very little in reply; but I could see, by the almost benignant sorrow expressed upon his countenance, that he evidently pitied me for the temerity that would doubtless lead me into the jaws of the insatiable monster of the *Herald.* The next morning I observed that the advertisement of my entertainments with my Museum Company at Winter Garden was left out of the *Herald* columns. I went directly to the editorial rooms of the *Herald;* and learning that Bennett was not in, I said to Mr. Hudson, then managing editor:

"My advertisement is left out of the *Herald;* is there a screw loose?"

"I believe there is," was the reply.

"What is the matter?" I asked.

"You must ask the Emperor," said Mr. Hudson, meaning of course Bennett.

"When will the 'Emperor' be in?" I inquired; "next Monday," was the answer.

"Well, I shall not see him," I replied; "but I wish to have this thing settled at once. Mr. Hudson, I now tender you the money for the insertion of my Museum advertisement on the same terms as are paid by other places of amusement, will you publish it?"

"I will not," Mr. Hudson peremptorily replied.

"That is all," I said. Mr. Hudson then smilingly and blandly remarked, "I have formally answered your formal demand, because I suppose you require it; but you know, Mr. Barnum, I can only obey orders." I assured him that I understood the matter perfectly, and attached no blame to him in the premises. I then proceeded to notify the Secretary of the "Managers' Association" to call the managers together at twelve o'clock the following day; and there was a full meeting at the appointed time. I stated the facts in the case in the *Herald* affair, and simply remarked, that if we did not make common cause against any newspaper publisher who excluded an advertisement from his columns simply to gratify a private pique, it was evident that either and all of us were liable to imposition at any time.

One of the managers immediately made a motion that the entire association should stop their advertising and bill printing at the *Herald* office, and have no further connection with that establishment. Mr. Lester Wallack advised that this motion should not be adopted until a committee had waited upon Bennett, and had reported the result of the interview to the Association. Accordingly, Messrs. Wallack, Wheatley and Stuart were delegated to go down to the *Herald* office to call on Mr. Bennett.

The moment Bennett saw them, he evidently suspected the object of their mission, for he at once commenced to speak to Mr. Wallack in a patronizing manner; told him how long he had known, and how much he respected his late father, who was "a true English gentleman of the old school," with much more in the same strain. Mr. Wallack replied to Bennett that the three managers were appointed a committee to wait upon him to ascertain if he insisted upon excluding from his columns the Museum advertisements,—not on account of any objection to the contents of the advertisements, or to the Museum itself, but simply because he had a private business disagreement with the proprietor?—intimating that such a proceeding, for such a reason, and no other, might lead to a rupture of business relations with other managers. In reply, Mr. Bennett had something to say about the fox that had suffered tailwise from a trap, and thereupon advised all other foxes to cut their tails off; and he pointed the fable by setting forth the impolicy of drawing down upon the Association the vengeance of the *Herald.* The committee, however, coolly insisted upon a direct answer to their question.

Bennett then answered: "I will not publish Barnum's advertisement; I do my business as I please, and in my own way."

"So do we," replied one of the managers, and the committee withdrew.

The next day the Managers' Association met, heard the report, and unanimously resolved to withdraw their advertisements from the *Herald,* and their patronage from the *Herald* job establishment, and it was done. Nevertheless, the *Herald* for several days continued to print gratuitously the advertisements of Wallack's Theatre and Niblo's Garden, and inordinately puffed these establishments, evidently in order to ease the fall, and to convey the idea that some of the theatres patronized the *Herald,* and perhaps hoping by praising these managers to draw them back again, and so to nullify the agreement of the Association in regard to the *Herald.* Thereupon, the managers headed their advertisements in all the other

New York papers with the line, "This Establishment does not advertise in the New York *Herald*," and for many months this announcement was kept at the top of every theatrical advertisement and on the posters and playbills.

The *Herald* then began to abuse and vilify the theatrical and opera managers, their artists and their performances, and by way of contrast profusely praised Tony Pastor's Bowery show, and Sundry entertainments of a similar character, thereby speedily bringing some of these side-shows to grief and shutting up their shops. Meanwhile, the first-class theatres prospered amazingly under the abuse of Bennett. Their receipts were never larger, and their houses never more thronged. The public took sides in the matter with the managers and against the *Herald*, and thousands of people went to the theatres merely to show their willingness to support the managers and to spite "Old Bennett." The editor was fairly caught in his own trap; other journals began to estimate the loss the *Herald* sustained by the action of the managers, and it was generally believed that this loss in advertising and job printing was not less than from $75,000 to $100,000 a year. The *Herald's* circulation also suffered terribly, since hundreds of people, at the hotels and elsewhere, who were accustomed to buy the paper solely for the sake of seeing what amusements were announced for the evening, now bought other papers. This was the hardest blow of all, and it fully accounted for the abuse which the *Herald* daily poured out upon the theatres.

But the more Bennett raved the more the people laughed, and the more determined did they seem to patronize the managers. Many people came to the Museum, who said they came expressly to show us that the public were with us and against the *Herald*. The other managers stated their experience to be the same in this respect. In fact, it was a subject of general remark, that, without exception, the associated managers never had done such a thriving business as during the two years in which they gave the *Herald* the cold shoulder.

Bennett evidently felt ashamed of the whole transaction; he would never publish the facts in his columns, though he once stated in an editorial that it had been reported that he had been cheated in purchasing the Broadway property; that the case had gone to court, and the public would soon know all the particulars. Some persons supposed by this that Bennett had sued me; but this was far from being the case. The owner of the lots sued Bennett, to compel him to take the title and pay for the property as per agreement; and that was all the "law" there was about it. He held James Gordon Bennett's bond, that he would pay him half a million of dollars for the land, as follows: $100,000 cash, and a bond and mortgage upon the premises for the remaining $400,000. The day before the suit was to come to trial, Bennett came forward, took the deed, and paid $100,000 cash and gave a bond and mortgage of the entire premises for $400,000. That lien still exists against the *Herald* property.

Had I really taken back the lease as Bennett desired, he would have been in a worse scrape than ever; for having been compelled to take the property, he would have been obliged, as my landlord, to go on and assist in building a Museum for me according to the terms of my lease, and a Museum I should certainly have built on Bennett's property, even if I had owned a dozen Museums up town. As it was, Bennett was badly beaten on every side, and especially by the managers, who forever established the fact that the *Herald's* abuse was profitable, and its patronage fatal to any enterprise; and who taught Mr. Bennett personally the lesson of his own insignificance, as he had not learned it since the days when gentlemen used to kick and cowhide him up and down the whole length of Nassau Street. In the autumn of 1868, the associated managers came to the conclusion that the punishment of Bennett for two years was sufficient, and they consented to restore their advertisements to the *Herald*. I was then associated with the Van Amburgh Company in my new Museum, and we concluded that the cost of advertising in the *Herald* was more than it was worth, and so we did not enter into the new arrangement 'made by the Managers' Association.

CHAPTER XLII.

Public Lecturing.

During the summer of 1866, Mr. Edwin L. Brown, Corresponding Secretary of the "Associated Western Literary Societies," opened a correspondence with me relative to delivering, in the ensuing season, my lecture on "Success in Life," before some sixty lyceums, Young Men's Christian Associations, and Literary Societies belonging to the union which Mr. Brown represented. The scheme embraced an extended tour through Pennsylvania, Ohio, Indiana, Illinois, Wisconsin, Missouri and Iowa, and I was to receive one hundred dollars for every repetition of my lecture, with all my travelling expenses on the route. Agreeing to these terms, I commenced the engagement at the appointed time, and, averaging five lectures a week, I finished the prescribed round just before New Year's. Before beginning this engagement, however, I gave the lecture for other associations at Wheeling, Virginia, Cincinnati, Ohio, and Louisville, Kentucky. I also delivered the lecture in Chicago, for Professor Eastman, who at that time had one of his Business Colleges in that city. He engaged the celebrated Crosby Opera House for the occasion, and I think, with, perhaps, two exceptions, I never spoke before so large and intelligent an audience as was there assembled. It was estimated that from five to six thousand ladies and gentlemen were gathered in that capacious building; and nearly as many more went away unable to obtain admission. I was glad to observe by the action of the audience, and by the journals of the following day, that my efforts on that occasion were satisfactory. Indeed, though it is necessarily egotistical, I may truly say that with this lecture I always succeeded in pleasing my hearers. I may add, that I have invariably, as a rule, devoted to charitable purposes every penny I ever received for lecturing, except while I was under the great Jerome Clock cloud in England, when I needed all I could earn.

My western tour was delightful; indeed it was almost an ovation. I found, in fact, that when I had strayed so far from home, the curiosity exhibitor himself became quite a curiosity. On several occasions, in Iowa, I was introduced to ladies and gentlemen who had driven thirty miles in carriages to hear me. I insisted, however, that it was more to see than to hear; and I asked them if that was not really the case. In several instances they answered in the affirmative. In fact, one quaint old lady said: "Why, to tell you the truth, Mr. Barnum, we have read so much about you, and your Museum and your queer carryings-on, that we were not quite sure but you had horns and cloven feet, and so we came to satisfy our curiosity; but, la, me! I don't see but what you look a good deal like other folks, after all."

While at the West, I visited my sister, Mrs. Minerva Drew, and her family, at Bristol, Wisconsin, where they reside on a farm which I presented to her about twenty years ago. Her children having grown up and married, all except her son, Fairchild B. Drew, who had just attained his majority, his father (Ezekiel Drew) wished to retain his services on the farm. Fairchild, however, felt that the farm was not quite large enough for his aspirations. I found also that he coveted a neighboring farm, which, with its stock, was for sale for less than five thousand dollars. I bought it for him, on condition that he should continue the care of the old farm, and that the two should be worked together. I trust that the arrangement will prove beneficial to all concerned; for there is great pleasure in helping others who try to help themselves; without such effort on their part, all good offices in their favor are thrown away,—it is simply attempting to make a sieve hold water.

On my tour, in attempting to make the connection from Cleveland, Ohio, to Fort Wayne, Indiana, via Toledo, I arrived at the latter city at one o'clock, P. M., which was about two hours too late to catch the train in time for the hour announced for my lecture that evening. I went to Mr. Andrews, the superintendent of the Toledo, Wabash and Western Railway, and told him I wanted to hire a locomotive and car to run to Fort Wayne, as I must be there at eight o'clock at night.

"It is an impossibility," said Mr. Andrews; "the distance is ninety-four miles, and no train leaves here till morning. The road is much occupied by freight trains, and we never run extra trains in this part of the country, unless the necessity is imperative."

I suppose I looked astonished, as well as chagrined. I knew that if I missed lecturing in Fort Wayne that evening, I could not appoint another time for that purpose, for every night was engaged during the next two months. I also felt that a large number of persons in Fort Wayne would be disappointed, and I grew desperate. Drawing my wallet from my pocket, I said:

"I will give two hundred dollars, and even more, if you say so, to be put into Fort Wayne before eight o'clock to-night; and, really, I hope you will accommodate me."

The superintendent looked me thoroughly over in half a minute, and I fancied he had come to the conclusion that I was a burglar, a counterfeiter, or something worse, fleeing from justice. My surmise was confirmed, when he slowly remarked:

"Your business must be very pressing, sir."

"It is indeed," I replied; "I am Barnum, the museum man, and am engaged to speak in Fort Wayne tonight."

He evidently did not catch the whole of my response, for he immediately said:

"Oh, it is a show, eh? Where is old Barnum himself?"

"I am Barnum," I replied, "and it is a lecture which I am advertised to give to-night; and I would not disappoint the people for anything."

"Is this P. T. Barnum?" said the superintendent, starting to his feet.

"I am sorry to say it is," I replied.

"Well, Mr. Barnum," said he, earnestly, "if you can stand it to ride to Fort Wayne in the caboose of a freight train, your well-established reputation for punctuality in keeping your engagements shall not suffer on account of the Toledo, Wabash and Western Railroad."

"Caboose!" said I, with a laugh, "I would ride to Fort Wayne astride of the engine, or boxed up and stowed away in a freight car, if necessary, in order to meet my engagement."

A freight train was on the point of starting for Fort Wayne; all the cars were at once ordered to be switched off, except two, which the superintendent said were necessary to balance the train; the freight trains on the road were telegraphed to clear the track, and the polite superintendent pointing to the caboose, invited me to step in. I drew out my pocket-book to pay, but he smilingly shook his head, and said: "You have a through ticket from Cleveland to Fort Wayne; hand it to the freight agent on your arrival, and all will be right." I was much moved by this unexpected mark of kindness, and expressing myself to that effect, I stepped into the caboose, and we started.

The excited state of mind which I had suffered while under the impression that the audience in Fort Wayne must be disappointed now changed, and I felt as happy as a king. In fact, I enjoyed a new sensation of imperial superiority, in that I was "monarch of all I surveyed," emperor of my own train, switching all other trains from the main track, and making conductors all along the line wonder what grand mogul had thus taken complete possession and control of the road. Indeed, as we sped past each train, which stood quietly on a side track waiting for us to pass, I could not help smiling at the glances of excited curiosity which were thrown into our car by the agent and brakemen of the train which had been so peremptorily ordered to clear the track; and always stepping at the caboose door, I raised my hat, receiving in return an almost reverent salute, which the occupants of the waiting train thought due, no doubt, to the distinguished person for whom they were ordered by special telegram to make way.

I now began to reflect that the Fort Wayne lecture committee, upon discovering that I did not arrive by the regular passenger train, would not expect me at all, and that probably they might issue small bills announcing my failure to arrive. I therefore prepared the following telegram which I despatched to them on our arrival at Napoleon, the first station at which we stopped:

> Lecture Committee, Fort Wayne:—Rest perfectly tranquil. I am to be delivered at Fort Wayne by contract by half-past seven o'clock—special train.

At the same station I received a telegram from Mr. Andrews, the superintendent, asking me how I liked the caboose. I replied:

> The springs of the caboose are softer than down; I am as happy as a clam at high water; I am being carried towards Fort Wayne in a style never surpassed by Caesar's triumphal march into Rome. Hurrah for the Toledo and Wabash Railroad!

At the invitation of the engineer, I took a ride of twenty miles upon the locomotive. It fairly made my head swim. I could not reconcile my mind to the idea that there was no danger; and intimating to the engineer that it would be a relief to get where I could not see ahead, I was permitted to crawl back again to the caboose.

I reached Fort Wayne in ample time for the lecture; and as the committee had discreetly kept to themselves the fact of my non-arrival by the regular train, probably not a dozen persons were aware of the trouble I had taken to fulfil my engagement, till in the course of my lecture, under the head of "perseverance," I recounted my day's adventures, as an illustration of exercising that quality when real necessity demanded. The Fort Wayne papers of the next day published accounts of "Barnum on a Locomotive," and "A Journey in a Caboose"; and as I always had an eye to advertising, these articles were sent marked to newspapers in towns and cities where I was to lecture, and of course were copied,—thus producing the desired effects, first, of informing the public that the "showman" was coming, and next, assuring the lecture committee that Barnum would be punctually on hand as advertised, unless prevented by "circumstances over which he had no control."

The managers of railroads running west from Chicago pretty rigidly enforce a rule excluding from certain reserved cars all gentlemen travelling without ladies. As I do not smoke, I avoided the smoking cars; and as the ladies' car was sometimes more select and always more comfortable than the other cars, I tried various expedients to smuggle myself in. If I saw a lady about to enter the car alone, I followed closely, hoping thus to elude the vigilance of the brakeman, who generally acted as doorkeeper. But the car Cerberus is pretty well up to all such dodges, and I did not always succeed. On one occasion, seeing a young couple, evidently just married, and starting on a bridal tour, about to enter the car, I followed closely, but was stopped by the door-keeper, who called out:

"How many gentlemen are with this lady?"

I have always noticed that young newly-married people are very fond of saying "my husband" and "my wife;" they are new terms which sound pleasantly to the ears of those who utter them; so in answer to the peremptory inquiry of the door-keeper, the bridegroom promptly responded:

"I am this lady's husband."

"And I guess you can see by the resemblance between the lady and myself," said I to Cerberus, "that I am her father."

The astonished husband and the blushing bride were too much "taken aback" to deny their newly-discovered parent, but the brakeman said, as he permitted the young couple to pass into the car:

"We can't pass all creation with one lady."

"I hope you will not deprive me of the company of my child during the little time we can remain together," I said with a demure countenance. The brakeman evidently sympathized with the fond "parient" whose feelings were sufficiently lacerated at losing his daughter through her finding a husband, and I was permitted to pass. I immediately apologized to the young bride and her husband, and told them who I was, and my reasons for the assumed paternity, and they enjoyed the joke so heartily that they called me "father" during our entire journey together. Indeed, the husband privately and slyly hinted to me that the first boy should be christened "P. T." My friend the Rev. Dr. Chapin, by the by an inveterate punster, is never tired of ringing the changes on the names in my family; he says that my wife and I are the most sympathetic couple he ever saw, since she is "Charity" and I am "Pity" (P. T.) On one occasion, at my house in New York, he called my attention to the monogram, P. T. B., on the door and said, "I did it," "Did what," I asked: "Why that," replied the doctor, "P. T. B.,—Pull The Bell, of course," thus literally ringing a new change on my initials.

At another time during my western lecturing trip, I was following closely in the wake of a lady who was entering the favorite car, when the brakeman exclaimed: "You can't go in there, sir!"

"I rather guess I can go in with a lady," said I, pointing to the one who had just entered.

"Not with that lady, old fellow; for I happen to know her, and that is more than you do; we are up to all these travellers' tricks out here; it's no go."

I saw indeed that it was "no go," and that I must try something else; "Look here, my dear fellow," said I; "I am travelling every day on the railroads, on a lecturing tour throughout the West, and I really hope you will permit me to take a seat in the ladies' car. I am Barnum, the Museum man from New York."

Looking sharply at me for an instant, the altogether too wide-awake brakeman exclaimed: "Not by a d—n sight you ain't! I know Barnum!"

I could not help laughing; and pulling several old letters from my pocket, and showing him the directions on the envelopes, I replied:

"Well, you may know him, but the 'old fellow' has changed in his appearance, perhaps. You see by these letters that I am the 'crittur.'"

The brakeman looked astonished, but finally said: "Well, that is a fact sure enough. I know you when I come to look again, but really I did not believe you at first. You see we have all sorts of tricks played on us, and we learn to doubt everybody. You are very welcome to go in, Mr. Barnum, and I am glad to see you," and as this conversation was heard throughout the car, "Barnum, the showman," was the subject of general observation and remark.

I fulfilled my entire engagement, which covered the lecturing season, and returned to New York greatly pleased with my Western tour. Public lecturing was by no means a new experience with me; for, apart from my labors in that direction in England, and occasional addresses before literary and agricultural associations at home, I had been prominently in the field for many years as a lecturer on temperance. My attention was turned to this subject in the following manner:

In the fall of 1847, while exhibiting General Tom Thumb at Saratoga Springs, where the New York State Fair was then being held, I saw so much intoxication among men of wealth and intellect, filling the highest positions in society, that I began to ask myself the question, What guarantee is there that *I* may not become a drunkard? and I forthwith pledged myself at that time never again to partake of any kind of spirituous liquors as a beverage. True, I continued to partake of wine, for I had been instructed, in my European tour, that this was one of the innocent and charming indispensables of life. I however regarded myself as a good temperance man, and soon began to persuade my friends to refrain from the intoxicating cup. Seeing need of reform in Bridgeport, I invited my friend, the Reverend Doctor E. H. Chapin, to visit us, for the purpose of giving a public temperance lecture. I had never heard him on that subject, but I knew that on whatever topic he spoke, he was as logical as he was eloquent.

He lectured in the Baptist Church in Bridgeport. His subject was presented in three divisions: The liquor-seller, the moderate drinker, and the indifferent man. It happened, therefore, that the second, if not the third clause of the subject, had a special bearing upon me and my position. The eloquent gentleman overwhelmingly proved that the so-called respectable liquor-seller, in his splendid saloon or hotel bar, and who sold only to "gentlemen," inflicted much greater injury upon the community than a dozen common groggeries—which he abundantly illustrated. He then took up the "moderate drinker," and urged that he was the great stumbling-block to the temperance reform. He it was, and not the drunkard in the ditch, that the young man looked at as an example when he took his first glass. That when the drunkard was asked to sign the pledge, he would reply, "Why should I do so? What harm can there be in drinking, when such men as respectable Mr. A, and moral Mr. B drink wine under their own roof?" He urged that the higher a man stood in the community, the greater was his influence either for good or for evil. He said to the moderate drinker: "Sir, you either do or you do not consider it a privation and a sacrifice to give up drinking. Which is it? If you say that you can drink or let it alone, that you can quit it forever without considering it a self-denial, then I appeal to you as a man, to do it for the sake of your suffering fellow-beings." He further argued that if it was a self-denial to give up wine-drinking, then certainly the man should stop, for he was in danger of becoming a drunkard.

What Doctor Chapin said produced a deep impression upon my mind, and after a night of anxious thought, I rose in the morning, took my champagne bottles, knocked off their heads, and poured their contents upon the ground. I then called upon Doctor Chapin, asked him for the teetotal pledge, and signed it. He was greatly surprised in discovering that I was not already a teetotaler. He supposed such was the case, from the fact that I had invited him to lecture, and he little thought, at the time of his delivering it, that his argument to the moderate drinker was at all applicable to me. I felt that I had now a duty to perform,—to save others, as I had been saved, and on the very morning when I signed the pledge, I obtained over twenty signatures in Bridgeport. I talked temperance to all whom I met, and very soon commenced lecturing upon the subject in the adjacent towns and villages. I spent the entire winter and spring of 1851-2 in lecturing through my native State, always travelling at my own expense, and I was glad to know that I aroused many hundreds, perhaps thousands, to the importance of the temperance reform. I also lectured frequently in the cities of New York and Philadelphia, as well as in other towns in the neighboring States.

While in Boston with Jenny Lind, I was earnestly solicited to deliver two temperance lectures in the Tremont Temple, where she gave her concerts. I did so; and though an admission fee was charged for the benefit of a benevolent society, the building on each occasion was crowded. In the course of my tour with Jenny Lind, I was frequently solicited to lecture on temperance on evenings when she did not sing. I always complied when it was in my power. In this way I lectured in Baltimore, Washington, Charleston, New Orleans, Cincinnati, St. Louis, and other cities, also in the ladies' saloon of the steamer Lexington, on Sunday morning. In August, 1853, I lectured in Cleveland, Ohio, and several other towns, and afterwards in Chicago, Illinois, and in Kenosha, Wisconsin. An election was to be held in Wisconsin in October, and the friends of prohibition in that State solicited my services for the ensuing month, and I could not refuse them. I therefore hastened home to transact some business which required my presence for a few days, and then returned, and lectured on my way in Toledo, Norwalk, Ohio, and Chicago, Illinois. I made the tour of the State of Wisconsin, delivering two lectures per day for four consecutive weeks, to crowded and attentive audiences.

My lecture in New Orleans, when I was in that city, was in the great Lyceum Hall, in St. Charles Street, and I lectured by the invitation of Mayor Crossman and several other influential gentlemen. The immense hall contained more than three thousand auditors, including the most respectable portion of the New Orleans public. I was in capital humor, and had warmed myself into a pleasant state of excitement, feeling that the audience was with me. While in the midst of an argument illustrating the poisonous and destructive nature of alcohol to the animal economy, some opponent called out, "How does it affect us, externally or internally?"

"*E*-ternally," I replied.

I have scarcely ever heard more tremendous merriment than that which followed this reply, and the applause was so prolonged that it was some minutes before I could proceed.

On the first evening when I lectured in Cleveland, Ohio, (it was in the Baptist Church,) I commenced in this wise: "If there are any ladies or gentlemen present who have never suffered in consequence of the use of intoxicating drinks as a beverage, either directly, or in the person of a dear relative or friend, I will thank them to rise." A man with a tolerably glowing countenance arose. "Had you never a friend who was intemperate?" I asked.

"Never!" was the positive reply.

A giggle ran through the opposition portion of the audience. "Really, my friends," I said, "I feel constrained to make a proposition which I did not anticipate. I am, as you are all aware, a showman, and I am always on the lookout for curiosities. This gentleman is a stranger to me, but if he will satisfy me to-morrow morning that he is a man of credibility, and that no friend of his was ever intemperate, I will be glad to engage him for ten weeks at $200 per week, to exhibit him in my American Museum in New York, as the greatest curiosity in this country."

A laugh that was a laugh followed this announcement.

"They may laugh, but it is a fact," persisted my opponent with a look of dogged tenacity.

"The gentleman still insists that it is a fact," I replied. "I would like, therefore, to make one simple qualification to my offer, I made it on the supposition that, at some period of his life, he had friends. Now if he never had any friends, I withdraw my offer; otherwise, I will stick to it."

This, and the shout of laughter that ensued, was too much for the gentleman, and he sat down. I noticed throughout my speech that he paid strict attention, and frequently indulged in a hearty laugh. At the close of the lecture he approached me, and extending his hand, which I readily accepted, he said, "I was particularly green in rising to-night. Having once stood up, I was determined not to be put down, but your last remark fixed me!" He then complimented me very highly on the reasonableness of my arguments, and declared that ever afterwards he would be found on the side of temperance.

Among the most gratifying incidents of my life have been several of a similar nature to the following: After a temperance speech in Philadelphia, a man about thirty years of age came forward, signed the teetotal pledge, and then, giving me his hand, he said, "Mr. Barnum, you have this night saved me from ruin. For the last two years I have been in the habit of tippling, and it has kept me continually under the harrow. This gentleman (pointing to a person at his side) is my partner in business, and I know he is glad I have signed the pledge to-night."

"Yes, indeed I am, George, and it is the best thing you ever did," replied his partner, "if you'll only stick to it."

"That will I do till the day of my death; and won't my dear little wife Mary cry for joy to-night, when I tell her what I have done!" he exclaimed in great exultation. At that moment he was a happy man, but he could not have been more so than I was.

Sir William Don—who came to this country and acted in several theatres, afterwards going to Australia, and dying, I believe, soon after his return to England—once heard me lecture, and immediately afterwards came forward and signed the pledge. He kept it for a short period only, although when he signed, he said that strong drink was the bane of his life. It is the one bane of too many brilliant men, who but for this one misfortune might attain almost every desirable success in life.

I may add, that I have lectured in Montreal, Canada, and many towns and cities in the United States, at my own expense. One of the greatest consolations I now enjoy is that of believing I have carried happiness to the bosom of many a family. In the course of my life I have written much for newspapers, on various subjects, and always with earnestness, but in none of these have I felt so deep an interest as in that of the temperance reform.

Were it not for this fact, I should be reluctant to mention, that besides numerous articles for the daily and weekly press, I wrote a little tract on "The Liquor Business," which expresses my practical view of the use and traffic in intoxicating drinks. In every one of my temperance lectures since the beginning of the year 1869, I have regularly read the following report, made by Mr. T. T. Cortis, Overseer of the Poor in Vineland, New Jersey:

Though we have a population of 10,000 people, for the period of six months no settler or citizen of Vineland has required relief at my hands as Overseer of the Poor. Within seventy days, there has only been one case among what we call the floating population, at the expense of $4.00. During the entire year, there has only been but one indictment, and that a trifling case of assault and battery, among our colored population. So few are the fires in Vineland, that we have no need of a fire department. There has only been one house burnt down in a year, and two slight fires, which were soon put out. We practically have no debt, and our taxes are only one per cent on the valuation. The police expenses of Vineland amount to $75.00 per year, the sum paid to me; and our poor expenses a mere trifle. I ascribe this remarkable state of things, so nearly approaching the golden age, to the industry of our people, and the absence of King Alcohol. Let me give you, in contrast to this, the state of things in the town from which I came, in New England. The population of the town was 9,500—a little less than that of Vineland. It maintained forty liquor shops. These kept busy a police judge, city marshal, assistant marshal, four night watchmen, six policemen. Fires were almost continual. That small place maintained a paid fire department, of four companies, of forty men each, at an expense of $3,000.00 per annum. I belonged to this department for six years, and the fires averaged about one every two weeks, and mostly incendiary. The support of the poor cost $2,500.00 per annum. The debt of the township was $120,000.00. The condition of things in this New England town is as favorable in that country as that of many other places where liquor is sold.

It seems to me that there is an amount of overwhelming testimony and unanswerable argument in this one brief extract, that makes it in itself one of the most perfect and powerful temperance lectures ever written.

CHAPTER XLIII.

The New Museum.

My new Museum on Broadway was liberally patronized from the start, but I felt that still more attractions were necessary in order to insure constant success. I therefore made arrangements with the renowned Van Amburgh Menagerie Company to unite their entire collection of living wild animals with the Museum. The new company was known as the "Barnum and Van Amburgh Museum and Menagerie Company," and as such was chartered by the Connecticut Legislature, the New York Legislature having refused us a charter unless I would "see" the "ring," a thousand dollars' worth, which I declined. I owned forty per cent and the Van Amburgh Company held the remaining sixty per cent in the new enterprise, which comprehended a large travelling menagerie through the country in summer, and the placing of the wild animals in the Museum in winter. The capital of the company was one million of dollars, with the privilege of doubling the amount. As one of the conditions of the new arrangement, it was stipulated that I should withdraw from all active personal attention to the Museum, but should permit my name to be announced as General Manager, and I was also elected President of the company. This arrangement gave me the comparative tranquillity which I now began to desire. I spent most of my time in Bridgeport, except in winter, when I resided in New York. I usually visited the Museum about once a week, but sometimes was absent for several months.

Meanwhile, immense additions were made to the curiosity departments of the new Museum. Every penny of the profits of this Museum and of the two immense travelling menageries of wild animals was expended in procuring additional attractions for our patrons. Among other valuable novelties introduced in this establishment was the famous collection made by the renowned lion-slayer, Gordon Cummings. This was purchased for me by my faithful friend, Mr. George A. Wells, who was then travelling in Great Britain with General Tom Thumb. The collection consisted of many hundreds of skins, tusks, heads and skeletons of nearly every species of African animal, including numerous rare specimens never before exhibited on this continent. It was a great Museum in itself, and as such had attracted much attention in London and elsewhere, but it was a mere addition to our Museum and Menagerie; and was exhibited without extra charge for admission.

In the summer of 1867, I saw in several New York papers a thrilling account of an immense gorilla, which had arrived from Africa in charge of Barnum's agent, for the Barnum and Van Amburgh Company. The accounts described the removal of the savage animal in a strong iron cage from the ship, and his transportation up Broadway to the museum. His cries and roarings were said to have been terrible, and when he was taken into the menagerie, he was reported to have bent the heavy iron bars of his cage, and in his cage to have seized a poker which was thrust at him, and to have twisted it as if it had been a bit of wire. Nothing so startlingly sensational in the line of zoölogical description had appeared since the *Tribune's* famous report of the burning of the American Museum, in 1865.

For several years I had been trying to secure such an animal, and several African travellers had promised to do their best to procure one for me; and I had offered as high as $20,000 for the delivery in New York of a full-grown, healthy gorilla. From the minute description now given by the reporters, I was convinced that, at last, the long-sought prize had been secured. I was greatly elated, and at once wrote from Bridgeport to our manager, Mr. Ferguson, advising him how to exhibit the valuable animal, and particularly how to preserve its precious life as long as might be possible. I have owned many ourang-outangs, and all of them die ultimately of pulmonary disease; indeed, it is difficult to keep specimens of the monkey tribe through the winter in our climate, on account of their tendency to consumption. I therefore advised Mr. Ferguson to have a cage so constructed that no draught of air could pass through it, and I further instructed him in methods of guarding against the gorilla's taking cold.

A few days later I went to New York expressly to see the gorilla, and on visiting the Museum, I was vexed beyond measure to find that the animal was simply a huge baboon! He was chained down, so that he could not stand erect, nor turn his back to visitors. His keeper could easily irritate him, and when the animal was excited, he would seize the iron bars with both hands, and, uttering horrid screams, would shake the cage so fiercely that it could be heard, and "felt" in the adjoining saloons. No doubt many of the visitors recalled Du Chaillu's accounts of the genuine gorilla, and were convinced that the veritable animal was before them. But I had been too long in the business to be caught by such chaff, and approaching the keeper, I asked him why he did not lengthen the chain, so that the animal could stand up?

"Because, if I do, he will show his tail," the keeper confidentially whispered in my ear.

The imposition was so silly and transparent that I did not care how soon it was exposed. As usual, however, I looked at the funny side of the matter, and immediately enclosed a ticket to my friend Mr. Paul Du Chaillu, who was then stopping at the Fifth Avenue Hotel, at the same time writing to the great African traveller, that, much as he had done, the Barnum and Van Amburgh Company had done more, since he had only killed gorillas, while we had secured a living one, and brought the monster safely from Africa to America. I informed him, moreover, that all the gorillas he had seen and described were tailless, while our far more remarkable specimen had a tail full four feet long!

Mr. Du Chaillu came into the Museum that afternoon, in great glee, with my open letter in his hand.

"Ah, Mr. Barnum," he exclaimed, "this is the funniest letter I ever received. Of course, you know your 'gorilla' is no gorilla at all, but only a baboon. I will not look at him, for when people ask me about 'Barnum's gorilla,' I prefer to be able to say that I have not seen him."

"On the contrary," said I, "I particularly desire that you should see the animal, and expose it. The imposition is too ridiculous."

"True; but I think your letter is more curious than your animal."

"Then I give you full leave to read the letter to all who ask you about the 'gorilla.' "

"Thank you," said Du Chaillu, "and I wish you would let me read it in my lectures at the West, where I am soon going on a tour."

I consented that he should do so, and I afterwards heard that he was delighting as well as enlightening western audiences on the subject of Manager Ferguson's management of the great "gorilla" in the Barnum and Van Amburgh Museum and Menagerie.

The menagerie of living animals was superior in extent to any other similar collection in America, embracing, as it did, almost every description of wild animal ever exhibited, including the smallest African elephant, and the only living giraffe then in the United States. The collection of lions and royal Bengal tigers was superb. There was a cage full of young lions that attracted great attention, and the whole menagerie was an exceedingly valuable one. When I say that to these attractions was added an able dramatic company, which performed every afternoon and evening, and that the admission to the entire establishment was but thirty cents, with no extra charge, except for a few front seats and private boxes, it is no wonder that this immense building, five stories high, and covering ground seventy-five by two hundred feet in area, was thronged "from sunrise to ten P. M.," and from top to bottom, with country and city visitors, of both sexes and all ages. The public was soon thoroughly convinced of the facts; first, that never before was such an outlay made for so great an assemblage of useful and amusing attractions, combining instruction with amusement, and thrown open to the people at so small a charge for admission; and second, that the surest way of deriving the greatest profit, in the long run, is to give people as much as possible for their money. That these facts were fully impressed upon our patrons is instanced in the monthly returns made to the United States Collector of Internal Revenue for the district, which showed that our receipts were larger than those of Wallack's Theatre, Niblo's Garden, or any other theatre or place of amusement in New York, or in America.

Anxious to gather curiosities from every quarter of the globe, I sent Mr. John Greenwood, junior, (who went for me to the isle of Cyprus and to Constantinople, in 1864,) on the "Quaker City" excursion, which left New York June 8, 1867, and returned in the following November. During his absence Mr. Greenwood travelled 17,735 miles, and brought back several interesting relics from the Holy Land, which were duly deposited in the Museum.

Very soon after entering upon the premises, I built a new and larger lecture room, which was one of the most commodious and complete theatres in New York, and I largely increased the dramatic company. Our collection swelled so rapidly that we were obliged to extend our premises by the addition of another building, forty by one hundred feet, adjoining the Museum. This addition gave us several new halls, which were speedily filled with curiosities. The rapid expansion of the establishment, and the immense interest excited in the public mind led me to consider a plan I had long contemplated, of taking some decided steps towards the foundation of a great free institution, which should be similar to and in some respects superior to the British Museum in London. "The Barnum and Van Amburgh Museum and Menagerie Company," chartered with a capital of $2,000,000 had, in addition to the New York establishment, thirty acres of land in Bridgeport, whereon it was proposed to erect suitable buildings and glass and wire edifices for breeding and acclimating rare animals and birds, and training such of them as were fit for public performances. In time, a new building in New York, covering a whole square, and farther up town, would be needed for the mammoth exhibition, and I was not without hopes that I might be the means of establishing permanently in the city an extensive zoölogical garden.

It was also my intention ultimately to make my Museum the nucleus of a great free national institution. When the American Museum was burned, and I turned my attention to the collection of fresh curiosities, I felt that I needed other assistance than that of my own agents in America and Europe. It occurred to me that if our government representatives abroad would but use their influence to secure curiosities in the respective countries to which they were delegated, a free public Museum might at once be begun in New York, and I proposed to offer a part of my own establishment rent-free for the deposit and exhibition of such rarities as might be collected in this way. Accordingly, a week after the destruction of the American Museum, a memorial was addressed to the President of the United States, asking him to give his sanction to the new effort to furnish the means of useful information and wholesome amusement, and to give such instructions to public officers abroad as would enable them, without any conflict with their legitimate duties, to give efficiency to this truly national movement for the advancement of the public good, without cost to the government. This memorial was dated July 20, 1865, and was signed by Messrs. E. D. Morgan, Moses Taylor, Abram Wakeman, Simeon Draper, Moses H. Grinnell, Stephen Knapp, Benjamin R. Winthrop, Charles Gould, Wm. C. Bryant, James Wadsworth, Tunis W. Quick, John A. Pitkin, Willis Gaylord, Prosper M. Wetmore, Henry Ward Beecher, and Horace Greeley. This memorial was in due time presented, and was indorsed as follows:

"EXECUTIVE MANSION, WASHINGTON, D. C.
April 27, 1866.
The purpose set forth in this Memorial is highly approved and commended, and our Ministers, Consuls and commercial agents are requested to give whatever influence in carrying out the object within stated they may deem compatible with the duties of their respective positions, and not inconsistent with the public interests.

ANDREW JOHNSON."

I went to Washington myself, and had interviews with the President, Secretaries Seward, McCulloch and Welles, and also with Assistant Secretary of the Navy, G. V. Fox, who gave me several muskets and other "rebel trophies." During my stay at the capital I had a pleasant interview with General Grant, who told me he had lately visited my Museum with one of his sons, and had been greatly gratified. Upon my mentioning, among other projects, that I had an idea of collecting the hats of distinguished individuals, he at once offered to send an orderly for the hat he had worn during his principal campaigns. All these gentlemen cordially approved of my plan for the establishment of a National Museum in New York.

But before this plan could be put into effective operation, an event occurred which is now to be narrated: The winter of 1867–68 was one of the coldest that had been known for years, and some thirty severe snowstorms occurred during the season. On Tuesday morning, March 3d, 1868, it was bitter cold. A heavy body of snow was on the ground, and as I sat at the breakfast table with my wife and an esteemed lady guest, the wife of my excellent friend Rev. A. C. Thomas, I read aloud the general news from the morning papers. Leisurely turning to the local columns, I said, "Hallo! Barnum's Museum is burned."

"Yes," said my wife, with an incredulous smile, "I suspect it is."

"It is a fact," said I, "just listen; 'Barnum's Museum totally destroyed by fire.' "

This was read so coolly, and I showed so little excitement, that both of the ladies supposed I was joking. My wife simply remarked:

"Yes, it was totally destroyed two years ago, but Barnum built another one."

"Yes, and that is burned," I replied; "now listen," and I proceeded very calmly to read the account of the fire. Mrs. Thomas, still believing from my manner that it was a joke, stole slyly behind my chair, and looking over my shoulder at the newspaper, she exclaimed:

"Why, Mrs. Barnum, the Museum is really burned. Here is the whole account of it in this morning's paper."

"Of course it is," I remarked, with a smile, "how could you think I could joke on such a serious subject!"

It was indeed too true, and the subject was no doubt "serious" enough; in fact the pecuniary blow was perhaps even heavier than the loss of the other Museum, especially as there was probably no Bennett around who would give me $200,000 for a lease! But during my whole life I had been so much accustomed to operations of magnitude for or against my interests, that large losses or gains were not apt to disturb my tranquillity. Indeed, my second daughter calling in soon after, and seeing how coolly I took the disaster, said that her husband had remarked that morning, "Your father wont care half so much about it as he would if his pocket had been picked of fifty dollars. That would have vexed him, but he will take this heavier loss as simply the fortune of war."

And this was very nearly the fact. Yet the loss was a large one, and the complete frustration of our plans for the future was a serious consideration. But worse than all were the sufferings of the poor wild animals which were burned to death in their cages. A very few only of these animals were saved. Even the people who were sleeping in the building barely escaped with their lives, and next to nothing else, so sudden was the fire and so rapid its progress. The papers of the following morning contained full accounts of the fire; and editorial writers, while manifesting much sympathy for the proprietors, also expressed profound regret that so magnificent a collection, especially in the zoölogical department, should be lost to the city.

The cold was so intense that the water froze almost as soon as it left the hose of the fire engines; and when at last everything was destroyed, except the front granite wall of the Museum building, that and the ladder, signs, and lamp-posts in front, were covered in a gorgeous framework of transparent ice, which made it altogether one of the most picturesque scenes imaginable. Thousands of persons congregated daily in that locality in order to get a view of the magnificent ruins. By moonlight the ice-coated ruins were still more sublime; and for many days and nights the old Museum was "the observed of all observers," and photographs were taken by several artists.

When the Museum was burnt, I was nearly ready to bring out a new spectacle, for which a very large extra company had been engaged, and on which a considerable sum of money had been expended in scenery, properties, costumes, and especially in enlarging the stage. I had expended altogether some $78,000 in building the new lecture-room, and in refitting the saloons. The curiosities were inventoried by the manager, Mr. Ferguson, at

$288,000. I bought the real estate only a little while before the fire, for $460,000, and there was an insurance on the whole of $160,000; and in June, 1868, I sold the lots on which the building stood for $432,000. The cause of the fire was a defective flue in a restaurant in the basement of the building.

Thus by the destruction of Iranistan, and two Museums, about a million of dollars' worth of my property had been destroyed by fire, and I was not now long in making up my mind to follow Mr. Greeley's advice on a former occasion, to "take this fire as a notice to quit, and go a-fishing."

We all know how difficult it is for a person to stop when he is engaged in business, and how seldom it is that we find a man who thinks he has accumulated money enough, and is willing to cease trying to make more. An active business life, like everything else, becomes a habit, and the strife for success in business, through all the changes of fortune, and ups and downs of trade, becomes an infatuation akin to that which spurs the gambler. Hence, men often pursue their money-getting occupations long after the necessity therefor has ceased. Of course, by wedding themselves to this one ambition they forego many of the higher pleasures of life, and though they have a vague idea of that "good time coming," when they are going to take things easy and enjoy themselves, that time never comes. Men who are entirely idle are the most miserable creatures in the world; but when by arduous toil they have secured a competence, and especially when they have reached a point in life where they are conscious of a waning of their vital energies, we must admit that they are unwise if they do not slip out of active business, and devote a large portion of their time to intellectual pursuits, social enjoyments, and, if they have not done so through life, to serious reflections on the ends and aims of human existence.

It is, perhaps, possible that notwithstanding the active life I have led, I have after all a lazy streak in my composition; at all events, I confess it was with no small degree of satisfaction that by this last burning of the Museum, notwithstanding the serious pecuniary loss it proved to me, I discovered a way open through which I could retire to a more quiet and tranquil mode of life. I therefore at once dissolved with the Van Amburgh Company, and sold out to them all my interest in the personal property of the concern. I was, however, beset on every side to start another Museum, and men of capital offered to raise a million of dollars if necessary, for that purpose, provided I would undertake its management. My constant reply was, "lead me not into temptation." I felt that I had enough to live on, and I earnestly believed the doctrine laid down in my lecture on "Money Getting," in regard to the danger of leaving too much property to children.

As I now had something like real leisure at my disposal, in the summer of 1868 I made my third visit to the White Mountains. To me, the locality and scene are ever fresh and ever wonderful. From the top of Mount Washington, one can see on every side within a radius of forty miles peaks piled on peaks, with smiling valleys here and there between, and, on a very clear day, the Atlantic Ocean off Portland, Maine, is distinctly visible—sixty miles away. Beauty, grandeur, sublimity, and the satisfaction of almost every sense combine to remind one of the ejaculation of that devout English soul who exclaims: "Look around with pleasure, and upward with gratitude." . . .

CHAPTER XLVI.

Sea-Side Park.

From the time when I first settled in Bridgeport and turned my attention to opening and beautifying new avenues, and doing whatever lay in my power to extend and improve that charming city, I was exceedingly anxious that public parks should be established, especially one where good drive-ways, and an opportunity for the display of the many fine equipages for which Bridgeport is celebrated, could be afforded. Mr. Noble and I began the movement by presenting to the city the beautiful ground in East Bridgeport now known as Washington Park,—a most attractive promenade and breathing place and a continual resort for citizens on both sides of the river, particularly in the summer evenings, when one of the city bands is an additional attraction to the pleasant spot. Thus our new city was far in advance of Bridgeport proper in providing a prime necessity for the health and amusement of the people.

Our park projects in the city date as far back as the year 1850. At that time, by an arrangement with Deacon David Sherwood, who lived in Fairfield, a few rods west of the Bridgeport line, and who owned land adjoining mine, we agreed to throw open a large plot of ground free to the public, provided State Street, in Bridgeport, was continued west so as to pass through this land. But a few "old fogies" through whose land the street would pass, thereby improving their property thousands of dollars in value, stupidly opposed the project in the Fairfield town-meeting, and the measure was defeated. Seventeen years afterwards, in 1867, after a long sleep, these same old fogies managed to awake, as did the citizens of Fairfield generally, and then State Street was extended without opposition; but property, to some extent, had changed hands and had largely increased in value, so that the chance of having a free park in that locality was forever lost, and the town was actually obliged to pay Deacon Sherwood for the privilege of continuing the highway through his land. How many similar opportunities for benefiting the public and posterity in all coming time are carelessly thrown away in every town, through the mere stupidity of mole-eyed land-owners, who stand as stumbling-blocks not only in the way of public improvements, but directly in opposition to their individual interests, and thus for scores of years rob the community of the pleasures to be derived from broad avenues lined with shade-trees and from open and free public grounds.

Up to the year 1865, the shore of Bridgeport west of the public wharves, and washed by the waters of Long Island Sound, was inaccessible to carriages, or even to horsemen, and almost impossible for pedestrianism. The shore edge in fact was strewn with rocks and boulders, which made it, like "Jordan" in the song, an exceedingly "hard road to travel." A narrow lane reaching down to the shore enabled parties to drive near to the water for the purpose of clamming, and occasionally bathing; but it was all claimed as private property by the land proprietors, whose farms extended down to the water's edge. On several occasions at low tide, I endeavored to ride along the shore on horseback for the purpose of examining "the lay of the land," in the hope of finding it feasible to get a public drive along the water's edge. On one occasion, in 1863, I succeeded in getting my horse around from the foot of Broad Street in Bridgeport to a lane over the Fairfield line, a few rods west of "Iranistan Avenue," a grand street which I have since opened at my own ex-

pense, and through my own land. From the observations
I made that day, I was satisfied that a most lovely park
and public drive might be, and ought to be opened along
the whole water-front as far as the western boundary line
of Bridgeport, and even extending over the Fairfield line.

Foreseeing that in a few years such an improvement
would be too late, and having in mind the failure of the
attempt in 1850 to provide a park for the people of
Bridgeport, I immediately began to agitate the subject in
the Bridgeport papers, and also in daily conversations
with such of my fellow-citizens as I thought would take
an earnest and immediate interest in the enterprise. I
urged that such an improvement would increase the tax-
able value of property in that vicinity many thousands of
dollars, and thus enrich the city treasury; that it would
improve the value of real estate generally in the city;
that it would be an additional attraction to strangers
who came to spend the summer with us, and to those who
might be induced from other considerations to make the
city their permanent residence; that the improvement
would throw into market some of the most beautiful
building-sites that could be found anywhere in Connecticut; and I dwelt upon the absurdity, almost criminality,
that a beautiful city like Bridgeport, lying on the shore of
a broad expanse of salt water, should so cage itself in, that
not an inhabitant could approach the beach. With these
and like arguments and entreaties I plied the people day
in and day out, till some of them began to be familiarized
with the idea that a public park close upon the shore of
the Sound was at least a possible if not probable thing.

But certain "conservatives," as they are called, said:
"Barnum is a hair-brained fellow, who thinks he can open
and people a New-York Broadway through a Connecticut wilderness"; and the "old fogies" added: "Yes, he is
trying to start another chestnut-wood fire for the city to
blow forever; but the city or town of Bridgeport will not
pay out money to lay out or to purchase public parks. If
people want to see green grass and trees, they have only

to walk or drive half a mile either way from the city limits, and they will come to farms where they can see either or both for nothing; and, if they are anxious to see salt water, and to get a breath of the Sound breeze, they can take boats at the wharves, and sail or row till they are entirely satisfied."

Thus talked the conservatives and the "old fogies," who unhappily, even if they are in a minority, are always a force in all communities. I soon saw that it was of no use to expect to get the city to pay for a park. The next thing was to see if the land could not be procured free of charge, or at a nominal cost, provided the city would improve and maintain it as a public park. I approached the farmers who owned the land lying immediately upon the shore, and tried to convince them that, if they would give the city free, a deep slip next to the water, to be used as a public park, it would increase in value the rest of their land so much as to make it a profitable operation for them. But it was like beating against the wind. They were 'not so stupid as to think that they could become gainers by giving away their property.' Such trials of patience as I underwent in a twelvemonth, in the endeavor to carry this point, few persons who have not undertaken like almost hopeless labor can comprehend. At last I enlisted the attention of Messrs. Nathaniel Wheeler, James Loomis, Francis Ives, Frederick Wood, and a few more gentlemen, and persuaded them to walk with me over the ground, which to me seemed in every way practicable for a park. These gentlemen, who were men of taste as well as of enterprise and public spirit, very soon coincided in my ideas as to the feasibility of the plan and the advantages of the site; and some of them went with me to talk with the land-owners, adding their own pleas to the arguments I had already advanced. At last, after much pressing and persuading, we got the terms upon which the proprietors would give a portion and sell another portion of their land which fronted on the water, provided the land thus disposed of should forever be appropriated to the purposes of a public park. But unfortunately a part of the land it was desirable to include was the small Mallett farm, of some thirty acres, then belonging to an unsettled estate, and neither the administrator nor the heirs could or would give away a rod of it. But the whole farm was for sale,—and, to overcome the difficulty in the way of its transfer for the public benefit, I bought it for about $12,000, and then presented the required front to the park. I did not want this land or any portion of it for my own purposes or profit, and I offered a thousand dollars to any one who would take my place in the transaction; but no one accepted, and I was quite willing to contribute so much of the land as was needed for so noble an object. Indeed, besides this, I gave $1,400 towards purchasing other land and improving the park; and, after months of persistent and personal effort, I succeeded in raising, by private subscription, the sum necessary to secure the land needed. This was duly paid for, deeded to and accepted by the city, and I had the pleasure of naming this new and great public improvement, "Sea-side Park."

Public journals are generally exponents of public opinion; and how the people viewed the new purchase, now their own property, may be judged by the following extracts from the leading local newspapers, when the land for the new enterprise was finally secured:

OUR SEA-SIDE PARK.
[*From the "Bridgeport Standard," August* 21, 1865.]
Bridgeport has taken another broad stride of which she may well be proud. The Sea-side Park is a fixed fact. Yesterday Messrs. P. T. Barnum, Captain John Brooks, Mr. George Bailey, Captain Burr Knapp, and Henry Wheeler generously donated to this city sufficient land for the Park, with the exception of seven or eight acres, which have been purchased by private subscriptions. Last night the Common Council appointed excellent Park Commissioners, and work on the sea-wall and the avenues surrounding the Park will be commenced at once.

Besides securing the most lovely location for a park to be found between New York and Boston, which for all time will be a source of pride to our city and State, there is no estimating the pecuniary advantage which this great improvement will eventually prove to our citizens. Plans are on foot and enterprises are agitated in regard to a park hotel, sea-side cottages, horse railroad branch, and other features, which, when consummated, will serve to amaze our citizens to think that such a delightful sea-side frontage has been permitted to lie so long unimproved. To Mr. P. T. Barnum, we believe, is awarded the credit of originating this beautiful improvement, and certainly to his untiring, constant, and persevering personal efforts are we indebted for its being finally consummated. Hon. James C. Loomis was the first man who heartily joined with Barnum in pressing the plan of a sea-side park upon the attention of our citizens, but it is due to our citizens themselves to say that, with an extraordinary unanimity, they have not only voted to appropriate $10,000 from the city treasury to making the avenues around the Park, and otherwise improving it, but they have also generously aided by private contributions in purchasing such land as was not freely given for the Park. Of course, we shall not only, at an early day, publish the names of such citizens as have subscribed money for this purpose, but they will also be handed down to posterity, as they will richly deserve, in the publication of the Park Commissioners.

[*From the "Bridgeport Standard," August* 21, 1865.]

The names of P. T. Barnum, Capt. John Brooks, Mr. George Bailey, Capt. Burr Knapp and Henry Wheeler have gone into history as the generous contributors to the best enterprise ever attempted for the benefit of our city; and the city has accepted the trust with the most commendable promptness, and appointed its commissioners, who have already entered upon their duties. We shall watch now with eager interest the unfolding and development of such a park as can nowhere be found on either side of the Sound, and one which shall be "a thing of beauty and a joy forever" to our city.

It needs but the hand of a skilful art, assisted by

a proper public spirit, to render the Sea-side Park a
charmed spot of delightful resort for public drives or
private walks. The commissioners chosen to superintend
the inauguration of the laying out and improvements
of the grounds are men of correct taste, of good judgment and of liberal and comprehensive views as to the
wants and demands of a growing city like Bridgeport.
They understand that Nature is here to be made so attractive by Art, that all classes shall be drawn hither not
merely for the pleasure of enjoying a favorite resort but
also for the profit which comes to the nobler impulses of
our nature, by the contemplation of cunning handicraft
upon the landscape, as God left it for man to adorn and
beautify. Here will be planted trees of every variety that
will endure the temperature of this latitude, and flowers
of every hue and perfume; here will walks serpentine
through shady groves, and anon lead to behold the broad
expanse of the beautiful Sound.

Some one has aptly said, that one work of art was
worth a thousand lectures on art. Here, then, let the stat-
ues of the artist be placed, to educate the masses by their
silent teachings, and win them to higher ideas and better
views of life by their mute eloquence. One feature of
American parks is especially worthy of mention; they are
essentially and emphatically democratic. They are made
for the people, and are in turn appreciated by the people.
They are open alike to the millionnaire with his coach-
and-six, and the poor pedestrian without a penny. The
advantages possessed by Bridgeport as a manufacturing
city are becoming daily more and more appreciated by
business-men from various portions of the country.
There is no city in the State which can compare with ours
in the recent erection of large and permanent manufacturing establishments. This fact brings into our midst a
large industrial population, for which, even now, the
supply of dwellings is inadequate to the demand. This
population, commingling and combining with our own,
and possessing energy, enterprise, business tact and intelligence, will rapidly develop the resources of our city
and its surroundings for mechanical pursuits, and the productions of the various manufacturing establishments

already erected, or in process of erection. To such a class, the benefits of a Park, possessing such facilities for recreation and improvement as the Sea-side Park will present, will be incalculable, in fostering the health, promoting the happiness, and elevating the taste of all who can avail themselves of its beneficial influences.

To the public-spirited gentlemen who have so generously donated to the city the land for the Sea-side Park, Bridgeport owes a debt of gratitude which she can never repay. Their names will descend to posterity, and be remembered with pride and exultation as among the noblest of public benefactors, so long as the flowers bloom and the waves wash the margin of the Sea-side Park. No citizen of Bridgeport, identified with her growth and prosperity, and having the future welfare of the city at heart, should fail to contribute, in such a manner as best he may, to such a grand improvement. Let our citizens take hold of this noble enterprise with that large and liberal spirit in which it has been conceived and thus far consummated, and Bridgeport will ere long possess an attraction which will draw hither for permanent residence much of the wealth and intelligence, refinement and virtue of the great metropolis, which now sequesters itself along the banks of the Hudson, or among the sand-knolls of New Jersey.

Thus was my long-cherished plan at length fulfilled; nor did my efforts end here, for I aided and advised in all important matters in the laying out and progress of the new park; and in July, 1869, I gave to the city several acres of land, worth at the lowest valuation $5,000, which were added to and included in this public pleasure-ground, and now make the west end of the park.

At the beginning, the park on paper and the park in reality were two quite different things. The inaccessibility of the site was remedied by approaches which permitted the hundreds of workmen to begin to grade the grounds, and to lay out the walks and drives. The rocks and boulders over which I had more than once attempted to make my way on foot and on horseback were devoted to the building of a substantial sea-wall, under the able superintendence of Mr. David W. Sherwood. Paths were opened, shade-trees were planted; and fortunately there was in the very centre of the ground a beautiful grove of full growth, which is one of the most attractive features of this now charming spot; and a broad and magnificent drive follows the curves of the shore and encircles the entire park. Although work is constantly going on and much remains to be done, yet a considerable portion of the park presents a finished appearance: a large covered music-stand has been built; and, on a rising piece of the ground, a substantial foundation has been built for a Soldiers' Monument. The corner-stone of this monument was laid with impressive ceremonies and a military display, in the presence of a large concourse of citizens and soldiers, among whom were Major-General Alfred H. Terry, U.S.A.; Major-General and Governor Joseph H. Hawley; Adjutant-General Charles T. Stanton; Quartermaster-General Julius S. Gilman; Surgeon-General Philo G. Rockwell; Paymaster-General William B. Wooster; Aides-de-Camp and Colonel John H. Burnham, Alford P. Rockwell, William H. Mallory, Charles M. Coit, General S. W. Kellogg, of the First Brigade; Colonel S. E. Merwin, jr., Colonel Crawford, and other officers of the Governor's staff, and of the Connecticut State Militia.

The branch horse-railroad already reaches one of the main entrances, and brings down crowds of people every day and evening, and especially on the evenings in which the band plays. At such times the avenues are not only thronged with superb equipages and crowds of people, but the whole harbor is alive with row-boats, sail-boats and yachts. The views on all sides are charming. In the rear is the city, with its roofs and spires; Black Rock and Stratford lights are in plain sight; to the eastward and southward stretches "Old Long Island's sea-girt shore"; and between lies the broad expanse of the salt water, with its ever "fresh" breezes, and the perpetual panorama of sails and steamers. I do not believe that a million dollars to-day would compensate the city of Bridgeport for the loss of what is confessed to be the most delightful public pleasure-ground between New York and Boston.

For these magnificent results, accomplished in so short a time, the people of Bridgeport are indebted to the park commissioners, and especially to Mr. Nathaniel Wheeler, whose untiring energy and exquisite taste have been mainly instrumental in bringing this work forward to its present state of completion.

There is easy and cheap access to this ground by means of the horse-railroad from East Bridgeport and Fairfield, and numerous avenues open directly upon the park from Bridgeport. It is the daily resort of thousands, who go to inhale the salt sea-air; and the main drive is already, on a lesser scale, to the citizens of Bridgeport, what the grand avenue in Central Park is to the people of New York; with this priceless advantage, however, in favor of Sea-side Park, of a frontage on the Sound, and a shore on which the waves are ever breaking, and sounding the grand, unending story of the mysteries of the great deep.

On the western and northern margins of this public ground, in sight of the Sound and in full view of every part of the park, will hereafter be built the villas and mansions of the wealthiest citizens, and, when the hand that now pens these lines is stilled forever, and thousands look from these sea-side residences across the water to Long-Island shore, and over the groves and lawns and walks and drives of the beautiful ground at their feet, it may be a source of gratification and pride to my posterity to hear the expressions of gratitude that possibly will be expressed to the memory of their ancestor who secured to all future generations the benefits and blessings of Sea-side Park.

CHAPTER XLVII.

Waldemere.

What I can call, without undue display of egotism or vanity, my "public life," may be said to have closed with my formal and final retirement from the managerial profession, when my second Museum was destroyed by fire, March 3, 1868. But he must have been a careless reader of these pages, which record the acts and aspirations of a long and industrious career, who does not see that what, in opposition to my "public life," may be considered my "private life," has also been largely devoted to the comfort, convenience, and permanent prosperity of the community with which so many of my hopes and happiest days are thoroughly identified. I speak of these things, I trust, with becoming modesty, and yet with less reluctance than I should do, if my fellow-citizens of Bridgeport had not generally and generously awarded me sometimes, perhaps, more than my need of praise for my unremitting and earnest efforts to promote whatever would conduce to the growth and improvement of our charming city.

When I first selected Bridgeport as a permanent residence for my family, its nearness to New York and the facilities for daily transit to and from the metropolis were present and partial considerations only in the general advantages the location seemed to offer. Nowhere, in all my travels in America and abroad, had I seen a city whose very position presented so many and varied attractions. Situated on Long Island Sound, with that vast water-view in front, and on every other side a beautiful and fertile country with every variety of inland scenery, and charming drives which led through valleys rich with well-cultivated farms, and over hills thick-wooded with far-stretching forests of primeval growth,—all these natural attractions appeared to me only so many aids to the advancement the beautiful and busy city might attain, if public-spirit, enterprise, and money grasped and improved the opportunities the locality itself extended. I saw that what Nature had so freely lavished must be supplemented by yet more liberal Art.

Consequently, and quite naturally, when I projected and established my first residence in Bridgeport, I was exceedingly desirous that all the surroundings of Iranistan should accord with the beauty and completeness of that place. I was never a victim to that mania which possesses many men of even moderate means to "own everything that joins them," and I knew that Iranistan would so increase the value of surrounding property that none but first-class residences would be possible in the vicinity. But there was other work to do, which, while affording advantageous approaches to my property, would at the same time be a lasting benefit to the public; and so I opened Iranistan Avenue, and other broad and beautiful streets, through land which I freely purchased and as freely gave to the public, and these highways are now the most convenient as well as charming in the city.

To have opened all these new avenues, in their entire length, at my own cost, and through my own ground, would have required a confirmation of Miss Lavinia Warren's opinion, that what little of the city of Bridgeport and the adjacent town of Fairfield was not owned by General Tom Thumb, belonged to P. T. Barnum. It is true that, apart from my East Bridgeport property, I became a very large owner of real estate on the other side of the river, in Bridgeport proper and in Fairfield, my purchases in Fairfield lying on and so near to the boundary line—Division Street—as virtually to be in Bridge-port. Everywhere through my own lands I laid out and threw open to the public, streets of the generous width which distinguished the old "King's roads" in the colonies, before grasping farmers and others encroached upon, and fenced in as private property, land that really belonged to the public forever; and on both sides of every avenue I laid out and planted a profusion of elms and other trees. In this way, I have opened miles of new streets, and have planted thousands of shade-trees in Bridgeport; for I think there is much wisdom in the advice of the Laird of Dumbiedikes, in Scott's "Heart of Mid-Lothian," who sensibly says: "When ye hae naething else to do, ye may be aye sticking in a tree; it will be growing when ye're sleeping." But, in establishing new streets, too often, when I had gone through my own land, the project came literally to an end, some "old fogy" blocked the way,—my way, his own way, and the highway,—and all I could do would be to jump over his field, and continue my new street through land I might own on the other side, till I reached the desired terminus in the end or continuation of some other street; or till, unhappily, I came to a dead stand-still at the ground of some other "old fogy," who, like the original owners of what is now the shorefront of Sea-side Park, "did not believe there was money to be made by giving away their property."

And this is the manner in which these old fogies talked: "We do n't believe in these improvements of Barnum's. What's the use of them? We can get to the city by the old road or street, as we have done for forty years. The new street will cut the pasture or mowing-lot in two, and make a checkerboard of the farm. It was bad enough to have the railroad go through, and we would have prevented that if we could; but this new street business is all bosh!" And then, singularly enough, every old fogy would wind up with: "I declare, I believe the whole thing is only to benefit Barnum, so that he can sell land, which he bought anywhere from sixty to two hundred dollars an acre, at the rate of five thousand dollars an acre in building-lots, as he is actually doing to-day."

It is strange indeed that these men, who could see the benefit to "Barnum's property" by opening new streets which would immediately convert cheap farm and pasture land into choice and high-priced building-lots, should not see that precisely the same thing would proportionately increase the value of their own property. Conservatism may be a good thing in the state, or in the church, but it is fatal to the growth of cities; and the conservative notions of old fogies make them indifferent to the requirements which a very few years in the future will compel, and blind to their own best interests. Such men never look beyond the length of their noses, and consider every investment a dead loss unless they can get the sixpence profit into their pockets before they go to bed. My own long training and experience as a manager impelled me to carry into such private enterprises as the purchase of real estate that best and most essential managerial quality of instantly deciding, not only whether a venture was worth undertaking, but what, all things considered, that venture would result in. Almost any man can see how a thing will begin, but not every man is gifted with the foresight to see how it will end, or how, with the proper effort, it may be made to end. In East Bridgeport, where we had no "conservatives" to contend with, we were only a few years in turning almost tenantless farms into a populous and prosperous city. On the other side of the river, while the opening of new avenues, the planting of shade-trees, and the building of many houses, have afforded me the highest pleasures of my life, I confess that not a few of my greatest annoyances have been occasioned by the opposition of those who seem to be content to simply vegetate through their existence, and who looked upon me as a restless, reckless innovator, because I was trying to remove the moss from everything around them, and even from their own eyes.

In the summer of 1867, the health of my wife continuing to decline, her physician directed that she should remove nearer to the sea-shore; and, as she felt that the care of a large establishment like Lindencroft was more than she could bear, I sold that place. I have already spoken of my building of this residence. It was emphatically a labor of love. All that taste and money could do was fairly lavished upon Lindencroft; so that, when all was finished, it was not only a complete house in all respects, but it was a perfect home. And a home I meant it to be, in every and the best sense of the word, for my declining years. Consequently, from basement to attic, everything was constructed, by days' work, in the most perfect manner possible. Convenience and comfort were first consulted, and thereafter, with no attempt at ostentation, elegance, pure and simple, predominated and permeated everywhere. No first-class house in the metropolis was more replete with all that goes to constitute a complete dwelling-place. Under this new roof I gathered my library, my pictures, my souvenirs of travel in other lands, and assembled my household "gods"; while the surrounding grounds, adorned with statuary and fountains, displayed also, in the walks, the arbors, the lawns, the garden, the piled-up rocks even, the profusion of trees and shrubbery, and the wealth of rare and beautiful flowers, my wife's exquisite taste, which in times past had made the grounds of our loved and lost Iranistan so celebrated as well as charming. It was hard indeed to tear ourselves from this fascinating spot, but there are times when even the charms of home must be sacrificed to the claims of health.

Lindencroft was sold July 1, 1867, and we immediately removed for a summer's sojourn to a small farmhouse adjoining Sea-side Park. During the hot days of the next three months we found the delightful seabreeze so bracing and refreshing that the season passed like a happy dream, and we resolved that our future summers should be spent on the very shore of Long Island Sound. I did not, however, perfect my arrangements in time to prepare my own summer residence for the ensuing season; and during the hot months of 1868 we resided in a new and very pretty house I had just completed on State Street, in Bridgeport, and which I subsequently sold, as I intended doing when I built it. But, towards the end of the summer, I added by purchase to the Mallett farm, adjoining Sea-side Park, a large and beautiful hickory grove, which seemed to be all that was needed to make the site exactly what I desired for a summer residence. It will be remembered that I bought this Mallett farm, not for myself, but so that a portion of it could be devoted to the public park; and, a generous slice having been thus given away, there were several acres remaining which were admirably adapted to one or more residences, and the purchase of the grove property made the location nearly perfect.

But there was a vast deal to do in grading and preparing the ground, in opening new streets and avenues as approaches to the property, and in setting out trees near the proposed site of the house; so that ground was not broken for the foundation till October. I planned a house which should combine the greatest convenience with the highest comfort, keeping in mind always that houses are made to live in as well as to look at, and to be "homes" rather than mere residences. So the house was made to include abundant room for guests, with dressing-rooms and baths to every chamber; water from the city throughout the premises; gas, manufactured on my own ground; and that greatest of all comforts, a semi-detached kitchen, so that the smell as well as the secrets of the cuisine might be confined to its own locality. The stables and gardens were located far from the mansion, on the opposite side of one of the newly opened avenues, so that in the immediate vicinity of the house, on either side and before both fronts, stretched large lawns, broken only by the grove, single shade-trees, rock-work, walks, flower-beds and drives. The whole scheme as planned was faithfully carried out in less than eight months. The first foundation stone was laid in October, 1868; and we moved into the completed house in June following, in 1869.

It required a regiment of faithful laborers and mechanics, and a very considerable expenditure of money, to accomplish so much in so short a space of time. Those who saw a comparatively barren waste thus suddenly converted to a blooming garden, and, by the successful transplanting and judicious placing of very large and full-grown forest trees, made to seem like a long-settled place, considered the creation of my new summer home almost a work of magic; but there is no magic when determination and dollars combine to achieve a work. When we moved into this new residence, we formally christened the place "Waldemere,"—literally, but not so euphoniously, "Waldammeer," "Woods-by-the-Sea,"— for I preferred to give this native child of my own conception an American name of my own creation.

On the same estate, and fronting the new avenue I opened between my own property and the public park, I built at the same time two beautiful cottages, one of which is known as the "Petrel's Nest," and the other, occupied by my eldest daughter, Mrs. Thompson, and my youngest daughter, Mrs. Seeley, as a summer residence, is called "Wavewood." From the east front of Waldemere, across the sloping lawn, and through the reaches of the grove, these cottages are in sight, and before the three residences stretches the broad Sound, with nothing to cut off the view, and nothing intervening but the western portion of Sea-side Park. Sea-side and sea-breezes, however, do not include the sum of rural felicities in summer; and so I still keep possession of the fine farm which, years ago, was the scene of the elephant-plowing feats. On this property, which is in charge of a judicious farmer, I have some very fine imported stock, including several head. of the celebrated white-blanket "Dutch cattle," which excite the curiosity and attract the attention of all who see them. These cattle are black, with a distinctly defined white "blanket" around their bodies, giving them a very unique appearance; and when they struck my fancy in Holland, some years ago, I imported several of them: nor is their singular appearance their best recommendation, for they are excellent milkers, and my dairy and farm products keep my table constantly supplied with fresh fruits and vegetables, poultry, and that choicest of country luxuries, pure cream.

Amid such comforts, advantages, and luxuries the summer months speed swiftly and sweetly by. My well-supplied stables afford the means of enjoying the numberless delightful drives which abound in the vicinity; and my salt-water-loving friend, Mr. George A. Wells, is always ready to minister to the pleasure of myself or my guests by tendering the use of anything in his Sound fleet, from a row-boat to a yacht. The five months in the year which I devote to rural rest seem all too short for the enjoyment which is necessarily compressed in the twenty weeks. But I can feel at the end of the season that it is a consolidation as well as compression, not only of pleasure, but of capital, in the way of health and vigor for the winter's campaign of city living and metropolitan excitement.

For, at my time of life, and especially for a man who has had so much to do with the metropolitan million as I have done, I am convinced that the city is the most congenial residence during the cooler season of the year. No matter how active may have been one's life, as a man grows older, if he does not become a little lazy, he at least learns to crave for comfortable ease and seeks for quiet. To such a man, the city in winter extends numberless pleasures. There is a sense of satisfaction even in the well-cleared sidewalks after a snow-storm, and an almost selfish happiness in looking out upon a storm from a well-warmed library or parlor window. One loves to find the morning papers, fresh from the press, lying upon the breakfast-table; and the city is the centre of attractions in

the way of operas, concerts, picture-galleries, libraries,
the best music, the best preaching, the best of everything
in æsthetical enjoyments. Having made up my mind to
spend seven months of every year in the city, in the
summer of 1867 I purchased the elegant and most eligi-
bly situated mansion, No. 438 Fifth Avenue, corner of
Thirty-ninth Street, at the crowning point of Murray
Hill, in New York, and moved into it in November. My
residence therein in the winter season has fully confirmed
my impressions in its favor. The house is replete with all
that can constitute a pleasant home, and the location is so
near to Central Park that we spend hours of every fine
day in that great pleasure-ground. While I am in town, it
is scarcely more than once or twice a week that I take
pains to ascertain by personal observation that I am living
on the edge of a toiling, excited city of a million inhabitants. My pecuniary interests in Connecticut and in New
York occupy my attention sufficiently to keep me from
ennui, and an extended correspondence—for which I do
not yet feel the need of a private secretary—employs an
hour or more of every day. I have had letters from New
Zealand, and other remote quarters of the globe, respecting curiosities, and addressed simply to "Mr. Barnum, America," and the post-office officials, knowing of
no other Barnum who would be likely to receive letters
from such out-of-the-way places, regularly put these
vaguely addressed letters in my New York box.

Yet I suppose that not less than two-thirds of all the
letters I receive are earnest petitions for pecuniary aid.
This begging-letter business began to persecute me as
long ago as the time of the Jenny Lind engagement, and
even before. Many of these letters ask money as a free
gift, and some of them demand assistance; while others
request temporary loans, or invite me to furnish the capital for enterprises which are certain to bring the richest
returns to all concerned therein. When I was travelling
with Jenny Lind, I received a letter from a woman in
Pittsburg, Pennsylvania, who informed me that she had

named her just-born boy-and-girl twins "P. T. Barnum"
and "Jenny Lind," coolly adding that we might send
$5,000 for their immediate wants, and make such provi-
sion for their future education and support as might be
determined upon at the proper time! In some of these
letters, the amusement afforded by the orthography and
grammar was almost a compensation for the annoyance
and impudence of the requests. One very bad speller,
referring me to a former employer of the letter-writer,
wrote: "I Can rePhurr you too Him"; another, urging his
petition, declared; "god Nose I am Poore"; and not long
ago I received a communication from an old man who
claimed to be too decrepid to earn a support, but he urged
that he was a religious man, and added: "I tak grait ple-
shur in Readin my bibel, speshily the Proffits"; and it did
look a little as if he had a sharp eye to the "Proffits."

I have said but little in these pages of the immediate
circle which is nearest and dearest to me. My wife, with
whom I have lived so many happy years, and who has
been my support in adversity and my solace in prosperity,
still survives. Our children are all daughters: Caroline C.,
the eldest, was married to Mr. David W. Thompson, October 19, 1852; Helen M., my second daughter, was
married to Mr. Samuel H. Hurd, October 20, 1857;
Frances J., the third daughter, was born May 1, 1842,
and died April 11, 1844; and Pauline T., the fourth
daughter, was married on her birthday, March 1, 1866,
to Mr. Nathan Seeley. For my eldest daughter I built and
furnished a beautiful house on ground near Iranistan, and
she moved into it immediately after her marriage, though
of late years she has resided in New-York in winter and in
Bridgeport in summer. For Helen and Pauline, I bought
and furnished handsome houses in Lexington Avenue, in
New-York, within a short distance of my own city residence in Fifth Avenue. A fine young rising generation of
my grandchildren is growing up around them and me.

I have written as little as might be, too, about my religious principles and profession, because I agree with the

man who, in answer to the pressing inquiry, declared that
he had "no religion to *speak* of"; and I believe with him
that true religion is more a matter of work than of words.
When I am in the city, I regularly attend the services and
preaching of the Rev. Dr. E. H. Chapin, and I usually go
to the meetings of the same denomination in Bridgeport.
"He builds too low who builds beneath the skies"; and I
can truly say that I have always felt my entire dependence
upon Him who is the dispenser of all adversity, as well as
the giver of all good. With a natural proclivity to look
upon the bright side of things, I am sure that under some
of the burdens—the Jerome entanglement, for instance—which have borne so heavily upon me, I should
have been tempted, as others have been, to suicide, if I
had supposed that my troubles were brought upon me by
mere blind chance. I knew that I deserved what I received; I had placed too much confidence in mere money
and my own personal efforts; I was too much concerned
in material prosperity; and I felt that the blow was wisely
intended for my ultimate benefit,—a chastening, which,
like the husks to the prodigal son, should cause me to
"come to myself," and teach me the lesson that there is
something infinitely better than money or position or
worldly prosperity in our "Father's house."

And I should be ungrateful indeed, if on my birthday,
this fifth of July, 1869, when I enter upon my sixtieth
year in full health and vigor, with the possibility of many
happy days to come, I did not reverently recognize the
beneficent Hand that has crowned me with so many
comforts, and surrounded me with so many blessings. It
is on this day, in my own beautiful home of Waldemere,
that I write these concluding lines, which record a long
and busy career, with the sincere hope that my experiences, if not my example, will benefit my fellow-men.

Rest Only Found in Action.

E very one knows the story of the Emperor Charles the Fifth. His ambition gratified to satiety in the conquest of kingdoms, and the firm establishment of his empire, he craved rest. He abdicated his throne, "retired from business," content to live on his laurels in the peaceful shades of the Cloister at Yustee. The tradition is that here he forgot the world without, withdrew in thought as in person from the cares and turmoils of State, and found rest and cheerfulness by alternating his devotions with the tinkering of clocks. Perhaps every one is not so familiar with the somewhat recent correction of this romantic story by Mr. Stirling. In fact, the Emperor was never so restless as when he was taking rest; was never so full of the perplexities of empire as when, in "due form," he had shaken them off. In the Cloister he was the same man that he was in the Camp and the Court; and when he sought to repress his energies, they simply tormented him.

Not denying that my egotism is equal to a good deal, I must beg my readers not to suppose that I assume for my own history a very extended similarity to that of the greatest monarch of his time. In fact, the points of difference are quite as striking as those of resemblance. It is true, we both tried the "clock business;" but I must claim that my tinkering in that way throws that of the Emperor entirely in the shade. I was not, however, fool enough to go into a cloister. Let not an illustration any more than a parable "run on all fours." But I want a royal illustration; and the history of Charles the Fifth, in the particular of abdicating for rest, I find very pertinent to my own experience. I took a formal, and as I then supposed a last adieu of my readers on my fifty-ninth birth-day. I was, as I had flattered myself, through with travel, with adventures, and with business, save so far as the care of my competence would require my attention. My book closed without a suspicion that in any subsequent edition "more of the same sort" would make possible an ADDITIONAL CHAPTER. It is with a sense of surprise, and withal a feeling akin to the ludicrous, that in this new edition, I cannot bring my career up to my sixty first birth-day, without filling a few more pages, in their contents not unlike in kind to those which make the bulk of my book.

As stated on page 359, my final retirement from the managerial profession closed with the destruction of my second Museum by fire, March 3d, 1868. But when I wrote that sentence I had not learned by a three years' cessation of business, how utterly fruitless it is to attempt to chain down energies which are peculiar to my nature. No man not similarly situated can imagine the *ennui* which seizes such a nature after it has lain dormant for a few months. Having "nothing to do," I thought at first was a very pleasant, as it was to me an entirely new sensation.

"I would like to call on you in the summer if you have any leisure, in Bridgeport," said an old friend.

"I am a man of leisure and thankful that I have nothing to do; so you cannot call amiss," I replied, with an immense degree of self-satisfaction.

"Where is your office down-town when you live in New York?" asked another friend.

"I have no office," I proudly replied. "I have done work enough, and shall play for the rest of my life. I don't go down-town once a week; but I ride in the Park every day, and am at home much of my time."

I am afraid I chuckled often when I saw rich merchants and bankers driving for their offices on a stormy morning, while I, looking complacently from the window of my cozy library, said to myself, "Let it snow and blow, there's nothing to call *me* out to-day." But Nature *will* assert herself. Reading is pleasant as a pastime; writing without any special purpose soon tires; a game of chess will answer as a condiment; lectures, concerts, operas, and dinner parties are well enough in their way, but to a robust, healthy man of forty years' active *business* life, something else is needed to satisfy. Sometimes like the truant school-boy I found all my friends engaged, and I had no play-mate. I began to fill my house with visitors, and yet frequently we spent evenings quite alone. Without really perceiving what the matter was, time hung on my hands, and I was ready to lecture gratuitously for every charitable cause that I could benefit.

Then I, who had traveled so many years, that all cities almost seemed to me as the same old "brick and mortar," began now to think I would like to travel. In 1869 an English friend and his daughter came to America specially to visit me. They wanted to see the "New World," and I was just in a state of mind to enjoy showing it to them. We first went to Niagara Falls, going by the Hudson River and Central Railroads; and returned by way of the Erie. I saw these scenes through the eyes of my English friends, and took a special pleasure in witnessing their surprise and delight. As they extolled the beautiful Hudson, that stream looked lovelier than ever; the Catskill Mountains were higher to me than ever before; Albany, Syracuse, and Rochester, were more lively than usual, for the same cause; the mammoth International Hotel at Niagara Falls looked capacious enough to bag up the whole islands of Great Britain; and the immense Cataract seemed large enough to drown all the inhabitants thereof. The Palace cars of the Erie Railroad astonished my friends and gave me great satisfaction. The contagion of their enthusiasm opened my eyes to marvels in spectacles which I had long dismissed as common-places!

They wanted to go to Cuba. I had been there twice; yet I readily agreed to accompany them. We took steamer from New York in January, 1870. We had a smooth, pleasant voyage, and did not even know when we passed Cape Hatteras. In three days we had doffed all winter clothing, and arrayed ourselves in white linen. Three weeks were most truly enjoyed among the novel scenes of Havana, and the peculiar attractions of Matanzas,—including a visit to the new and beautiful Cave a few miles from that city. We made a charming visit to a coffee plantation and orange orchard; another to a sugar plantation, where my English friends, as well as myself, were shocked to see the negro slaves, male and female, boys and girls, cutting and carrying the sugar cane under the lash of the mounted, booted, and spurred Spanish overseer.

But riding in our charming volantes from that plantation to the exceedingly beautiful valley of the Yumurri, caused us almost to forget the sad scene we had witnessed. We all agreed as we stood on the east side of this almost celestial valley and witnessed the sun dropping behind the hill, on whose summit the royal palms were holding up their beautiful plumes, that the valley below, interspersed with its cottages and streamlets, and its rich tropical trees, shrubs and flowers, was a scene of surpassing loveliness; and I was not surprised to see the tears of joy and gratitude roll down the cheeks of the young English lady. I enjoyed this scene hugely; but as one evidence that this pleasure was chiefly derived from the enjoyment it afforded my trans-Atlantic friends, I will say that when I was in Cuba with Jenny Lind in 1851, I witnessed the same scene without emotion, so absorbed was I in business at that time. And this is a fitting opportunity for saying that in order to enjoy traveling, and indeed almost anything else, it is of the very first importance that it be done with congenial companions.

We feasted upon oranges, pineapples, bananas, and other tropical fruits, and enjoyed the warm, mild days. The enjoyment was no doubt enhanced, or at least better appreciated, by our reading of the freezing condition of our New York friends. The quaint buildings, and the novel manners and customs of a nation speaking a different language from our own, of course are interesting for a short time.

We went to New Orleans by steamer. We stopped a few days at the St. Charles' Hotel; "did" the city; and then took passage for Memphis on a steamer which was so capacious and commodious that my English friends declared, that people at "home" would scarce believe it was a steamer. A few days' sail up the broad Mississippi was a real treat. The conversations which my English friend held with the Southern planters, and their manumitted slaves, caused him to somewhat change his opinions in regard to the merits of our late civil war.

From Memphis we went by rail to the Mammoth Cave of Kentucky; thence to Louisville, Cincinnati, Pittsburgh, Harrisburgh, Baltimore, and Washington. A few days sojourn at the best hotel in the world, "The Arlington," a visit to all the attractions in and around our national Capitol,—including attendance at Mrs. President Grant's Levee and a talk with the President, as well as numerous senators and members of Congress, terminated our visit. We then proceeded to Richmond; for my friend had a great desire to see the Confederate Capital, and especially Libby Prison, and "Castle Thunder." He was particularly indignant when he discovered that the latter institution was a tobacco warehouse, instead of being a great castellated fortress, such as his imagination had pictured it. From Richmond we visited Baltimore and Philadelphia, and returned to New York.

In April we made up a small, congenial party of ladies and gentlemen, and visited California via the Union and Central Pacific Railroads. And let me here say, that this trip is just one of the most delightful that I ever made.

The Pullman Palace Cars are so convenient and comfortable that ladies and gentlemen can make the trip to California, a distance of 3,000 miles, with no more real fatigue than they will experience in their own drawing-rooms. They can dress in dishabille, read, lounge, write, converse, play a social game, sleep, or do what they choose, while a great portion of the route affords a constant succession of novel and delightful scenes, to be witnessed no where else on the face of the earth. I say emphatically, that for every person who can afford it, the trip to California is one that ought by all means to be made. Like a thing of beauty it will prove "a joy forever."

When our party arrived at San Francisco, they all agreed in saying that if they were compelled to return home the next day, they should feel that they were well paid for their journey. In view of the strange and interesting scenes that we witnessed in Salt Lake City,—a place in many respects unlike any other in the world; and in fresh remembrance of the wild, bold rocky mountain scenery, the vast plains, the wild antelope, buffalo, and wolves, the mining districts, the curious snow sheds, and many other scenes and peculiar things brought to our notice,—I think my friends were right in their conclusions.

We took our journey leisurely. I lectured in Council Bluffs, at Omaha, and at Salt Lake City. We stopped several days in this celebrated Mormon city; and as I wished without prejudice to examine into the habits, customs, and opinions of the Mormons, we put up at the Townsend House—a very excellent hotel kept by Mr. Townsend, a New England Mormon, with three or more wives. One of the principal Mormons, an Alderman and an Apostle, had visited me in New York. He devoted his time to our party for several successive days; and through his courtesy and influence we were furnished facilities for obtaining information that not one stranger in a thousand ever enjoys. We not only visited the Tabernacle, and all the institutions, civil and religious, but were introduced into the families of several of the dignitaries. In turn, we were visited at our hotel by all the principal church officers. Without stopping to discuss their great error—a plurality of wives,—I must say that all of our party agreed that the Mormons of Salt Lake City were an industrious, quiet, seemingly conscientious, peaceable, God-fearing people. A serious defection has taken place in their church. The portion called the "Liberals" have renounced polygamy for the future; and this example, together with their rejection of certain theological superstitions, is giving them great influence and respect. This branch of the Mormons is growing rapidly; and I have no doubt that their influence, aided by the great influx of Gentiles, caused by the Pacific Railroad, will soon serve in exterminating the plurality wife system—unless, unhappily, fanatics and fools give this system renewed strength by recklessly persecuting its devotees to martyrdom.

I lectured in the Salt Lake Theatre—a large and commodious building belonging to the Mormons. A dozen or so of Brigham Young's wives, and scores of his children, were among the audience. As I came out of the theatre one of the Apostles introduced me to five of his wives in succession! The Mormon wives whom I visited in company of their husbands, expressed themselves pleased with their positions; but I confess I doubt their sincerity on this point. All whom our party conversed with (and some of our ladies talked with these Mormon wives in secret), expressed their solemn conviction, that polygamy was the only true domestic system sanctioned by the Almighty; although they confessed they wished it was right for a man to have but one wife.

I was introduced by her father to a girl of seventeen, named Barnum. The old man was an original Mormon. He had moved from Illinois with Brigham Young, and his disciples, when they were driven out and compelled to make that wonderful and fearful journey over the plains. The daughter was born in Salt Lake City, and of course knew nothing of any other religion. I asked her laughingly if she expected to have the fifth part of a man for her husband.

"I expect I shall. I believe it is right," she replied.

My apostolic friend took me to Brigham Young's house early in the morning. Mr. Young had gone to Ogden to accompany some Bishops whom he was sending abroad. I left my card with his Secretary, and said I would call at four o'clock. But before noon a servant from President Young brought a message for me to call on him at 1 o'clock. At the hour designated I called with my friends. Brigham Young was standing in front of one of his houses—the "Bee Hive," in which was his reception room. He received us with a smile, and invited us to enter. He was very sociable; asked us many questions, and promptly answered ours. Finally he said with a chuckle,

"Barnum, what will you give to exhibit me in New York and the Eastern cities?"

"Well, Mr. President," I replied, "I'll give you half the receipts, which I will guarantee shall be $200,000 per year, for I consider you the best show in America."

"Why did you not secure me some years ago when I was of no consequence?" he continued.

"Because, you would not have 'drawn' at that time," I answered.

Brigham smiled and said, "I would like right well to spend a few hours with you, if you could come when I am disengaged." I thanked him, and told him I guessed I should enjoy it; but visitors were crowding into his reception-room, and we withdrew.

I subsequently met him in the street driving his favorite pair of mules attached to a nice carriage. He raised his hat and bowed, which salutation I, of course, returned. I hope that Brigham's declining years will prompt him to receive a new "revelation," commanding a discontinuance of the wife plurality feature of the Mormon religion.

Arriving at Sacramento, where the train stopped for half an hour, I was "interviewed" for the first time in my life by a newspaper reporter. On the same evening, in the excellent Cosmopolitan Hotel, in San Francisco, I was again "interviewed" by the chief editor of a morning paper, accompanied by his reporter. By this time I had got accustomed to this business, and when the gentlemen informed me they wanted to interview me, I asked them to be seated, pulled up an extra chair, on which to rest my feet, and said,

"Go a-head, gentlemen; I am ready."

Well, they did "go a-head," asking me every conceivable question, on every conceivable subject. I felt jolly and "spread myself." The consequence was, three columns of "Barnum Interviewed" appeared next morning with a "To be continued" at the bottom; and the succeeding morning appeared three columns more. This conspicuous advertisement prepared the way for a lecture, which I gave in Pratt's large hall, which was well attended.

It took us a week to "do" San Francisco with its suburbs, including Oakland, Woodward's celebrated and beautiful Gardens, and "Seal Rock." When I saw that small rocky island lying only ten rods off, covered with Sea Lions weighing from eight hundred to two thousand pounds, the "show fever" began to rise. I offered fifty thousand dollars to have ten of the large sea lions delivered to me alive in New York, so that I could fence in a bit of the East River near Jones' Wood, and give such an exhibition to citizens and strangers in that city.

The Chinese quarters,—where were their shops, restaurants, and laundries, their Joss House, and the Chinese Theatre,—gave us a new sensation, and were quite sufficient to quench a lingering desire which I had long felt to visit China and Japan. The Chinese servants and laborers are diligent, peaceable, clean, and require no watching. When I remembered how many thousands of dollars I had paid to "eye servants" for not doing what I hired them to do, I did not feel sorry that there was a prospect of the "Celestials" extending their travels to the Eastern states.

We visited "the Geysers," and when we witnessed the bold mountain scenery through which we passed to get there, and then saw and heard the puffing, steaming, burning, bubbling acres of hot springs emitting liquids of a dozen different minerals, and of as many different colors, we said, "This would pay for coming all the way from New York, if we saw nothing else,"—and it would.

In returning from the Geysers to Calistoga we fell into the hands of the celebrated stage-driver, Foss. He had been "laying" for me several days, and had said he would "give Barnum a specimen of stage driving that would astonish him." He did it! Foss is by far the greatest stage-driver of modern times. The way he handles the reins seems marvelous; and although he dashes his six-horse team, under full gallop, down the most precipitous mountain roads, making one's hair continually to stand on end, his horses are as docile as lambs, and they know every tone of Foss's voice and obey accordingly. I suppose that this New Hampshire Jehu is, after all, as safe a driver as ever held the ribbons.

Calistoga lies chiefly on made ground. Dig down five feet and you find water wherein an egg will boil hard in five minutes. A Japanese tea plantation is started here with prospects of success.

We devoted a fortnight to visiting the great Yo Semite Valley. We went by way of Mariposa where we saw the Mariposa grove of "big trees," whence I sent to New York a piece of bark thirty-one inches thick! That bark was taken from a tree 102 feet in circumference, over three hundred feet high, and according to its annual layers, 837 years old. The Yo Semite has been so often and so well described that I shall not attempt a new description. Suffice it to say it is one of those great and real things in nature that goes in reality far beyond any previous conception. From the moment I got a bird's eye view of this wonderful valley from "Inspiration Point," until a week afterwards, when we mounted our horses to emerge from it, I could not help oft repeating, "wonderful, wonderful, sublime, indescribable, incomprehensible; I never before saw anything so truly and appallingly grand; it pays me a hundred times over for visiting California."

On returning to Stockton, I lectured for a Methodist church pursuant to an agreement made to that effect when I left for the Yo Semite twelve days before.

On our return home we stopped at Cheyenne and took the Branch Railroad to Denver, Colorado, afterwards going fifty miles by stage to the mines at Georgetown, Golden City, Central City, and other notable places.

Returning from Denver, we stopped at the truly wonderful town of Greeley, where when we left home in April not ten persons resided, but where was now settled the "Union Colony." This Company then numbered six hundred. Greeley is now a city, nearly a year old, containing thousands of inhabitants, increasing at a rate totally unexampled. There is no community of interests here except in such public works as the irrigating canals, and the school-houses. Each inhabitant owns whatever lands and buildings he or she pays for; and real estate and other property rises in value according to the increase in the number of inhabitants. Here are millions of acres of rich valley land, which needed only the irrigation which the great Platte river is giving through the canals of the Union Colony. This model town of Greeley will ever have peace and prosperity within its borders; for no title can inhere to any land or building where intoxicating drinks are permitted to be sold. It is a city of refuge from the curse of strong drink; and to it for generations to come will whole families congregate as their paradise guarded by flaming swords of sobriety and order where they can live rationally, happily, and prosperously.

From Greeley we returned to New York, and my family removed to our summer quarters in Bridgeport the last of June. Here we were visited by numerous noble friends. The late Alice Cary spent several weeks with us at Waldemere, and although her health was feeble she enjoyed the cool breezes as well as the fine drives, clambakes, etc., for which Bridgeport is specially renowned. Indeed, my own house was the last which this good and gifted lady ever entered except her own in New York, to which I accompanied her from Bridgeport.

But the restless spirit of an energetic man of leisure prompted me again to travel. I went with friends to Montreal, Quebec, the Saginaw River, and the regions round about. Returning by way of Saratoga Springs, my English friends again had occasion to open their eyes at the large Union Hotel, and Congress Hall, where fifteen hundred persons dine at one time, and two thousand lodge under a single roof without crowding.

"Well, this *is* a big country, and you Americans do everything on a big scale that's a fact," was the expression for the thousandth time of my Anglo-Saxon companions.

In September, I made up a party of ten, including my English friend, and we started for Kansas on a grand buffalo hunt. General Custar, commandant at Fort Hayes, was apprized in advance of our anticipated visit, and he received us like princes. He fitted out a company of fifty military horsemen, furnishing us with horses, arms and ammunition. We were taken to an immense herd of buffaloes, quietly browsing on the open plain. We charged on them, and during an exciting chase of a couple of hours, we slew twenty immense bull buffaloes. We might have killed as many more had we not considered it wanton butchery. Every man had killed his buffalo, some had killed two, and we were satisfied. We had plenty of buffalo and antelope meat, and on the whole our ten days' sport afforded another "sensation,"—a feeling so necessary to one in my state. But "sensations" cannot be made to order every day. I am, therefore, taught by an experience of three years "retirement" from business, that it is better to be moderately engaged in some legitimate occupation so long as health and energy permit. If a man is regularly in "harness," though he may do but a small portion of the drawing, he may at least so far occupy his mind as not to need spasmodic excitements.

Hence, although my worldly possessions, trivial indeed in comparison with those of some of New York's millionaires, are nevertheless as ample as I care to acquire, I, at this present writing, and from the necessity of my active nature, am embarking in a great show enterprise, requiring five hundred men and horses to transport and sustain it through the country. My chief object in setting on foot this great travelling Exhibition is to establish a safety-valve for my present pent-up energies. The next object is to please the public.

My third and final object is not to lose money by the operation, but I can truly affirm that this object hardly contemplates the making of money. I am far more anxious to put before the community a grand and triumphant show, than I am to add a penny to my competence. To make my great traveling Museum, Menagerie, and Hippodrome co-extensive in splendor with the patronage of my fellow citizens, so that it shall be simply self-sustaining, is the height of my ambition. That it may continue to increase in magnitude and merit in exact proportion to its financial receipts will be the satisfactory result. In this way I have the satisfaction at the start of putting on wheels and exhibiting at a merely nominal price of admission the most colossal series of Exhibitions ever before transported through the country. My ambition will be sufficiently satisfied in the anticipation that the great show, combining valuable instruction with innocent amusement, shall become at once an institution worthy of its originator and of the country which gave him birth.

FOR THE BEST IN PAPERBACKS, LOOK FOR THE

In every corner of the world, on every subject under the sun, Penguin represents quality and variety—the very best in publishing today.

For complete information about books available from Penguin—including Pelicans, Puffins, Peregrines, and Penguin Classics—and how to order them, write to us at the appropriate address below. Please note that for copyright reasons the selection of books varies from country to country.

In the United Kingdom: For a complete list of books available from Penguin in the U.K., please write to *Dept E.P., Penguin Books Ltd, Harmondsworth, Middlesex, UB7 0DA.*

In the United States: For a complete list of books available from Penguin in the U.S., please write to *Dept BA, Penguin*, Box 120, Bergenfield, New Jersey 07621-0120.

In Canada: For a complete list of books available from Penguin in Canada, please write to *Penguin Books Ltd, 2801 John Street, Markham, Ontario L3R 1B4.*

In Australia: For a complete list of books available from Penguin in Australia, please write to the *Marketing Department, Penguin Books Ltd, P.O. Box 257, Ringwood, Victoria 3134.*

In New Zealand: For a complete list of books available from Penguin in New Zealand, please write to the *Marketing Department, Penguin Books (NZ) Ltd, Private Bag, Takapuna, Auckland 9.*

In India: For a complete list of books available from Penguin, please write to *Penguin Overseas Ltd, 706 Eros Apartments, 56 Nehru Place, New Delhi, 110019.*

In Holland: For a complete list of books available from Penguin in Holland, please write to *Penguin Books Nederland B.V., Postbus 195, NL-1380AD Weesp, Netherlands.*

In Germany: For a complete list of books available from Penguin, please write to *Penguin Books Ltd, Friedrichstrasse 10-12, D-6000 Frankfurt Main 1, Federal Republic of Germany.*

In Spain: For a complete list of books available from Penguin in Spain, please write to *Longman, Penguin España, Calle San Nicolas 15, E-28013 Madrid, Spain.*

In Japan: For a complete list of books available from Penguin in Japan, please write to *Longman Penguin Japan Co Ltd, Yamaguchi Building, 2-12-9 Kanda Jimbocho, Chiyoda-Ku, Tokyo 101, Japan.*

FOR THE BEST IN CLASSICS, LOOK FOR THE

☐ HARD TIMES

Charles Dickens

A powerful portrait of a Lancashire mill town in the 1840s, *Hard Times* stigmatized the prevalent philosophy of Utilitarianism which allowed human beings to be enslaved to machines and reduced to numbers.

328 pages   *ISBN: 0-14-043042-3*   **$2.25**

☐ GREAT EXPECTATIONS

Charles Dickens

In the story of the orphan Pip and the mysterious fortune which falls into his lap, Dickens developed a theme that would preoccupy him towards the end of his life — How do men know who they are?

512 pages   *ISBN: 0-14-043003-2*   **$2.95**

☐ WALDEN & CIVIL DISOBEDIENCE

Henry David Thoreau

"If a man does not keep pace with his companions, perhaps it is because he hears a different drummer." Conveying Thoreau's wonder at the commonplace and his yearning for spiritual truth and self-reliance, *Walden* is both a naturalist's and a Transcendentalist's account of the beauty of solitude.

432 pages   *ISBN: 0-14-039044-8*   **$2.95**

☐ JANE EYRE

Charlotte Brontë

One of the most widely read of all English novels, *Jane Eyre* depicts the refusal of a spirited and intelligent woman to accept her appointed place in society with unusual frankness and with a passionate sense of the dignity and needs of women.

490 pages   *ISBN: 0-14-043011-3*   **$2.25**

FOR THE BEST IN CLASSICS, LOOK FOR THE

☐ **WUTHERING HEIGHTS**

Emily Brontë

An intensely original work, this story of the passionate love between Cathy and Heathcliff is recorded with such truth, imagination, and emotional intensity that it acquires the depth and simplicity of ancient tragedy.

372 pages   ISBN: 0-14-043001-6   **$2.95**

☐ **UTOPIA**

Thomas More

Utopia revolutionized Plato's classical blueprint of the perfect republic, and can be seen as the source of Anabaptism, Mormonism, and even Communism. Witty, immediate, vital, prescient, it is the work of a man who drank deep of the finest spirit of his age.

154 pages   ISBN: 0-14-044165-4   **$2.95**

☐ **THE SCARLET LETTER**

Nathaniel Hawthorne

Publicly disgraced and ostracized by the harsh Puritan community of seventeenth-century Boston, Hester Prynne draws on her inner strength to emerge as the first true heroine of American fiction.

284 pages   ISBN: 0-14-039019-7   **$2.25**

☐ **WINESBURG, OHIO**

Sherwood Anderson

Introduced as "The Tales and the Persons," this timeless cycle of short stories lays bare the lives of the friendly but solitary people of small town America at the turn of the century.

248 pages   ISBN: 0-14-039059-6   **$4.95**

☐ **CANDIDE**

Voltaire

One of the glories of eighteenth-century satire, *Candide* was the most brilliant challenge to the prevailing thought that held "all is for the best in the best of all possible worlds."

144 pages   ISBN: 0-14-044004-6   **$2.25**

☐ **PRIDE AND PREJUDICE**

Jane Austen

While Napoleon transformed Europe, Jane Austen wrote a novel in which a man changes his manners and a young lady her mind. In Austen's world of delicious social comedy, the truly civilized being maintains a proper balance between reason and energy.

400 pages   ISBN: 0-14-043072-5   **$2.25**

FOR THE BEST IN CLASSICS, LOOK FOR THE

☐ **THE ODYSSEY**

Homer

E. V. Rieu's best-selling prose translation captures both the delicacy and drama of the hero Odysseus's journey and allows the freshness and excitement of Homer's well-knit plot to delight us as much as it did the ancient Greeks.

368 pages　ISBN: 0-14-044001-1　**$2.95**

☐ **THE PRINCE**

Niccolo Machiavelli

This treatise on statecraft — in which the author uncompromisingly proposes what most governments do but none profess to do — holds such power to shock that at one time Machiavelli was identified with Satan himself.

154 pages　ISBN: 0-14-044107-7　**$2.25**

☐ **HEART OF DARKNESS**

Joseph Conrad

Written in the last year of the nineteenth century, *Heart of Darkness* represents in many ways the first twentieth-century novel. Conrad's story of Marlow's search for Mr. Kurtz provides an extraordinary exploration of human savagery and despair.

122 pages　ISBN: 0-14-043168-3　**$1.95**

☐ **THE CANTERBURY TALES**

Geoffrey Chaucer

Told by a motley crowd of pilgrims journeying from Southwark to Canterbury, these tales — bawdy, pious, erudite, tragic, comic — reveal a picture of four-teenth-century England which is as robust as it is representative.

526 pages　ISBN: 0-14-044022-4　**$2.95**

FOR THE BEST IN CLASSICS, LOOK FOR THE

☐ THE RED BADGE OF COURAGE

Stephen Crane

Certainly one of the greatest novels written about the heat of battle, Crane's story ultimately concerns the battle waged in young Henry Fleming's mind as he reacts to "reality," confronts duty and fear, and comes to terms with himself and the world.

222 pages   ISBN: 0-14-039021-9   **$2.95**

☐ McTEAGUE

Frank Norris

This searing portrait of the downfall of a slow-witted dentist and his avaricious wife is a novel of compelling narrative force and a powerful and shocking example of early American realism.

442 pages   ISBN: 0-14-039017-0   **$5.95**

☐ SELECTED ESSAYS

Ralph Waldo Emerson

With these essays calling for harmony with nature and reliance on individual integrity, Emerson unburdened his young country of Europe's traditional sense of history and showed Americans how to be creators of their own circumstances.

416 pages   ISBN: 0-14-039013-8   **$4.50**

☐ SISTER CARRIE

Theodore Dreiser

This unsparing story of a country girl's rise to riches as the mistress of a wealthy man is a pioneering work of naturalism, especially so in this unexpurgated edition which follows Dreiser's original manuscript.

500 pages   ISBN: 0-14-039002-2   **$4.95**

☐ UNCLE TOM'S CABIN

Harriet Beecher Stowe

A powerful indictment of slavery that brought the abolitionists' message to the White House and beyond, *Uncle Tom's Cabin* was hailed by Tolstoy as "one of the greatest productions of the human mind."

630 pages   ISBN: 0-14-039003-0   **$3.95**

☐ THE ADVENTURES OF HUCKLEBERRY FINN

Mark Twain

"All modern American literature comes from one book by Mark Twain called *Huckleberry Finn*," wrote Ernest Hemingway. An incomparable adventure story and a classic of American humor, no book has a better claim to the title of The Great American Novel.

336 pages   ISBN: 0-14-039046-4   **$1.95**